Key Concepts in Migration

Recent volumes include:

Key Concepts in Sociology
Peter Braham

Key Concepts in Youth Studies
Mark Cieslik and Donald Simpson

Key Concepts in Race and Ethnicity
Nasar Meer

The SAGE Key Concepts series provides students with accessible and authoritative knowledge of the essential topics in a variety of disciplines. Cross-referenced throughout, the format encourages critical evaluation through understanding. Written by experienced and respected academics, the books are indispensable study aids and guides to comprehension.

Key Concepts in Migration

DAVID BARTRAM, MARITSA V. POROS
AND PIERRE MONFORTE

SAGE

Los Angeles | London | New Delhi
Singapore | Washington DC

SAGE

Los Angeles | London | New Delhi
Singapore | Washington DC

SAGE Publications Ltd
1 Oliver's Yard
55 City Road
London EC1Y 1SP

SAGE Publications Inc.
2455 Teller Road
Thousand Oaks, California 91320

SAGE Publications India Pvt Ltd
B 1/I 1 Mohan Cooperative Industrial Area
Mathura Road
New Delhi 110 044

SAGE Publications Asia-Pacific Pte Ltd
3 Church Street
#10-04 Samsung Hub
Singapore 049483

Editor: Chris Rojek
Editorial assistant: Gemma Shields
Production editor: Katherine Haw
Copyeditor: Rose James
Marketing manager: Michael Ainsley
Cover design: Wendy Scott
Typeset by: C&M Digitals (P) Ltd, Chennai, India
Printed by: Ashford Colour Press Ltd, Gosport, Hampshire.

MIX
Paper from responsible sources
FSC® C011748
FSC www.fsc.org

First published 2014

Library of Congress Control Number: 2013950108

British Library Cataloguing in Publication data

A catalogue record for this book is available from the British Library

ISBN 978-0-85702-078-9
ISBN 978-0-85702-079-6 (pbk)

contents

about the authors

David Bartram received his PhD in sociology from the University of Wisconsin–Madison following a BA from Kenyon College. He is currently Senior Lecturer in Sociology at the University of Leicester. His current research explores the connection between migration and happiness; other topics include migrant workers in Israel and migration to Israel more generally. He has held grants from the Economic and Social Research Council (UK), the Social Science Research Council (USA), the Nuffield Foundation (UK), and the Hebrew University of Jerusalem.

Maritsa V. Poros is Associate Professor of Sociology and International Studies at The City College and Graduate Center of the City University of New York. She received her PhD from Columbia University, followed by a postdoctoral fellowship at the US Census Bureau. Her research has been funded by the US National Science Foundation and examines the social networks of immigrants and the inequalities they experience in the labour market, their communities and everyday life.

Pierre Monforte is Lecturer in Sociology at the University of Leicester. He received his PhD from the European University Institute in Florence (Italy) and was a postdoctoral fellow at the Université de Montréal. His research explores the dynamics of protest of migrants in different political contexts. He has carried out empirical research in France, Germany, Canada and the UK. He also explores the process of construction of European immigration and asylum policies.

1 Introduction

Few if any topics are more fundamental to the social sciences than international migration. We cannot usefully speak about a 'society' without knowing something about its membership and boundaries. That point has particular force in the contemporary period when most societies are defined in relation to nations: one usually thinks by default of *British* society or *American* society. Matters might be simpler if the membership of societies were fixed, static, and thus obvious and uncontested – if we all could easily know who counts as 'British', etc. But when societies experience immigration in non-trivial numbers (as virtually all countries now do) it becomes plain that societies are inevitably quite fluid and perhaps even chronically indistinct. The observation holds not just for social science research but for the experience of everyday life: the basis for social solidarity and cooperation is sometimes less secure than some would like, though the point has as much to do with the preferences (and sometimes the prejudices) of some natives as it does with the inflows of immigrants themselves.

For research and teaching in the social sciences, then, immigration and immigrants are ignored at one's peril even when focusing on topics that might at first glance appear to have nothing to do with immigration. The study of entrepreneurship cannot overlook the strong tendency of immigrants to create their own businesses. Research on elections and voting behaviour would flounder in many contexts without attention to the distinctive patterns of particular immigrant groups; Florida and California are obvious examples in this respect, but the assertion is no less true of France – to say nothing of the emphasis some parties put on immigration as a campaign issue. Perhaps a sociologist could investigate the Amish in the USA without worrying too much about immigrants – but that suggestion demonstrates by way of contrast a broader point about the sociology of religion. In each case, immigrants are not simply a distinctive group: they are a key part of the whole, with far-reaching implications for how we understand important aspects of 'us'.

The centrality of migration in the social sciences is of course matched by its political salience. Migration is a highly challenging policy area in most wealthy countries (and in some poorer ones as well). In many countries there is widespread public opposition to (or, at a minimum, uneasiness about) immigration that reaches any significant numbers. Many people fear, usually with little justification, that migrants will 'take our jobs'. Having defined migrants as not 'part of us', some people also worry about provision of certain public services: instead of seeing the issue simply in terms of numbers (additional demand that can be satisfied via expanded supply, drawing on the added economic contributions immigrants make), many natives identify immigrants as the source of any and all difficulties they experience in gaining access to health care, education, public housing, etc. Political leaders in democratic countries then face a difficult choice: either be led by public opinion, or attempt to lead by trying to educate voters about a highly complex and emotive topic. As in many policy areas, politicians often punt (in the American-football sense), trying to manage expectations by creating an appearance of acting on voters' concerns about immigration, while bending policy to the wishes of powerful interests such as lobbyists and campaign donors. It is usually difficult to describe the resulting policy approaches as rational and coherent.

It hardly needs saying that efforts to improve policy-making on migration depend heavily on the development of a better understanding of migration, among policy-makers and the public alike. A well-known example illustrates the point. In 2006, the American government began extending a large fence (in certain places, a 21-foot-high steel wall) along its border with Mexico, reinforced by electronic sensors, cameras, etc. (Previously, only limited portions of the border had anything more than basic barbed wire.) The logic was simple: to reduce 'illegal immigration', one simply had to prevent entry, making it more difficult to cross the border except at designated places. What the politicians didn't know – indeed, what they failed to learn despite the efforts of migration researchers to help them learn – is that a fence inhibiting entry would discourage the tendency of many migrants (especially those lacking authorization) to engage in 'circular migration'. Some migrants are employed in seasonal jobs, and they often return home of their own accord – and then re-enter the USA for the next relevant season. When the fence was built, many migrants worried that they would be unable to re-enter, and so they refrained from returning home: their presence in the USA became *more* permanent rather than less. On top of that, many 'illegal immigrants' do not acquire that status by sneaking across the border; instead, they enter by posing as tourists, or they begin with a temporary work permit but then do not leave when it expires. It is not difficult to see, then, that the Americans' fence did little if anything to inhibit illegal immigration; at best, its simple logic was beneficial only in giving the impression that the government was responsive to voters' concerns. One might say that we are still waiting for American policy-makers to absorb some lessons readily available in migration research.

The demands we as citizens and voters try to impose on policy-makers are rooted in our own understanding of migration, and in that respect social science research has a great deal to offer. Courses on migration have become a staple of degree programmes in most social science disciplines, and in addition to the primary research there is now a good selection of texts designed to help students gain entry to the field. The exposition in most instances is historical and /or explanatory (i.e., with respect to particular historical or sociological developments). There is usually direct treatment of a limited number of core concepts (e.g. integration, ethnicity), but in general the concepts relevant to the study of migration are embedded in historical or analytical discussions and are thus not readily accessible to those seeking to understand the concepts themselves. Indeed, in some instances the historical/analytical discussions presume an understanding of the concepts, and so a neglect of concepts per se potentially results in an underdeveloped appreciation of concepts and history/analysis alike. The logic of a 'key concepts' book is thus quite attractive: one can have direct access to a focused (and relatively brief) treatment of a wide range of the concepts that underpin more conventional forms of writing. We say 'wide range' and not 'complete set' because the porous boundaries of migration studies as a field mean that any claim we might make here for the latter would inevitably run up against someone's sense that we have omitted something important.

Writing this book was a much less onerous task than we initially imagined. While it took a great deal of work, the work was rewarding insofar as it led us to read more widely than we normally would in our more circumscribed research efforts. In certain instances we found ourselves asking questions like 'Okay, what *does* integration mean?' We suspect that sort of experience is quite common, given the wide range of concepts migration scholars use together with the tendency to do quite specific research. This reasoning leads us to expect that the book will be useful not only for students but for other researchers as well; we have each learned a great deal from contributions written by the others.

In addition to our own research and teaching, the book is informed to a degree by our own personal histories of migration, which have been useful insofar as we have tried to write about concepts in a way that connects to lived experience. After all, concepts (and theories) do not exist for their own sake but to help us understand the world we live in and our place in it. While our own migration experiences are distinctive in that most migrants are not academics moving with relative ease among the world's wealthiest countries, all three of us have a 'grounded' sense of what at least some of these concepts mean. For what it's worth: Bartram is originally from the USA but has lived in the UK for twelve years; he is now a British citizen, after passing the 'Life in the UK' test, participating in a citizenship ceremony and paying an extortionate fee to the British government. He also lived for extended periods in Israel, and for part of that time he was arguably an 'illegal immigrant' by virtue of doing paid work (editing someone else's manuscript), probably in violation of the student visa he then held (again, though, hardly a typical illegal immigrant). Poros is a second-generation American, born to Greek parents; her partner lives in London and holds Greek citizenship, which has afforded her an EEA (European Economic Area) permit and residence in the UK on the basis of European Union mobility provisions. Her pursuit of Greek citizenship has turned out to be far more complicated. And Monforte is originally from France but now lives in the UK (having also spent an extended period in Canada) on the basis of EU mobility provisions.

We have benefited enormously from the feedback and suggestions of colleagues in a wide range of countries. We are particularly grateful to Rutvica Andrejasevic, Loretta Baldassar, Paolo Boccagni, Richard Courtney, Antje Ellermann, Russell King, Peter Kivisto, Marco Martiniello, Laura Morales, Aubrey Newman, Mary Savigar, Kelly Staples, Carlos Vargas-Silva, Gustavo Verduzco and Catherine Wihtol de Wenden. Poros also wishes to thank Taressa Dalchand for her diligent assistance on several chapters. Finally, we are very grateful for the support and forbearance of our editors at SAGE – especially Martine Jonsrud and Chris Rojek – who responded with unfailing patience to our messages about the competing demands of very small children.

2 Migration

Definition: international migration is the movement of people to another country, leading to temporary or permanent resettlement; in the aggregate it commonly raises questions about national identities and social membership.

In a perspective that is content with common sense, migration is the relocation of individuals to some distant place, i.e., at least beyond one's own city or town. In these basic terms, it is primarily a geographic phenomenon. It is also a very common experience: as is often noted, migration is a universal feature of human history, reaching back many thousands of years.

This book focuses mainly on international migration, however, and the definition in the previous paragraph is then too broad. What really matters about international migration – the reason many people find it interesting (and some find it challenging) – is the international part. Internal (domestic) migration is much more common, especially in the USA: every year significant percentages of Americans move between cities or states. But migration to another country is different – often more difficult, more fraught, and arguably more consequential despite the lower numbers of people who do it (relative to internal migration). The geographic nature of migration is hardly unimportant, but international migration is better understood more broadly as a *social* phenomenon that connects with a comprehensive range of life domains – politics, economics, culture, identity, etc.

To understand international migration at a conceptual level, consider that at the heart of the word 'international' is the word 'nation'. Migration from one country to another is usually consequential because of differences in nationality, or because of differences among people that are understood to correspond to nationality. An immigrant in any particular destination country is often noticeable, meriting attention as unusual, for being 'foreign'. This is a form of difference typically perceived as highly salient, one that marks 'immigrants' as distinct from those who migrate within a country; in some cases this perception contributes to a feeling that people who are immigrants are 'out of place' and really belong elsewhere (i.e., not 'here').

The word 'perceived' in the previous sentence is important. Immigrants are not different from natives in some sort of essential or inherent way; in many respects they can have a great deal in common with natives.[1] But in modern societies where nation-states are core institutions, nationality and 'foreignness' are *constructed* as central points of difference (Waldinger and Lichter 2003). People latch onto these points of difference, endowing them with meaning and significance, often reinforcing them in the process (see Gilroy 1993). As Martin et al. (2006) argue, international migration is a *response* to differences between countries (e.g. economic inequality, or variations in political freedom or repression): individuals migrate because they want something not available in their own country. But the point can be taken further: the concept of international migration is *animated by* (perceptions of) difference. Again, differences are identified and labelled in terms relating to nationality but are understood to correspond to other forms of difference – social, economic, cultural, etc. As a matter of intuition, someone moving to New York from El Salvador is defined as different in ways that someone moving from Cleveland (Ohio) is not.

We can appreciate the utility of the conception provided here by considering instances of international migration that depart in interesting ways from more typical cases. The population of Israel consists of a very high percentage of immigrants; almost one million people migrated to Israel in the 1990s alone, adding more than 20 per cent to the population. Israel is very keen to welcome Jewish immigrants, even to the point of offering virtually unconditional citizenship to Jews upon arrival, prior to leaving the airport. Jewish immigrants are then eligible for substantial benefits and support for integration and settlement. The apparent contrast with other countries, where quite restrictive attitudes and policies prevail, could hardly be greater. Even in Canada immigrants are desired only to a point: one's chances of admission are higher if one is relatively young, well-educated, etc. In Israel the age and education of immigrants are unimportant at least in policy terms, as are other characteristics that might affect one's economic prospects (Cohen 2009).

What is important, however, is being Jewish. The reason Jewish immigrants are welcome in Israel – indeed, are eagerly sought – is that Jews who live in other countries are not considered foreign. Instead, insofar as Israel is the 'Jewish state', Jews everywhere are already considered part of the Israeli/Jewish nation (what matters here is Jewishness not as religious practice but as national identity/belonging). This point is apparent in the way certain words are used to describe the immigration of Jews. Many people do not use the Hebrew word for immigration (*hagirah*) when discussing Jewish immigrants (Shuval and Leshem 1998). Instead, the term used in normal conversation and official discourse alike is *aliyah*, meaning ascent: Jews who move to Israel are 'going up'. The term has highly positive connotations, not least for the fact that it also describes the ancient practice of ascent to Jerusalem for religious festivals when the Temple was standing; it also denotes being called to recite a blessing before and after a Torah reading during synagogue services.

From this perspective, in being so welcoming to Jewish immigrants Israel is not quite the exception it might otherwise appear to be. Again, in most countries immigrants are 'foreigners', and the presence of large numbers of foreigners amounts to an anomaly that (for many) requires resolution, e.g. via departure or integration/naturalization. For Israel, it is the fact that Jews are living somewhere else that (for many) constitutes an anomaly, and immigration (of Jews) is the resolution of the anomaly.[2] The law regulating Jewish immigration to Israel is the 'Law of Return': Jews who move to Israel are understood to be 'returning' to the land of their ancestors. In English one sometimes speaks of the diaspora – but the Hebrew term *galut* (meaning exile) carries a stronger connotation of not being where one belongs. From a mainstream Zionist point of view, Israel is where Jews belong, even if they are also members of other nations. From this perspective, the movement of Jews to Israel is hardly international migration at all.

That perspective is in certain respects a peculiar one, and it overstates the differences between Israel and other cases in some unhelpful ways. (Similar points apply to '*Aussiedler*'/ 'returnees' in Germany, where the notion of 'return' informs policies and attitudes but should not lead us to perceive something other than immigration.) From a point of view that does not begin with mainstream Zionism, Jewish immigrants in Israel are indeed immigrants, and they share certain characteristics and experiences with immigrants elsewhere. But the Israeli/Zionist way of looking at these matters is useful for our consideration here, because it shows how important perceptions of national belonging vs. foreignness are to the concept of international migration. If one already belongs to the nation, then perhaps one is not quite an 'immigrant' in the way 'foreigners' are. By the same token, foreignness is a key component of the definition of international migration. International migration is thus necessarily specific to the (modern) period characterized by the dominance of nation-states (Joppke 1999a).

Israel is not the only country that helps makes this point. At the risk of provoking ire among Canadians: consider whether migration from Detroit to Windsor is 'international migration' in the same way that that term applies to migration from China to Canada. In legal terms, the two flows are similar: the USA and Canada are distinct nation-states, and the citizens of one cannot legally migrate to the other without the latter's permission. But in some respects the differences between American and Canadian national identity are not so great, and someone who moves across the Detroit River into Ontario is perhaps less of an 'immigrant' than someone who moves there from Hong Kong.[3] (No doubt some Canadians and others with a broadly cosmopolitan outlook would disagree.) Legal status (e.g. citizenship) is not as important (for conceptual purposes, at least) as perceptions of culture and nationality – a point evident also in the experience of many immigrants in the UK who in earlier decades arrived from the 'New Commonwealth' as British citizens but who were nonetheless surely 'immigrants' (Entzinger 1990; see Hansen 2000). International migration involves crossing borders, but some borders matter more than others (and matter differently for different people as well).

This at any rate is how immigration figures in many people's experiences, and those experiences matter insofar as they form part of the context for the way immigration is identified as such a significant issue in social, political and economic terms. In modern societies, populations and socio-political processes are defined, to a great extent, with reference to nation-states. A key element of identity is one's nationality: individuals are different (via self-definition and/or perception) by virtue of being British, not French, or Korean, not Japanese. Moreover, nationality is often 'sticky': when someone migrates from France to Britain, one does not instantly become British. Indeed, some immigrants find that the identity associated with their country of origin becomes deeper after moving to another country (see Ryan 2010: 'Becoming Polish in London').

International migration is thus defined primarily with reference to national differences and a world of sovereign nation-states. Even so, these differences and institutions are not immutable. On the contrary: migration presents a significant challenge to the nation-state (Joppke 1998, 1999a), as well as a challenge to a wide range of other institutions in both destination and origin countries (Koslowski 2000). Mass migration to the wealthy democracies, in particular, has resulted in a diversification of legal statuses (e.g. citizenship) and identities; Castles (2010) argues persuasively that migration is a key component of 'social transformation' more generally. While some migration scholars perceive the emergence of a 'post-national' period (Soysal 1994), a more moderate view sees nation-states as altered by migration but nonetheless resilient in response to it (Joppke 1999a).

For many people, the salience of national identity is very much a matter of regret, in part because of its consequences for how immigrants are sometimes treated by natives. In addition, modern nationalism has fed vicious wars and other actions ranging from individual acts of cruelty to instances of genocide in Germany, Armenia and Rwanda. In a cosmopolitan orientation, national identity does not matter: we are all equal as individuals, as 'global citizens' – and nationalism is something to be resisted or suppressed, particularly when one considers its consequences in places like Bosnia. That orientation is perhaps normatively compelling (though some advocates of a 'liberal nationalism' believe it is utopian and even undesirable), but it does not describe the world as it is, even if there are certain trends in that direction. Again, however, the idea is useful by way of contrast to a counterfactual: if we lived in a world where national identities and national borders did not matter, then 'international migration' would not be what it is in the world as it is.

In application to particular cases, the general concept of international migration often requires qualifications of various sorts, e.g. 'transnational' migration (connoting that immigration is often not a 'complete' process, as migrants sustain ties with the country of origin). Most of these qualifications are dealt with here as separate chapters exploring the more specific concepts. Any number of additional cautions are useful, to avoid some common misconceptions. For example, many people in the USA believe that there is rampant 'illegal' immigration from Mexico – when in fact Mexicans are increasingly likely to migrate internally and net migration from Mexico to the USA in recent years has fallen dramatically, perhaps even to zero (Cave 2011, 2012). (Mexico itself is becoming a significant destination for migrants from other countries, including the USA, Germany and South Korea, Cave 2013.) Analogous concerns in the UK might be alleviated if there were better understanding that a large proportion of 'immigrants' are students, most of whom do leave the UK soon after their studies are completed. We would also want to avoid drawing 'global' conclusions via analysis of 'Western' countries only, and so many of the chapters to follow consider migration experiences in middle-income and poorer countries as well. As with any social phenomenon it is possible to discern patterns and trends, but contemporary international migration is characterized by relentlessly increasing complexity and change (Castles and Miller 2009), so that it resists simplification even at a conceptual level.

NOTES

1 As Castles and Miller (2009) note, nation-states themselves are typically characterized by considerable internal heterogeneity. Benedict Anderson's (1983) analysis of nation-states as 'imagined communities' is an important corrective to 'essentialist' understandings.

2 By contrast, many Palestinian/Arab citizens of Israel experience a lesser degree of social membership in Israel despite having been born there: they are citizens with formal equality, but they do not share the 'nationality' that underpins the Israeli nation-state.

3 By the same token, an American who moves to China is arguably more of an immigrant there than someone who moves from Taiwan to China. The point does not depend on any inherent qualities of Chinese people but rather on the salience of national differences in particular contexts.

KEY READINGS

Castles, S. and Miller, M.J. (2009) *The Age of Migration: International Population Movements in the Modern World*. London: Macmillan Press.

Joppke, C. (1999a) *Immigration and the Nation-state: the United States, Germany, and Great Britain*. Oxford: Oxford University Press.

Martin, P.L., Abella, M.I. and Kuptsch, C. (2006) *Managing Labor Migration in the Twenty-first Century*. New Haven, CT: Yale University Press.

3 Acculturation

Definition: A process by which the cultural patterns of distinct groups change when those groups come into contact with each other – sometimes resulting in the groups becoming less distinct culturally.

The concept of acculturation has a long and contentious history in migration studies. One might say the concept grew up with the history of migration to the USA, especially beginning with the second great wave of immigration at the turn of the twentieth century. The term has been used widely in the North American and European contexts, though increasingly with criticism, especially in societies that identify with a 'multiculturalist' ideology.

Early anthropologists and sociologists took an interactive approach to the concept of acculturation, defining it as a process by which the cultural patterns of distinct cultural groups change over time as they have contact with each other. Noted anthropologists Robert Redfield, Ralph Linton and Melville J. Herskovits (1936: 149), working as a subcommittee to the Social Science Research Council, defined acculturation as occurring 'when groups of individuals having different cultures come into continuous first-hand contact with subsequent changes in the original cultural patterns of either or both groups'. These early definitions of acculturation were criticized in the 1960s by Milton Gordon in his seminal book, *Assimilation and American Life* (Gordon 1964). Gordon reviewed numerous definitions of the term acculturation and its close cousin, assimilation, concluding that most of these definitions lacked a structural perspective regarding how distinct groups interact. Gordon was expressly interested in prejudice and discrimination and therefore understood acculturation to be an unequal exchange or interaction between cultures where one culture holds a dominant structural position, i.e., a position of power. Unlike earlier investigators, Gordon conceptualized acculturation via emphasis on the social relationships of native and minority groups. Gordon's view had great influence on subsequent definitions of acculturation (not to mention assimilation), such as those in the work of Herbert Gans and Richard Alba, leading to the notion that acculturation was generally a one-way process in which ethnic minorities adopted the cultural patterns dominant in their host societies (e.g. Gans 1979, 1998; Alba and Nee 2003). Elements of those cultural patterns as described by Gordon ranged from language, dress, emotional expression and personal values to musical tastes and religion. The reference group for these cultural behaviours was middle-class, white, Anglo-Saxon Protestants.

Herb Gans and Richard Alba and his associates have been perhaps the strongest proponents of Gordon's legacy. Their studies built on Gordon's definition of acculturation to measure the acculturation processes of first-generation immigrants in American society. Language acquisition became the principal measure of acculturation among the first generation in studies since the 1970s. Although much of the early research argued that first-generation 'whites' had acculturated and, indeed, assimilated into American society by the 1970s, much of the debate today relates to the so-called 'new' immigration: people from Latin America, the Caribbean, Asia and Africa, who have made up the vast majority of immigration flows to the USA since 1965. For instance, Alba and Nee (2003) found that the earlier generations of Irish, Italians, Eastern Europeans, etc., acculturated (and assimilated) over time by acquiring the practices and customs of the American 'mainstream' – principally, proficiency or even fluency in English. The 'new' immigrants, on the other hand, present a more mixed picture, with different rates of acculturation for different groups. Still, conventional views hold that acculturation precedes assimilation and that language acquisition is the first (and necessary) step towards creating and maintaining primary relationships with individuals and institutions in the host society. Along with this uni-directional process lies the notion that the binary relationship between the 'hosts' and 'minorities' of a society reflects social realities more accurately than a multifaceted approach.

Critics of the concepts of acculturation and assimilation have identified faults associated with both assumptions. In general, these critical arguments promote the idea of ethnic difference and of multiple reference groups within society as against a binary relationship between host and immigrant/minority (Alba and Nee 1997). These criticisms have been based largely on ideologies of multiculturalism found most prominently in countries such as Canada and the UK. They argue that multiculturalist societies have become so heterogeneous that the binary model of acculturation (and assimilation) hardly applies any more. Nor can one legitimately argue that acculturation must precede assimilation, as many 'new' immigrants have arrived in their host societies with greater human capital (education, English-language proficiency, etc.) than their predecessors upon which the older definitions of acculturation were based.

Questions about acculturation also arise for the native-born children of immigrants (the 'second generation'), though the concept takes on a different meaning for them. Alejandro Portes and his associates developed several acculturation concepts to capture differences in the ways the immigrant second generation managed acculturation, particularly as a relationship between themselves and their parents (Portes et al. 2009). Variants included 'consonant', 'selective', and 'dissonant' acculturation. Consonant acculturation occurs when parents and children simultaneously learn the language and become accommodated to the customs and culture of the host society. Selective acculturation occurs when parents and children learn the language and culture of the host society and, at the same time, retain significant elements of their 'original' culture or remain part of their ethnic communities (see also Waters et al. 2010). Finally, dissonant acculturation occurs when children reject the values and culture of their parents for those of the host society (Portes et al. 2009) or learn and adopt host society values and culture far faster than their parents (Waters et al. 2010). The perceived difficulties of second-generation adaptation through language acculturation and ultimately assimilation have been found to be much less problematic than is imagined by immigration sceptics. Indeed, Waters et al. (2010) found that 'selective assimilation' is by far the most common outcome of second-generation adaptation. The children of immigrants seem to be quite skilled at learning and adopting the host society language and culture while at the same time retaining important elements of their parents' culture, which provide them with sometimes crucial ethnic resources and social capital. This 'best of both worlds' position may even give them significant advantages over their native-born peers.

Still, whether applied to the first or second generation, these concepts of acculturation often remain static, especially as language and generational status remain the primary measures for assessing whether acculturation has taken place. Thus, both approaches to acculturation (the linear/binary version and the multicultural version) have been criticized. Critics argue that the concept of acculturation (and related ideas such as assimilation and ethnic retention) are inherently weak because they measure acculturation in terms of a set of static characteristics one must possess (Waldinger 2003). In contrast, Waldinger espouses a relational perspective (see Barth 1969; Brubaker 2004) in that he sees 'immigrants', 'natives', 'ethnics', etc., not as bounded groups that one can take for granted, but rather as parts of webs of relationships that form a multidimensional continuum describing the extent to which 'acceptability' of persons in society is a possibility. Social life, and indeed ethnic life, therefore, constitute dynamic processes that only rarely enclose categories of people in all situations. In particular, the relational perspective challenges the idea that there could be an identifiable 'mainstream' toward which one might be acculturating or assimilating (to say nothing of the underlying normative tone of the idea). After all, the term 'mainstream' seems to be just another way of talking about a white, middle-class reference group, as Gordon unabashedly identified over fifty years ago. The relational perspective also challenges the idea that immigrants or minorities could belong to an 'authentic' or identifiable ethnic group without experiencing all of the usual cleavages of class, region, religion, etc., that are inherent in such groupings. The tendency (in the older views) to reify ethnicity in theories of acculturation and assimilation comes apart in favour of a more process-oriented, dynamic understanding of how individuals move in and out of 'groupness', in Waldinger's words. Acculturation, then, becomes a process by which individuals and groupings of individuals change through their exchange of culture (its practices, tools, symbols, ideas, values, etc.) over time.

The concept of acculturation varies in use across disciplines and to some extent across place. It has been widely used in anthropology, sociology, psychology and social work and in North America, the UK and Europe. As noted, it has also frequently been criticized, most recently in the context of highly diverse immigration inflows in 'immigration countries'. A more apt and challenging way to understand acculturation lies with the relational perspective, which asks us to locate and observe the relationships within which cultural change takes place and to understand change as a process that itself continually shifts in time and place.

See also: *Ethnicity and ethnic minorities; Second generation; Integration; Assimilation; Multiculturalism*

KEY READINGS

Alba, R.D. and Nee, V. (2003) *Remaking the American Mainstream: Assimilation and Contemporary Immigration.* Cambridge, MA: Harvard University Press.

Barth, F. (ed.) (1969) *Ethnic Groups and Boundaries: The Social Organization of Culture Difference.* Bergen and London: Little Brown.

Gans, H.J. (1998) 'Toward a reconciliation of "assimilation" and "pluralism": the interplay of acculturation and ethnic retention', in C. Hirschman, P. Kasinitz and J. DeWind (eds), *The Handbook of International Migration.* New York: Russell Sage Foundation, pp. 161–71.

Gordon, M.M. (1964) *Assimilation in American Life: The Role of Race, Religion, and National Origins.* New York: Oxford University Press.

Portes, A., Fernández-Kelly, P. and Haller, W. (2009) 'The adaptation of the immigrant second generation in America: a theoretical overview and recent evidence', *Journal of Ethnic and Migration Studies*, 35 (7): 1077–104.

4 Alien/Foreigner

Definition: The terms alien and foreigner refer to a person who is a member of some **other** *society, a non-citizen, someone who is a stranger or outsider, e.g. by virtue of having been born in another country.*

Referring to an immigrant as a foreigner or alien implies (in the case of alien, quite strongly) that that person is not in fact a member of their new society. Foreignness is not an inherent quality of a person; instead it is a relation, defined by particular contexts: I am only a foreigner there, not here (Saunders 2003). The concepts thus lead us to consider the basis for membership and belonging: who belongs, who does not belong, and how do we reach such determinations? Given that national identity is a primary basis for belonging in societies/countries defined as nation-states, the answers have much to do with whether it is possible for someone to join the nation that dominates in the country to which they have migrated. Etymology is revealing even if not all-determining: the word 'nation' derives from a Latin root connected with birth (compare the Spanish word 'nació', meaning 'he/she was born'). For someone born elsewhere – or born 'here' but to the 'wrong' parents – one's prospects for gaining a new national membership and shedding one's foreignness cannot be taken for granted.

The question of belonging is addressed to an extent via citizenship, but determining who is a foreigner or alien is not as simple as identifying those who are not citizens. As Georg Simmel long ago remarked in his essay on 'The Stranger', the condition of the stranger is to be *in* a society but not *of* it; the stranger is both insider and outsider simultaneously (Simmel 1964 [1908]). This peculiar position is the hallmark of the foreigner/alien, and it profoundly shapes their integration into a new society – it is a condition that for many immigrants is not remedied even with naturalization. There is a disjuncture between citizenship and foreignness with respect to immigrants: one can have formal citizenship and yet still be considered a foreigner, particularly if in racial or ethnic terms one stands out as different in a context where these characteristics are held to be significant. Or, one can lack formal citizenship and yet be considered essentially 'one of us', as with Jewish visitors to Israel.

At first blush, the terms imply a dichotomy: one is either 'one of us' or a foreigner. In reality, matters are more complex. The populations of most nation-states are far from homogeneous in regard to national identity; a dominant national identity is typically contested or rejected by members of subordinate groups. In that sort of context, immigrants might not feel or be defined as foreign to any great degree when living among those who arrived and settled earlier; examples include new Cuban immigrants arriving in Miami, or people from any number of origins arriving in London. National identity itself can change via mass immigration. Some natives in dominant groups might accept the redefinition of national identity entailed by immigration, such that new immigrants quickly become part of 'us' regardless of ethnic differences; others might feel that their 'own' country is itself becoming foreign to them.

For most immigrants, foreignness remains a key aspect of their encounters with the destination society. Many natives take for granted the notion that immigrants are 'different' in ways that really matter; foreignness is then normally a lower position in a hierarchy (Saunders 2003). Taking a longer historical view, Booth (1997) notes that ideas about alienage have become 'suspect', and it is indeed more difficult now than in earlier eras to assert that the treatment of outsiders is not a matter for moral concern. Even so, his claim that concern with the 'special bonds' of citizenship is 'almost vestigial' rings at least slightly hollow. Other indications of attitudes can be found by comparing the connotations of the two words. While the terms are synonyms to a degree, one's choice about which to use is typically determined by one's attitude towards immigration (Sassen 1999). Those who want to minimize immigration inflows are typically more inclined to use alien, as with Peter Brimelow's screed *Alien Nation* (1996) lamenting 'America's immigration disaster', or Pat Buchanan's *State of Emergency* (2006) decrying the 'Third World Invasion and the conquest of America' (with the term 'illegal alien' appearing on virtually every page). Some authors no doubt rely on readers making a connection to 'alien' in the sense of hypothetical beings from another planet, fostering an impression that immigrants are irredeemably different from 'us'.

These popular uses of the word alien have only heightened the historical stigma against foreigners developed in the law, particularly in France and the United States. In pre-revolutionary France, the alien's inability to inherit or pass down property to one's heirs was considered a stain or blot on one's moral character (Sahlins 2004). In United States law, alien denoted similar legal deficiencies and prohibitions, often connected to notions of racial belonging. The 1789 naturalization law declared that only 'free white persons' were eligible for citizenship (during that period, they became eligible after only one year of residence). By the late 1800s, specific exclusionary laws were directed at Chinese, Japanese, Filipinos, and Mexicans – in short, racial 'others'. The term alien acquired derogatory connotation also as it became attached to 'illegality', as in 'illegal alien'; one also sees the odd term 'alien citizens', i.e., those who were American citizens by birth but even so were considered 'foreign' by mainstream American culture and often by the state as well (Ngai 2004).

This type of exclusion was not unique to the USA. In the UK, for instance, immigrants from the 'New Commonwealth', such as the colonial citizens of the British Caribbean, were often regarded as foreign and marked racially as 'coloured' – as against the presumed Anglo-Saxon origins of people returning from ('old') Commonwealth countries such as Australia (McDowell 2003). Colonial citizenship was a kind of second-class citizenship denoting the 'foreignness' of subjects who belonged to the British Empire. We see this pattern clearly with the Ugandan Asians who tried to migrate to the UK en masse following their expulsion from Uganda by Idi Amin in 1972. Their United Kingdom 'D' passports initially made them ineligible for residence in the UK, although they were finally accepted after much political negotiation and the resignation of the British government (Gregory 1993; Poros 2013).

We might imagine that immigrants begin as foreigners and then progressively become less foreign, as they integrate and/or assimilate; their rights and membership often expand, e.g. if they gain permanent residence and then citizenship. But this is not always a one-way process. Non-citizen immigrants can also *lose* rights and in effect become more foreign: if they commit sufficiently serious crimes (or a sufficient number of quite minor crimes, as in the USA), they can easily find themselves subject to deportation, a rather definitive statement that one is completely a foreigner (Ngai 2004). Even citizens have not been exempt from this reversal: during World War II, the American government interned tens of thousands of native-born American citizens of Japanese ancestry (Cole 2003). As is often noted, worries (not to mention surveillance and enforcement) in the context of the post-9/11 'security' agenda cast a cloud over citizens belonging to particular racial and ethnic groups: British citizens who are Muslims are sometimes perceived as foreign in ways that American or Australian tourists in the UK are not.

The peculiar condition of the foreigner described above reflects a fundamental tension about citizenship and belonging more generally (Bosniak 2008). In liberal, democratic societies, principles of justice and equality are quite central, underpinning a tendency towards inclusion of immigrants. However, there are also countervailing processes that promote exclusion, especially via the selective process of entry to the nation-state. Thus, internal inclusiveness and external exclusiveness form the context in which immigrants are accepted into a society, and again the paradox of immigrant belonging is that immigrants are typically defined as outsiders (foreigners) even if they have become naturalized citizens.

Advocates and opponents of immigration tend to emphasize one side of this paradox and downplay the other. Advocates argue for internal inclusion, asserting that residents of a state or community must be treated with fairness and have rights despite lack of formal citizenship (even if they entered the country illegally). Opponents of immigration, by contrast, argue for external exclusion on the basis that the state has the ultimate right to define its political community through regulation of the national border. Michael Walzer attempts to reconcile these perspectives, arguing that they are not incompatible and that immigrants, once they reside within a territory, are no longer strangers. Discrimination against aliens within the internal sphere of a society violates democratic principles of justice and is nothing short of tyranny, claims Walzer (1983; see Bosniak 2008). For Walzer, the principles that govern admission, exclusion and deportation of immigrants constitute a separate sphere and cannot be used to exert pressure on processes governing membership of the internal community. Linda Bosniak argues that this separation of spheres is ultimately impossible, however. The exclusionary boundaries of communities often find expression internally as well. Immigrants exist within and across two competing spheres that contradict one another. Full inclusion in the community is a 'fantasy' (Bosniak 2008: 140): in a world constituted by national membership, the alienage of immigrants is an irremediable condition.

The contradictions of belonging are also laid bare by Saskia Sassen in her work *Territory, Authority, Rights*. Sassen (2008) argues that citizenship has always been an incompletely theorized contract with the state. Moreover, states have a deep interest in keeping it this way. The contradiction of being simultaneously an insider and outsider in a society emerges directly from the state's exercise of discretion (some would say arbitrariness) in determining citizenship and its treatment of immigrants within its own borders. Naturalized citizens, non-citizen residents, and unauthorized or illegal alien residents all experience the condition of outsider to varying degrees. All are also to some degree vulnerable to deportation, a prospect that hangs like a dark cloud over their rights and freedoms even in liberal, democratic societies. On the other hand, even undocumented immigrants enjoy significant rights in their host societies: in many respects the activities of their daily lives are similar to those of documented immigrants, naturalized citizens and native-born citizens, e.g. holding jobs, attending schools, raising families, driving vehicles, and participating to some degree in local civic life (Sassen 2008). Undocumented immigrants sometimes even become eligible for legal residence through demonstration of 'good conduct' and continuous presence. They are both insiders and outsiders from both a legal-political perspective and a social one. As long as the international state system (and its citizenship regime) persists as the main mode of organizing political and social life, the contradictions of belonging for foreigners and aliens are unlikely ever to be reconciled.

See also: *Citizenship; Integration; Undocumented/illegal immigration; Deportation*

KEY READINGS

Bosniak, L. (2008) *The Citizen and the Alien: Dilemmas of Contemporary Membership*. Princeton, NJ: Princeton University Press.

Ngai, M.M. (2004) *Impossible Subjects: Illegal Aliens and the Making of Modern America*. Princeton, NJ: Princeton University Press.

Sassen, S. (2008) *Territory, Authority, Rights: From Medieval to Global Assemblages*. Princeton, NJ: Princeton University Press.

Simmel, G. (1964) *The Sociology of Georg Simmel*, compiled and translated by Kurt Wolff. Glencoe, IL: Free Press.

5 Assimilation

Definition: The process by which immigrants become similar to natives – leading to the reduction (or possibly the disappearance) of ethnic difference between them.

The basic meaning of 'assimilation' is readily apparent from its root (and other words based on that root): immigrants assimilate when they become similar to natives. Differences between immigrants and natives are typically perceived as aggregating to *ethnic* difference, and so Alba and Nee define assimilation as 'the decline of an ethnic distinction and its corollary cultural and social differences' (2003: 11) – a definition exemplary for its clarity and conciseness, denoting a process that can emerge from change in the destination society as well as in the immigrants themselves. As noted in the chapter on integration, not all scholars work with such a clear and distinct sense of the concept, and it is easy to find analyses where the word is used to refer to processes arguably better described as integration. One can also perceive 'national' patterns of usage: American migration scholars have more commonly used 'assimilation' while many European observers prefer 'integration', even when addressing similar questions (there are of course exceptions in both contexts). Even so, as this is a book on concepts we take the view that there is a useful (and perhaps essential) distinction to be made, even if the ideas are clearly related: integration can occur without assimilation insofar as it is sometimes possible for immigrants to gain social membership (and even to achieve a degree of equality with natives) without becoming ethnically indistinguishable from natives.

The concept of assimilation has carried some heavy baggage which it has begun to shed only in the last two decades. The term can be used empirically, to describe what many immigrants actually do – but it can also be used normatively, to indicate what many natives *expect* immigrants to do (with such expectations typically rooted in ethnocentrism or even outright prejudice). For many years these two senses were thoroughly entangled, with the consequence that when observers began to reject the projection of assimilationist expectations onto immigrants they often rejected the word itself. In more recent years a number of scholars (e.g. Alba and Nee 1997, 2003; Morawska 1994) have identified assimilation as an indispensable concept for empirical understanding of what immigrants (and the destination societies) experience, while leaving its unsavoury normative implications firmly in the past.

These points are readily apparent in a trajectory followed by many immigration countries during the twentieth century and in particular in the American case. In early American notions of the 'melting pot', immigrants were expected to (and in some instances did) disappear as such, blending into the receiving society, deliberately adopting traits of the latter and leaving previous identities behind (e.g. Alba and Nee 1997). Observations of this pattern matured into classic notions of 'straight-line assimilation', an idea originating with Warner and Srole (1945), whose empirical findings were accompanied by the normative assumptions of the day: immigrants' cultural traits were 'inferior' and needed to be 'unlearned', particularly by their children. In another canonical treatment of this topic, Milton Gordon wrote of the 'middle-class cultural patterns of, largely, white Protestant, Anglo-Saxon origins' as the United States' 'core culture' (1964: 72), to which immigrants would assimilate. This perspective, rooted in the more general frame of modernization theory in which wealthy destination countries were also the most 'advanced', was properly identified as ethnocentric – just as immigrants and 'ethnics' generally became less inclined to 'melt' away. Immigrant-receiving countries in the late twentieth century became, to varying degrees, multicultural societies – at a minimum in demographic terms but in some places as a matter of attitudes and active policies (multiculturalism). Instead of becoming similar to natives in a comprehensive (and normatively mandated) way, immigrants' difference and diversity became grounds for celebration, a new way of perceiving 'us'.

This historical shift, and its valorization, led some observers to conclude that assimilation was an outmoded idea; in short, immigrants were no longer assimilating. That assertion was at best an exaggeration; it also constituted an excessively narrow understanding of what assimilation actually denotes. Again, a key point is that assimilation results in part from changes not just in immigrants but in the receiving society as well. The work of Alba and Nee (e.g. 2003) is particularly important in that regard. As Kivisto and Faist (2010) note, Alba and Nee drew on an article by Zolberg and Woon (1999 – itself building on Bauböck 1994a) to identify three distinct processes that result in assimilation. 'Boundary crossing' denotes the conventional mode of assimilation: individuals undergo substantial changes that amount to joining the mainstream, e.g. learning a new language and/or rejecting 'old' ethnic labels. While that mode leaves existing boundaries more or less intact, 'boundary blurring' describes a reduction in ethnic difference operating at a societal level rather than an individual level: boundaries between groups become less salient and more permeable, e.g. with greater acceptance of multiple/overlapping identities, bilingualism and dual citizenship. Immigration to the USA has clearly had this sort of transformative impact, while assimilation in this mode has not occurred to the same extent in many European countries (Alba 2005). The third process, 'boundary shifting', is a wholesale realignment of boundaries, either in a more exclusionary or more inclusionary direction. This far-reaching transformation is rarer, and some observers write about it in a speculative mode, as with Gans's (1999) suggestion that the black/white divide in the USA is perhaps being transformed into a black/non-black divide as 'Asians' are increasingly accepted as 'honorary whites'.

A redemption of assimilation as an empirical description is facilitated by an insightful observation from both Brubaker (2003) and Joppke and Morawska (2003) regarding the word's grammatical properties. Assimilation can be used as a transitive and an intransitive verb (the point applies to integration as well). In the former sense, some other actor (e.g. a state) does something to immigrants – via legal requirements, transmission of public attitudes, etc. – thus imposing assimilation on them. In the latter, assimilation describes what immigrants themselves do. The normative baggage of the term has to do with its transitive sense: many people object when governments or public attitudes lead immigrants to change their identities or actions in ways they would not themselves prefer. But the intransitive sense of assimilation amounts to a useful concept for empirical purposes: again, most immigrants do assimilate at least to some degree.

In a 'common-sense' perspective, assimilation is viewed as beneficial for immigrants in quite a broad way; the point might seem especially obvious regarding immigrants' children (the second generation) as their socialization takes place in the destination country. But research in several disciplines has established that the opposite conclusion (assimilation leads to deterioration in outcomes) is sometimes more appropriate. Rumbaut (1997) summarizes a number of findings regarding health and education in the USA: for example, there were lower rates of infant mortality and low birthweight among babies born to immigrant women from Mexico than among babies born to similarly situated native women – but that advantage did not persist for the babies of second-generation mothers, who in effect assimilated to the (worse) patterns of native women. Risky behaviours are also more prevalent among many second-generation youths than among immigrant (foreign-born) youths; that trajectory is not only intergenerational, but appears also in the increasing incidence of risky behaviours among foreign-born youths as length of residence increases.

The notion of 'segmented assimilation', developed by Portes and Zhou (1993), provokes doubts about the assumption of beneficial consequences in a more systematic way; it also offers an explanation for variation in outcome patterns for different groups. It is all too easy to imagine that assimilation is a universal process that pertains to immigrants and their children in general. In reality, different immigrants are situated in quite different ways, with far-reaching consequences for the type of assimilation they experience. For some, assimilation is in most respects beneficial, consisting of (or resulting in) acceptance and upward mobility. But this conventional assimilation pathway is often not open to members of the second generation who are marked in the terms of American racial categories as non-white and whose economic position relegates them to residence in disadvantaged neighbourhoods of inner cities. In that context, assimilation is typically 'downward': when immigrants' children assimilate under those conditions, they become members of the USA's disadvantaged minority groups, with significant consequences for their educational (and eventual occupational) attainment (Portes and Rumbaut 1996). In those circumstances, resisting assimilation – maintaining tight-knit ethnic communities that sustain a strong commitment to children's education – can lead to better outcomes.

It is perhaps tempting to think that immigrants adapt to their new circumstances in only one mode: either they assimilate or they maintain transnational ties that sustain ethnic identities and communities. As Morawska (2003) argues, however, these modes are typically concurrent: many immigrants assimilate in particular ways *while* maintaining transnational ties, and it is instructive to consider various combinations of patterns in both modes (see Kivisto 2003). Transnational ties might help sustain ethnic identities and communities – but there is no contradiction when we recall that assimilation is merely the *decline* of ethnic distinctions, not their disappearance. Following Kivisto (2003), we should expect to find a high degree of complexity in this field: ethnic distinctions decline in salience in part because dimensions of ethnicity come to mean different things to different groups and even to different individuals within groups. One would hardly expect immigrants to remain unchanged after arrival – but then the same point applies to the destination society as well. On those terms, assimilation is once again a lively topic in research on migration.

See also: *Integration; Acculturation; Multiculturalism*

KEY READINGS

Alba, R.D. and Nee, V. (2003) *Remaking the American Mainstream: Assimilation and Contemporary Immigration*. Cambridge, MA: Harvard University Press.

Joppke, C. and Morawska, E. (2003) 'Integrating immigrants in liberal nation-states: policies and practices', in C. Joppke and E. Morawska (eds), *Toward Assimilation and Citizenship: Immigrants in Liberal Nation-states*. Basingstoke: Palgrave Macmillan, pp. 1–36.

Kivisto, P. and Faist, T. (2010) *Beyond a Border: The Causes and Consequences of Contemporary Immigration*. London: Pine Forge Press.

Portes, A. and Rumbaut, R. (1996) *Immigrant America: A Portrait*. Berkeley, CA: University of California Press.

Rumbaut, R.G. (1997) 'Assimilation and its discontents: between rhetoric and reality', *International Migration Review*, 31: 923–60.

6 Borders

Definition: Geographical and political lines that divide and join countries, lines crossed by migrants and/or fortified with barriers of various types by states hoping to keep migrants out.

Although migration is a broadly social phenomenon rather than merely geographical, the geography of nation-states is nonetheless an important contextual factor for migration, and the borders between states help define the act of migration. Borders are not only the point of crossing (or exclusion) – they mark the spaces whose *differences* make migration a consequential act. The notion of differences is central to migration: in one space, an individual is at home, a member, a citizen; in another space that person is a 'foreigner', and the perception of foreignness is an essential component of the concept of 'immigrants' (as the introductory chapter makes clear).

A border, like most social institutions, is an idea that guides and constrains people's actions; sometimes that idea is marked with physical structures designed to express, implement or enforce it. The core of the idea here is: 'This space is ours, and you may not enter without our permission.' The claim that a border is primarily a social institution (and not primarily a physical feature or structure) is apparent in the fact that most borders exist by virtue of agreement between the two states separated by the border. Agreements can break down, as during wars, and borders can be changed and imposed by force – but in 'normal' periods borders function as a matter of agreement. States sometimes build walls and other barriers to try to prevent unauthorized crossings, but borders still exist when such structures are absent, and borders can deter unauthorized crossings even when there is no physical barrier. In short, borders are primarily social, not physical (see Migdal 2004; O'Dowd and Wilson 1996). This is not to suggest that borders are therefore 'soft': the willingness of some countries to enforce migration restrictions means that borders are sometimes sites of great violence and death. Until 1989 East German soldiers shot people trying to escape into West Berlin, and the militarization of parts of the US–Mexican border has contributed to thousands of deaths among would-be migrants whose attempts at crossing were displaced to more remote and dangerous border regions.

Some states make significant expenditures related to the symbolic nature of borders, in connection with migration. Andreas (2000) describes recent 'reinforcements' of the US–Mexico border as an exercise in 'symbolic politics' designed to reassure American voters that the US government has not lost control of its borders. Deployments of personnel and expensive technology in the 1990s, as well as construction of a ten-foot-high steel wall in places (the 'Iron Curtain'), do not function primarily as effective deterrents against the infiltration of illegal immigrants (particularly when people are equipped with a ladder...). Nor (if we ask why these methods were implemented during a particular period) do they come as responses to a demonstrably increased threat (unauthorized crossings from Mexico had taken place in large volume for many decades before the reinforcement projects). Instead, they are the actions of political entrepreneurs who hope to capture votes and other resources via a type of ritualized performance, a 'symbolic representation of state authority' (2000: 8) that arouses and then allays people's worries. Borders in this sense operate as much for the perceptions and feelings of natives as for the actions of would-be migrants.

The ours/yours dimension of borders is rooted in the modern nation-state, which is routinely connected to a particular territory (e.g. Malkki 1992). A nation can exist outside 'its' territory, but it is then a diaspora nation, not a nation-state (as Jewish history demonstrates, particularly before 1948). In a stylized understanding of geography familiar from the multicoloured maps used for example in schools, nation-states are clearly demarcated from one another; the dotted lines of Kashmir and Jerusalem are aberrations, anomalies demanding resolution (which is not always forthcoming). Gellner contrasts the political maps describing modern nations to an ethnographic map describing the distribution of peoples in an era prior to the age of nationalism: in the latter, one perceives a 'riot of diverse points of colour ... such that no clear pattern can be discerned in any detail' (1983: 139–40). The process of nation-state building brought some order to what might appear, from the vantage point of the present, to have been chaos: all of France is now French, Britain is British, and Ireland is *not* British (but perhaps it's best not to talk about Ulster). The maps used to teach geography to schoolchildren are misleading, however, insofar as they suggest excessively sweeping generalizations; English is the first language in most but not all of Britain, and most people in Ireland are fluent only in English (not Irish).

Even so, borders as they exist at any one point in time demarcate one nation-state from another and help invest certain instances of movement with the meaning that makes such movements 'inter*national* migration'. Moving (relocating) from Niagara Falls, New York, to Niagara Falls, Ontario is international migration, despite the very short distance involved (possibly less than a mile); moving from Buffalo to Detroit is not (though the shortest route from one to the other is via southern Ontario). Despite certain similarities, the US and Canada are different nation-states, with different norms and laws (the latter enforced by a different set of authorities) – and citizens of one may not cross the border without the latter's permission.

The 'power' of borders in connection with migration is demonstrated in a striking way when we observe situations in which people do not move but borders do – such that non-mobile individuals become 'foreigners' having much in common with immigrants in a more conventional sense. With the break-up of the Soviet Union in 1991, Estonia and Latvia once again became independent countries, and large numbers of Russians in both countries faced uncertain prospects for citizenship despite having been born there (in cases where their parents, not they, had been the 'immigrants') (Brubaker 1992b). The point is readily made even about the US, though it requires going back further in history: prior to the Mexican–American War of 1846–48, much of the American south-west was part of Mexico, and migration from (what is now) Sonora to Arizona only became 'international' after the US forced Mexico to sell very large parts of its northern territory. Histories with similar implications can be told for the break-up of the Austro-Hungarian Empire and the redrawing of maps in central and eastern Europe.

Borders can change in other ways (not just relocation), with significant consequences for migration. Processes of European integration within frameworks such as the European Union and the Nordic Common Labour Market have resulted in decreased salience of borders in ways that facilitate migration, even to the point of calling into question its international character. Travelling among countries that adhere to the Schengen Agreement is an experience interesting for what it does not require: heading east from Dunkerque on the E40 (A16) highway in France, one encounters only a small sign upon entering Belgium – all other physical manifestations of the border have been removed, and the crossing takes place at 130 km/h (or more). Migration from Oslo to Stockholm arguably has more in common with migration from Buffalo to Detroit than with migration from Santo Domingo to New York; the Norwegian/Swedish border has by no means been erased, but its salience has certainly been diminished, by design.

Some migration takes the form of daily border-crossing, where people work in a different country but do not change their residence. The Swiss cities of Basel and Geneva are right on the border with France (the Basel Airport is wholly within France), and French workers can earn the higher wages available in Switzerland but pay the lower costs of living (particularly for housing) in France. Similar situations can be found in many locations. For many years Palestinians in the West Bank and Gaza made daily crossings to work in Israel (Semyonov and Lewin-Epstein 1987), though the Israeli case involves a great deal more ambiguity and conflict, on several dimensions. It is now less common for Palestinians to work in Israel as defined by its pre-1967 borders (the 'Green Line'), but some workers commute to jobs in Israeli settlements in the West Bank. From the perspective of some Israelis, Ma'ale Adumim is a suburb of Jerusalem, part of Israel – and when Palestinians travel from the village of Jahalin to work in Ma'ale Adumim they perhaps cross an international border (they must pass through a checkpoint to do so). Others – not least the Palestinian workers themselves – take a quite different view.

Borders are often understood as lines – a concept that in mathematical terms has no width (only length). But we can also think of borders as zones (Gavrilis 2008), and a related concept of 'borderlands' draws attention to the fact that actions and institutions in spaces close to borders are often distinctive in certain ways. One expression of this point is the growth of 'maquiladoras', factories in Mexico near the northern border, producing goods for export to the USA under favourable trade and tax regimes. Rapid expansion of maquiladoras has drawn workers northwards – and once they are close to the border some of these workers come to see entry to the USA as a relatively small further step. Additionally, attempts to regulate migration, as well as migration itself, concentrate resources and attention (including intensified government surveillance) on 'foreigners' and borders alike, with consequences for identity and experience among those living in border regions (Lugo 2008; Stea et al. 2010; Romero 2008).

Some who write about globalization have declared that we now live in a 'borderless world' (e.g. Ohmae 1990). That declaration is a vast overstatement, particularly in connection with migration. Borders that control migration have decreased in salience in a limited set of instances, e.g. the European Union – but even in Europe borders retain a great deal of power to shape and sometimes inhibit migration. The legally guaranteed right of British citizens to live and work in France does not mean that migration between the two is entirely 'free' – on the contrary, it involves definable costs, including the overcoming of certain types of barriers (e.g. linguistic, social, cultural). The two countries remain different in significant ways, and migration from Britain to France has a specific meaning that internal migration within most countries would not have (though one could no doubt find exceptions on that latter point: perhaps Tibet to Shanghai). If there were truly no borders, then the specific notion of international migration would be meaningless – and that is plainly not the case.

See also: *Regional Integration and migration*

KEY READINGS

Andreas, P. (2000) *Border Games: Policing the U.S.–Mexico Divide*. Ithaca, NY: Cornell University Press.

Migdal, J. (ed.) (2004) *Boundaries and Belonging: States and Societies in the Struggle to Shape Identities and Local Practices*. Cambridge: Cambridge University Press.

7 Brain Drain/ Gain/Circulation

Definition: Brain drain refers to the loss of highly trained people through emigration, primarily from developing countries. Conversely, brain gain refers to the gain or immigration of highly trained people to developed countries from developing ones. Brain drain and brain gain are typically thought of as one-way flows, while brain circulation refers to a two-way flow of highly trained individuals between developing and developed countries, often accompanied by technology and capital.

In the 1960s and 1970s, the term 'brain drain' was used to describe the loss or emigration of highly educated and skilled individuals primarily from 'developing' countries to 'developed' ones. Developed countries were seen as winners in this process, gaining needed human capital to work in booming science and technology industries. These migration flows mainly comprised students and highly educated/highly skilled workers, who could transfer their skills to expanding industries in science, engineering and health care. For instance, the UN Economic Commission for Africa estimated that about 27,000 Africans migrated to the West (primarily to the USA and former colonial powers such as France, the United Kingdom, Portugal and Germany) from 1960–1975 (El-Khawas 2004). That number rose to 40,000 annually from 1975–1985 and then peaked at 80,000 in 1987. In the 1990s, about 20,000 highly skilled Africans were emigrating per year.

Brain drain often begins with students who pursue advanced degrees in industrialized countries and then stay there (rather than returning home as they might originally have intended) to work in their fields of expertise. For instance, about 20 per cent of Taiwanese students (college graduates) emigrated in the 1970s and 1980s to pursue advanced degrees (O'Neil 2003). In the 1960s and 1970s India experienced large-scale brain drain of students and highly qualified scientists, engineers and physicians. Many other countries have experienced and/or continue to experience significant loss of talent via emigration, e.g. China, the Philippines, Ukraine, Russia. The UN estimated that in the 1960s approximately 300,000 highly qualified personnel were part of brain drain flows to the West from developing countries (Saxenian 2005). In recent years, nearly one in ten persons with university or tertiary education originating in developing countries live in developed countries (Sriskandarajah 2005). The number is even higher for those educated in science and technology fields. Of course, immigration regimes and the policies of sending and receiving countries also matter to potential migrants, shaping the costs, benefits and ease of leaving one's country to move to a new one (Mahroum 2005). Many immigration regimes have promoted income, tax and other benefits along with flexible immigration laws designed to promote the immigration of students and highly skilled individuals. Policies of sending countries can also make emigration easier (or harder) for their most highly educated individuals.

Apart from immigration regimes and policies, some of the causes cited for brain drain include low wages, lack of opportunity, economic insecurity, poor scientific and technological infrastructures, political conflict and general instability. Brain drain has been associated with other aspects of development such as the sending of remittances. On the one hand, countries have perceived brain drain as a significant loss to their economies and societies, not only a loss of talent but also a loss of tax revenue and investments in education as talented individuals take their expertise out of the country. On the other hand, migrants' remittances worldwide have provided more capital to developing economies than development aid given by developed countries. Migrants of all sorts send remittances home, low-income workers and the highly skilled alike. The tension between gains in remittances and losses from brain drain may not be a zero-sum game, however. Increasing numbers of countries that once contained large reservoirs of highly educated and skilled labour (and which then lost some of those workers via brain drain) are capitalizing on their diasporas to recapture some of the benefits of that workforce now located abroad.

A number of these early developing countries have experienced huge growth in their economies in the past two decades, creating new dimensions to the brain drain phenomenon. In some instances, brain drain has turned into brain circulation as highly skilled professionals and entrepreneurs have returned 'home' to make a living in fast-developing economies such as Taiwan and India, or to conduct transnational business across two or more countries. The concept of brain circulation, then, challenges the core-periphery model of brain drain/gain where highly skilled individuals are seen as engaging in a one-way flow from developing to developed countries (with that flow benefiting only the developed countries). Significant numbers of highly trained individuals have been moving back to their home countries or between their home and host countries while engaged in entrepreneurship or other professional activities related to the industries that originally recruited them. These flows also blur the divide between so-called developed and developing countries.

Studies of brain circulation (e.g. Saxenian 2005) have also documented important transfers of technology and capital in these two-way flows, which were not previously apparent in concepts of brain drain/gain. Migrants involved in brain circulation invest capital, labour and technology as they conduct business in two or more countries where they have residence – a clear instance of transnationalism. Taiwanese and Indian information technology (IT) entrepreneurs in Silicon Valley are frequently cited as early participants in this brain circulation. These ethnic entrepreneurs make up some 20 per cent of Silicon Valley's labour force in IT. They have transferred knowledge, capital, technology and labour from Taiwan and China to the United States and from India to the United States in their cross-regional ventures. Taiwanese IT entrepreneurs were even among the earliest proponents of establishing venture capital firms in Taiwan (Saxenian 2005). Taiwan's government leaders also saw the value of financing science and technology initiatives in order to facilitate innovation and the establishment of a technology market niche. Thus, three Taiwanese spin-offs of American venture firms remain leading investors in Taiwan's and China's technology sector today.

India, too, developed its IT sector in part through the early initiatives of India-born entrepreneurs who had been living and working in Silicon Valley. Despite initial obstacles, including poor infrastructure and complicated bureaucratic procedures, Indian ethnic entrepreneurs brought venture capital firms to India to begin financing research in science and technology. Drawing on large pools of educated labour in India, these entrepreneurs helped create market niches in sectors such as software development technology (similarly to the Taiwanese).

Transnational entrepreneurs are often ideally positioned to operate across international markets because they have essential linguistic and cultural skills. The decentralized nature of ethnic entrepreneurship challenges earlier notions of brain drain as a process dominated by states and multinational or large corporations in search of specialized, high-skilled labour. As countries such as China and India develop and grow even more, we may see less and less migration or circulation of the highly skilled – particularly as more young people become highly educated in their own countries and succeed in finding work there. Both China and India have invested significant capital in their higher education systems in order to keep skilled personnel at home. These countries are also investing heavily in their diaspora networks to convince emigrant entrepreneurs and educated workers to return home.

Dozens of countries now have diaspora organizations that are sponsored by (or even form part of) their governments. Some of the earliest and most highly developed diaspora organizations involve the Philippines and Filipino migrants. The Philippines has been experiencing brain drain since the 1960s, primarily involving nurses, engineers, doctors and other scientists who went to the Middle East, Southeast Asia, the USA and the UK. The Commission of Filipinos Overseas, created in 1981, was the earliest of the three principal diaspora organizations in the Philippines. It promotes economic and cultural ties between the Philippines and its diaspora by engaging actively with diaspora organizations where Filipino migrants live. A separate body (also created in 1981), called the Overseas Workers Welfare Administration (OWWA), advocates for the labour rights of Filipino migrants abroad. And the Philippines Overseas Employment Administration (POEA), established the following year, is the government body that now regulates the movement of all Filipinos abroad. These three organizations cover the full range of Filipino migrants, not only the highly skilled workers conventionally considered part of the Philippines' brain drain.

Other countries' diaspora organizations focus mainly on encouraging the educated segment of its emigrant population to return or to participate in the country's development activities. Haiti, Serbia, Syria and Armenia have created organizations with such a focus (Agunias 2009). Serbia, for instance, formed an Economic Council comprising professionals and experts from the country itself and from its diaspora in order to begin to address the brain drain. The council held a Serbian diaspora medical conference in 2010. The government also plans to establish a virtual business network to disseminate information on investment opportunities, business partnerships and data on organizations and individuals.

The phenomena of brain drain since the 1960s and 1970s, and, later, brain circulation have prompted many individuals, organizations and governments to become more active in trying to harness the advantages of being part of a highly skilled diaspora. Today, the lines between developing and developed economies are blurring ever faster as brain circulation becomes more and more common for some countries. Nonetheless, brain drain has not gone away in the contemporary period. Poor economic conditions sometimes resurface and promote further brain drain. Today, for instance, southern European economies such as Spain, Italy and Greece are (again) sending thousands of workers to northern Europe, the US, Canada and Australia as they experience deepening recessions and painful austerity reforms. Many of these workers are the most highly educated in the workforce and have the networks and resources to gain new jobs and build new lives in other countries. The migration of the highly skilled includes enormous variations. Thus, the concepts of brain drain, brain gain and brain circulation are unlikely to lose their meaning or salience in the near future.

See also: *Diaspora; Remittances; Transnationalism*

KEY READINGS

El-Khawas, M.A. (2004) 'Brain drain: putting Africa between a rock and a hard place', *Mediterranean Quarterly*, 15 (4): 37–56.

Mahroum, S. (2005) 'The international policies of brain gain: a review', *Technology, Analysis & Strategic Management*, 17: 219–30.

O'Neil, K. (2003) *Brain Drain and Gain: The Case of Taiwan*. Washington, DC: Migration Policy Institute.

Saxenian, A.L. (2005) 'From brain drain to brain circulation: transnational communities and regional upgrading in India and China', *Studies in Comparative International Development*, 40 (2): 35–61.

Sriskandarajah, D. (2005) *Reassessing the Impacts of Brain Drain on Developing Countries*. Washington, DC: Migration Policy Institute.

8 Chain Migration

Definition: the process by which migrants encourage and facilitate the subsequent migration of family members and friends – sometimes resulting in the migration of all (or almost all) individuals from one locality to a single destination.

The notion that migration is more an extended social process than a single act (emphasized particularly by Castles and Miller 2009) is especially apparent in the concept of chain migration. After immigrants arrive and begin to make a life for themselves in their destination country, they sometimes encourage family members and friends in their country of origin to join them. Chain migration is however more precise than family migration or family reunification. The idea of a chain takes shape when the migrants who follow the 'pioneers' themselves encourage and facilitate migration by yet more people in their networks. On occasion, that process can take root to such an extent that an entire community or village might end up relocating to a particular destination. Some observers have worried that rights to sponsor family members might render chain migration uncontrollable. In reality, the extent of chain migration via legal sponsorship has not matched those worries; on the other hand, immigrants can also assist the migration of friends and family members in more informal ways, sometimes helping them evade legal restrictions.

The process of chain migration is rooted in *migrant networks* (Boyd 1989). Two aspects of networks are particularly salient here. One has to do with the legal rights that certain countries grant to individuals to sponsor relatives of specified types. In most instances citizens have fairly broad rights to be joined by a foreign-born spouse, though that right is usually not unlimited (Britain, for example, now requires demonstration of the prospective migrant's ability to speak and read English). If the spouse has minor children, they will typically be allowed to immigrate as well; sometimes there is similar provision for immigrants' adult children and/or parents. Other rights of 'reunification' sometimes pertain to siblings (currently the fourth preference of family-based immigration visas in the USA). Those latter rights are less prevalent in most wealthy destination countries (and even in the USA the sponsor must be a naturalized citizen), but they have at times formed the basis for chain migration precisely because the siblings might then also have the right to be joined by a foreign-born spouse (and perhaps his or her children and/or parents), at least upon gaining permanent residence.

These 'additional' migrants are able to enter the destination country as a matter of legal right based on specific family ties. But chain migration can result from other, more diffuse mechanisms that operate via migrant networks. Those mechanisms include: providing information on the availability of jobs, housing, quality of life, etc., in the destination; offering assistance in getting started, e.g. a place to stay upon arrival; and establishment of a genuine 'community' in the destination (particularly as the numbers of connected people there increase). Massey et al. (2003) extend the term sponsor beyond its legal sense to include assistance of this sort. The chain element of the migration flow emerges when communication and offers of assistance are extended to people in the place of origin who were not connected to the migrants who left initially. Family ties are often the starting point of chain migration, and those connections can help facilitate migration even when the legal rights described above do not exist and the migration in question is 'irregular' (Massey and Espinosa 1997; Staring 2004). As migration flows expand and deepen, the resources that flow via migrant networks might become available quite generally to members of the network who remain in the community of origin. These resource flows can become significant even when the connections that enable them do not involve family ties: other types of social bonds can sometimes be just as effective as family in facilitating additional migration (MacDonald and MacDonald 1964).

Worries about chain migration among natives in destination countries have at times been intense. Yu (2008: 5–6) cites a 1981 report from the Select Commission on Immigration and Refugee Policy (SCIRP), created by the American government to study migration issues:

> To illustrate the potential impact, assume one foreign-born married couple, both naturalized, each with two siblings who are also married and each nuclear family having three children. The foreign-born married couple may petition for the admission of their siblings. Each has a spouse and three children who come with their parents. Each spouse is a potential source for more immigration, and so it goes. It is possible that no less [sic] than 84 persons will become eligible for visas in a relatively short period.

This statement fomented further political concern (one might say grandstanding) and led to a significant amount of research attempting to provide an empirical base for evaluation. An early contribution from Jasso and Rosenzweig (1986) concluded that the 'immigration multiplier' – the extent to which migration fosters more migration via family sponsorship chains – was quite low: they estimated that for every immigrant who arrived on an employment-based visa an additional 1.2 immigrants arrived in the subsequent 10 years. The multiplier with respect to family-based entrants was 0.2. Subsequent research argued that those figures were underestimates (note that there is no 'true' figure: one's findings depend on decisions about measurement and the meaning of the concept itself). A more recent investigation (Yu 2008) found that the overall multiplier estimated over a 25-year period from 1972 was 2.2. Needless to say, these findings indicate that the extent of chain migration (at least in the sense of immigrants exercising the legal right to sponsor relatives) is quite limited in comparison to the worries some people were expressing.

Another key finding of research on chain migration is that the process and its extent are quite different for different migration flows. Filipino immigrants in the US arriving after the 1965 liberalization of immigration legislation sponsored additional relatives at a relatively high rate (Jasso and Rosenzweig 1989; Liu et al. 1991). Rates were higher for Asian countries in general. One likely contributor to chain migration from Asian countries such as the Philippines is the presence of US military bases there. In the USA, immigration via family-based visas is not primarily a matter of immigrants sponsoring immigrants: in the 1980s, almost two-thirds of people petitioning to be joined by relatives in the categories where no quotas applied were native-born citizens sponsoring their foreign-born spouses (Heinburg et al. 1989).

The concerns some people have about chain migration can be captured in the phrase 'migration begets migration'. This way of thinking about the concept is premised on the notion that migration is an individual act: one individual migrates, and then other individuals follow. In reality, migration is often a *household* decision and process (Stark and Bloom 1985; Massey 1990). In that frame, chain migration (at least insofar as it involves family members) is perhaps better described as 'delayed family migration' (MacDonald and MacDonald 1964). Under the right circumstances, the entire family might prefer to move together at one time – but if those circumstances are lacking (as they often are), migration of the family takes place in stages (Banerjee 1983). Of course, one might need to remember that 'family' in some cultures means *extended* families, not nuclear families as commonly understood in many wealthier countries. Even so, the research by Jasso and Rozenzweig (1986) shows that there are limits in the length of migration chains: earlier arrivals often sponsor family members, but those later arrivals sponsor subsequent migration at a much lower rate.

One likely reason that some people in countries such as the USA and the UK worry so much about chain migration is that they imagine that large proportions of people living elsewhere quite naturally want to move 'here'. Research on the immigration multiplier helps show that this notion is not well founded. Many immigrants who could become naturalized citizens do not do so (especially in the USA), and they are then not in a position to sponsor relatives in the higher preference categories such as siblings (Goering 1989). Even when immigrants are able to sponsor their relatives, they often choose not to do so – or the family member chooses not to come. Sometimes the decision to migrate via family sponsorship comes many years after such sponsorship becomes legally possible (Heinburg et al. 1989); sponsors might wait until they are in a position to offer genuine help such as a place to stay or assistance in finding a job. Some primary immigrants return home or move on to a different country (and then never sponsor anyone). One is tempted to conclude that some natives in wealthy countries are inclined to exaggerate the attractions of migration; potential migrants themselves are often more cautious: and it is worth recalling that most of the world's population never migrates internationally at all, and only about half go to the wealthiest countries.

Even so, networks and social capital do help facilitate migration and play a significant role in determining who migrates, even when legal sponsorship does not take place. Johnston et al. (2006) suggest that under conditions of globalization it has become easier to migrate without being preceded by family and friends – but chain migration certainly persists insofar as migrants continue to help those who do want to follow.

See also: *Cumulative causation; Family migration and reunification; Migrant networks; Undocumented (illegal) migration*

KEY READINGS

Boyd, M. (1989) 'Family and personal networks in international migration: recent developments and new agendas', *International Migration Review*, 23 (3): 638–70.

Goering, J.M. (ed.) (1989): 'Introduction and overview to special issue, the "explosiveness" of chain migration: research and policy issues', *International Migration Review*, 23 (4): 797–944.

Yu, B. (2008) *Chain Migration Explained: The Power of the Immigration Multiplier*. New York: LFB Scholarly Publishers.

9 Circular Migration

Definition: A pattern of regulated or unregulated mobility between two or more countries that is economically motivated, temporary and cyclical.

Circular migration has recently become popular in policy circles for its perceived potential to reduce permanent migration and promote development (see Vertovec 2007a; Newland 2009). Some states see it as a valuable policy to appease opponents of permanent immigration and to encourage economic development in the sending country via increased remittances, reduced brain drain, etc. International organizations such as the International Organization for Migration (IOM) and the Global Commission on International Migration (GCIM) of the United Nations have also embraced circular migration (see GCIM 2005; IOM 2005). However, states' views rarely if ever have taken into account the effects on migrants themselves or considered whether circular migration programmes can in fact advance the life goals of migrants. For some kinds of migrants, circular migration may go far in facilitating their trade and business activities, allowing them dual nationality or the ability to have the 'best of both worlds'. For others, circular migration is a necessary compromise where more permanent, stable migratory flows have become difficult or impossible.

Although there is no strong consensus among international organizations and states on the definition of circular migration, these flows are marked by several distinct characteristics (Newland 2009). Circular flows take place between two or more locations: a place of 'origin' and one or more destinations. They have a distinct temporal dimension, often involving short-term moves, such as seasonal movements. They can also involve longer-term moves up to a few years as for skilled, temporary workers, or life-cycle moves as with retirees, for instance. Circular flows are repetitive, involving more than one cycle between origin and destination(s). Circular flows are also meant to encourage development both for the origin and destination countries of migrants and for the migrants themselves. We might also add that circular moves are almost always economically motivated rather than for family reunification or some other primarily non-economic purpose.

Circular migration flows have existed for many centuries. Leslie Page Moch (2003) describes the circular flows of seasonal agricultural workers moving between the French highlands and Spain in the 1700s, and the Hollandsgänger since the early 1600s. The Hollandsgänger were mostly young men from Westphalia in Germany who travelled to Holland to work seasonally around capital-intensive dairy production there. They cut hay and peat, dug madder, and harvested grain on dairy farms that produced cheese for an international market. The landholdings of these Westphalians were very small (the Thirty Years Wars had decreased their landholdings substantially), allowing them to work most intensively during the summer months in Holland and then tend to their harvests back home. This North Sea system of circular migration involved almost 30,000 people by 1730 but was eventually cut short by new opportunities in the United States and in the industrial Rhine-Ruhr region.

Informal circular flows such as the Hollandsgänger were common and tolerated or encouraged for years before the implementation of strict border controls by states. Mexican agricultural workers circulated between Mexico and the United States for many years before the implementation of the Bracero programme, which provided some 4 million contracts for the temporary movement of Mexicans between 1942 and 1964 and allowed these workers to circulate back and forth between their homes and the United States according to seasonal agricultural demand. However, guestworker programmes such as the Bracero programme are not necessarily circular migration flows in the sense that they are designed only to benefit the labour needs of the destination country and even to prevent permanent settlement by migrants. The northern European guestworker programmes beginning in the 1950s were similar to the Bracero programme in not accounting for the needs or desires of the migrants themselves or for the development of the sending regions; they were created only for the economic benefits to the sponsoring countries. Nonetheless, guestworker programmes disrupted historical circular flows and made such future flows more difficult when the programmes were ended.

Circular migration is usually economically motivated and can take place under state-sponsored programmes or through informal mechanisms governed indirectly by states, employers and migrants themselves. In fact, there are relatively few state-sponsored circular migration programmes around the world. Under these programmes, states may facilitate circular migration through various types of policies such as extending voting and property rights to expatriates, easing or broadening visa requirements (e.g. raising caps or introducing multiple-entry visas), accepting dual citizenship, establishing investment incentives and information, and providing direct transportation and communication links between the countries of circulation (Newland 2009).

Circular migration has quite distinct gender patterns. Some examples of highly gendered circular flows include female caregivers for the elderly and domestics, seasonal agricultural workers (both male and female), and mostly male highly skilled IT workers. Even state-sponsored programmes have produced very gendered circular flows owing to prevailing beliefs about what constitutes men's or women's work. For instance, the Canadian Seasonal Agricultural Worker Program (SAWP) is composed almost entirely of men (95 per cent). However, in a unique case in Quebec, where only women are employed, they are essentially held hostage to the farm. Men are not allowed to enter; women must ask permission to leave; and women must be accompanied when they do leave the farm (Schwenken 2013). These conditions are quite similar to those endured by women who work as domestics in the Gulf countries. The 'kafala' sponsorship system there results in extreme dependence of women domestics on their employers. They must live in their employer's home and need their employer's permission to leave the home or to engage in non-work activities. Their inability to change employers also makes their conditions ripe for exploitation and abuse. In other less severe cases, such as Canada's Live-In Caregiver Programme, women may still be disadvantaged by taking part in circular migration schemes that call for lower skill levels and more flexible or temporary work conditions. Thus, many nurses and schoolteachers who may not meet Canada's criteria for the immigration of professionals have become part of this programme (Schwenken 2013).

Circular migration shares many features with transnationalism. Transnational migrants engage in back-and-forth movement between two or more countries to sustain their economic, political, or cultural interests and activities. They may have businesses that rely on markets or production processes located in more than one country. For instance, transnational wholesale and retail traders in the garment industry circulate between their factories in their 'home' countries and commercial markets in the 'destination' countries. Business owners in the IT sector and other related fields often locate subsidiaries in other countries or use venture capital in capital-rich destinations to fund their enterprises 'back home'. This 'brain circulation' benefits from liberal policies on trade, investment and dual nationality even when there are no formal programmes in place to govern or encourage such movement.

The majority of circular migration flows around the world, however, seem to involve mostly low-skilled domestic or service work and agricultural labour, reproduced informally through networks of migrants and the complicity or neutrality of governments and employers. Information about seasonal or temporary jobs spreads informally through the networks of circular migrants, who often support one another with short-term resources such as housing. The work circular migrants do to share information and obtain job opportunities also lowers the transaction costs of employers, who often turn a blind eye to immigration (and other) violations. In some cases, states have even become complicit in promoting informal circular migration by deregulating care work for families and the elderly, for instance. In Austria and Germany, these neo-liberal policies withdrew public programmes in favour of paying families an allowance to cover the costs of care, essentially removing the state's responsibility for providing such services. Those allowances have often gone to migrant women instead of the family members' relatives, who were initially targeted to do that work. Migrant carers often share the job of caring with friends from their countries of origin. These types of arrangements are advantageous to migrant women as they are able to send remittances and to care for their own families back home by returning for several months at a time.

Informal circular flows also tend to go hand in hand with undocumented or irregular status. Although doing so is always risky, undocumented circular migrants become adept at crossing borders illegally and often. Or, if they have entered a country legally, they might overstay their visas or make illegal crossings in future cycles. They might also be considered 'irregular' because of their economic activities in the destination. They are likely to work in the informal economy, for instance. Circular migrants, therefore, often have irregular legal status. As with other migrants, however, they are usually able to send significant remittances to their families and to provide other goods and resources on their return trips. The networks of these migrants also reduce many risks and provide crucial resources, including the very jobs circular migrants have moved to obtain. Nonetheless, circular migrants are often left vulnerable to abuse and exploitation by employers and become the targets of deportation efforts by government officials who want to show that they are 'doing something' about illegal immigration.

A healthy dose of scepticism thus seems appropriate when considering the recent promotion of circular migration schemes in immigration policy developments, especially in North America and Europe. These schemes are likely to reduce the choices of migrants (even while expanding some benefits), preventing them from accruing the years of continuous residence and/or work experience necessary to achieve long-term legal residence in most countries. This seems especially true for low-skilled workers who make up the majority if not a very large portion of circular migrants around the world. For instance, Basok's (2003) study of Mexican agricultural workers in Canada found that, although the Mexican workers clearly benefited from SAWP by gaining the ability to invest in land, businesses, children's education and health care in Mexico, their heavy dependence on employers and the programme itself made them vulnerable to abuse and reliant on it alone to fund all of their new investments. Other prospects, such as for naturalization and dual nationality, were far from the horizon of these migrants. Circular migration schemes seem to provide long-term benefits only for wealthier migrants, who are already well-positioned to reap the advantages of having a temporary presence in two or more countries.

See also: *Brain drain/gain/circulation; Chain migration; Guestworkers; Remittances; Undocumented (illegal) migration; Transnationalism*

KEY READINGS

Basok, T. (2003) 'Mexican seasonal migration to Canada and development: a community-based comparison', *International Migration*, 41 (2): 3–26.

Global Commission on International Migration (2005) *Migration in an Interconnected World: New Directions for Action*. Geneva: Global Commission on International Migration.

Moch, L.P. (2003) *Moving Europeans: Migration in Western Europe since 1650*, 2nd edn. Bloomington, IN: Indiana University Press.

Newland, K. (2009) *Circular Migration and Human Development*. Human Development Research Paper 2009/42. New York: United Nations Development Programme.

Vertovec, S. (2007) *Circular Migration: The Way Forward in Global Policy?* Oxford: International Migration Institute, University of Oxford.

10 Citizenship

Definition: A formal status denoting rights (political rights, in particular) and a more general concept for understanding social membership. Some immigrants become naturalized citizens; immigration has also transformed the meaning of citizenship itself.

For most people citizenship is understood as an identifier of national belonging, codified as a legal status and signalled by the passport one holds: 'I am a Canadian citizens.' Such belonging has complex and comprehensive ramifications, however – which means that citizenship as a concept functions at the core of several social science fields. Some conventional ways of thinking about citizenship – in particular, the ostensibly natural association between membership in a nation and the possession of a set of rights – have come under severe strain as a consequence of mass migration (e.g. Joppke 2010). In idealized understandings of the nation-state, individuals have a single, stable national membership that determines rights and constitutes identity (Gellner 1983; Castles and Davidson 2000). Large-scale immigration, however, poses a number of challenges that connect with citizenship: under what conditions can immigrants ('foreigners') become citizens? What consequences follow if immigrants can't or don't become citizens? What consequences follow when they can and do? Citizenship is also a means of exclusion (not only inclusion): lack of the relevant citizenship is, for many would-be immigrants, an insurmountable obstacle that prevents migration to the country they might choose.

Bosniak (2008) identifies four distinct components of citizenship, each with its own complexities and ambiguities (see Bloemraad et al. 2008; Jenson 2007). First, citizenship is a matter of formal legal status, as with the passport one holds (or could hold – a significant proportion of US citizens do not have one). Second, citizenship is a matter of rights – at an earlier stage, civil and political rights (e.g. to own property and to vote), and in the later Marshallian (1950) conception, social rights as well (the right to a minimal economic/material condition facilitating participation in the communal life of a society). Third, citizenship denotes active engagement or participation in democratic self-governance. In recent years, this 'participatory citizenship' has been located not just in the political sphere but in a wider range of institutions, including those conventionally considered 'private'. Fourth, citizenship has a subjective component that captures people's sense of identification and solidarity. This affective dimension helps bind members of a nation-state (typically on the basis of the common culture and language that help constitute the nation), but it also describes the ties felt by members of other types of collectivities, including some that reach beyond national borders. In all four dimensions one commonly finds distinct gender differences, with varying rights, roles and responsibilities for women vs. men (e.g. Lister 2003).

There are significant disjunctures among these four aspects of citizenship, and the disjunctures are highlighted and intensified by mass immigration, particularly in democratic countries where political legitimacy derives from the 'consent of the governed' (Bauböck 1994b). The possession and exercise of rights is not limited to those who hold citizenship as a formal status; Bosniak (2008) writes persuasively about the 'citizenship of aliens'. Non-citizens commonly have extensive (citizenship) rights, even some of the political rights that one might imagine are the distinctive preserve of (formal) citizens; with very few exceptions, non-citizens cannot vote in national elections (though in some countries they may vote in local/municipal ballots), but voting is only one political right among many and is arguably not the most important one. In addition, many natives, whose legal status affords them rights, do not exercise them, and some 'foreigners' have higher levels of actual political and civic engagement (e.g. helping with candidates' campaigns) than some status citizens – a point that extends even to undocumented immigrants, who sometimes engage in political mobilization despite insecure status and residence rights (Monforte and Dufour 2011). Immigration adds in obvious ways to the numbers of people for whom these ambiguities arise; it also extends affective identifications in ways that transcend national borders (thus transnational citizenship).

In some countries access to formal citizenship (via naturalization) is relatively easy, requiring little more than a sufficient period of legal residence, some language competence and a declaration of loyalty (as well as a typically hefty application fee). Canada, an 'immigration country' to an even greater degree than the US, actively encourages naturalization among immigrants and consequently experiences a higher rate of naturalization than in the US, where a laissez-faire approach prevails (Bloemraad 2006). Naturalization confers rights and benefits and, in the minds of many, is supposed to symbolize the achievement of a new national identity (as against a merely instrumental desire to gain the rights and benefits). States sometimes pass laws that have unintended consequences in this regard, as when the USA in 1996 reformed its welfare laws to exclude permanent residents who had not become citizens – resulting in an increase in naturalization applications (some of which no doubt did not reflect genuine adoption of a new loyalty). On the other hand, naturalization can result in the deepening of loyalties, rather than merely reflecting an already completed process (Schuck 1998).

In other settings the 'national' aspect of citizenship involves less permeable boundaries. For many years it was quite difficult for Turkish immigrants and their children to become naturalized German citizens, in part because of a more exclusive understanding of what it means to be German in a national/cultural sense (Brubaker 1992a; Nathans 2004). (This understanding was apparent by contrast in Germany's version of a 'Law of Return' extending immigration rights and easy access to citizenship to ethnic Germans in Eastern European countries.) Formal requirements for some application types are extensive (including a minimum of 15 years' residence in some cases), and even a successful application does not result in citizenship in the sense that one is accepted by the rest of the society as fully 'German'. The 1999 revisions to naturalization requirements amounted to a significant liberalization that had rapid consequences for application numbers, but the new law is more the beginning than the end of a project to reshape German citizenship in its identity sense (Nathans 2004). In some developing countries, on the other hand, acquisition of citizenship as formal status can be accomplished without naturalization as conventionally understood: the weak institutionalization of citizenship means that even undocumented/illegal immigrants manage to acquire documents that convincingly attest to formal citizenship (Sadiq 2009).

Naturalization raises the question of dual citizenship, which again challenges some core conventional notions about citizenship (Faist 2007). Again, historically citizenship was (and in many jurisdictions still is) tightly tied to a single national identity and nation-state. A significant (and varying) proportion of immigrants in most destination countries have remained outside the community of formal citizens – a situation that raised concerns about the depth of democratic governance. In some cases immigrants remained 'foreigners' because they could not satisfy the conditions for naturalization; in other contexts immigrants chose not to naturalize despite having the opportunity to do so – in part because their origin and/or destination country would have required renunciation of the origin's citizenship. These requirements have been abandoned in certain instances (e.g. Mexico in 1998), and in other countries they remain on the statute books but are not enforced (e.g. the USA); in recent years one thus sees a marked increase in naturalization applications among Mexicans in the USA.

Trends described above have led observers to offer apparently divergent conclusions about the evolution of citizenship in an 'age of migration'. In contrast to its grounding in the nation-state as conventionally understood, citizenship is sometimes said to have entered a 'post-national' phase (Soysal 1994), wherein the rights dimension of citizenship becomes detached from its (national) identity dimension. The consolidation of international human rights norms/laws (and their institutionalization in bodies such as the European Court of Human Rights) means that the rights that constitute a central aspect of citizenship are rooted in a universal notion of personhood rather than in membership of a particular nation, and in many countries formal citizenship status entails few rights not already held by permanent residents as well. Alternatively, migration leads to changes in practice that amount to a devaluation of citizenship (Jacobson 1996): when non-citizens have rights to such an extent that many are not inclined to become status citizens even when that option is available, then citizenship is no longer the defining principle of membership in nation-states – and indeed the nation-state itself is perhaps no longer a foundation for sovereignty and self-determination. These two perspectives are arguably different only in their premises; if one believes a priori that it is impossible to conceive meaningfully of citizenship without its national/identity component, then arguments such as Soysal's will appear objectionable (see Miller 2000). Both arguments can also be said to overstate the extent of recent change in citizenship practices (see Joppke 1999b).

From the perspective of immigrants (i.e., those already 'here'), citizenship is about inclusion (though some immigrants might experience 'second-class citizenship'). However, from the perspective of many non-migrants, citizenship is decidedly about exclusion (Brubaker 1992a; Shachar 2009): lacking citizenship of the country to which one would like to migrate is usually sufficient reason for that country to deny entry (not to mention permission for residence), particularly to those lacking family connections to citizens. The point can seem unremarkable because the practice seems so natural – but Shachar (2009) suggests that citizenship (i.e., of a wealthy/developed country) is akin to a valuable form of property, such that unrestricted inheritance of it (together with the migration-inhibiting consequences of that mode of transmission) is impossible to justify. Most countries grant citizenship at birth only to children who have at least one parent who is a citizen (*jus sanguinis* – as against *jus solis* laws that grant citizenship to all children born in that country's territory). This way of determining who is entitled to live in a particular country perpetuates a set of vast inequalities, and Shachar argues that if one wants to preserve the identity-sustaining component of citizenship, then its transmission via inheritance ('birthright citizenship') ought to be taxed, to redistribute some of the unearned opportunities that accrue to those born in wealthy countries and to compensate those whose migration ambitions will be frustrated by exclusions rooted in citizenship.

An extensive literature has emerged in recent years on notions of 'global citizenship' or 'cosmopolitan citizenship' (e.g. Carter 2001; Cabrera 2010). This idea is inspired in part by consideration of the impacts and implications of international migration (as well as globalization more generally). Some individuals actively embrace an identity as global citizens, and for a small cosmopolitan elite the idea can be realized in practice (in the sense that one can choose to live just about anywhere). But migration possibilities for most of the world's population remain quite restricted (whether by policy or poverty), and when most people are unable to live in much of the world outside their own national borders, the notion that they are 'global citizens' seems more than a bit dubious. Migration is typically considered the least advanced component of globalization (in comparison to trade and investment), and that point reflects some significant limits on the notion of global citizenship as well. Mass migration has had significant implications for citizenship (including its meaning for natives as well), but it is more reasonable to perceive an evolution of national citizenship rather than its demise and/or replacement.

See also: *Integration; Denizens*

KEY READINGS

Bloemraad, I. (2006) *Becoming a Citizen: Incorporating Immigrants and Refugees in the United States and Canada*. Berkeley, CA: University of California Press.

Bosniak, L. (2008) *The Citizen and the Alien: Dilemmas of Contemporary Membership*. Princeton, NJ: Princeton University Press.

Joppke, C. (2010) *Citizenship and Immigration*. Cambridge: Polity.

Sadiq, K. (2009) *Paper Citizens: How Illegal Immigrants Acquire Citizenship in Developing Countries*. Oxford: Oxford University Press.

Shachar, A. (2009) *The Birthright Lottery: Citizenship and Global Inequality*. Cambridge, MA: Harvard University Press.

11 Cumulative Causation

Definition: The process by which existing migration flows result in future flows, leading to the self-perpetuation and continuous growth of immigration from particular origins to particular destinations.

The general concept of cumulative causation was introduced by the economist Gunnar Myrdal (1957) to explain increasing economic inequalities between industrialized and developing countries. It was then adapted by Douglas Massey (1990) for the field of migration studies to explain more specifically the density and geography of migration flows. Cumulative causation has been used mainly to analyse migration flows from Mexican rural areas to the United States. But the concept has a more general scope that helps explain mechanisms of migration processes more broadly, shedding light on certain patterns of migration from Latin American countries (not only Mexico) to the USA (Fussell 2010), from China to the USA (Liang et al. 2008), and from rural to urban areas in Thailand (Curran et al. 2005; Korinek et al. 2005). One important limit of this concept, however, is that it is less relevant for explanations of migration flows originating in urban areas (Fussell and Massey 2004).

The concept of cumulative causation draws on analysis of change over time at multiple levels. It relates different socio-economic factors such as individual behaviour, household strategies and social capital to explain why a specific migration flow typically reproduces itself over time. According to this concept, the existence of a migration flow for a sufficient period of time will create the conditions for its self-perpetuation and continuous growth over time: an extended process of migration will emerge and become embedded. At the core of this process, one perceives that 'each act of migration alters the social context within which subsequent migration decisions are made, thus increasing the likelihood of additional movement' (Massey et al. 2003: 20). The alteration of this 'social context' relates to different dimensions.

First and foremost, a migration flow leads to the construction of social networks linking the migrant groups with their community (family members and friends) in the country of origin. This network facilitates the diffusion and accumulation of migration-related capital among those who remain in the origin, thus increasing the probability of their migration. This migration-related capital includes elements such as information on travel, employment or housing opportunities, and financial support after arrival; it also includes the psychological support of having social ties in the destination country. The accumulation of migration-related capital thus considerably reduces the uncertainties as well as the financial, social and psychological costs of migration. It also becomes a crucial element of household economic strategies (Massey 1990). For these reasons, the longer a migration flow is established, the larger and more diversified it will become. Initial migration flows often consist of younger men who have a relatively high level of resources, as evident in the case of immigrants moving from Mexican rural areas to the USA (Durand et al. 1999). As they became established in the destination country, individuals having a poorer socio-economic background could rely on these 'pioneers' and thus contemplate migration themselves. This process of diffusion and accumulation of social capital among the community of origin is the core mechanism of cumulative causation. It explains in particular why people in a community in which emigration has become significant will have higher probabilities of moving than those coming from a community in which emigration is rare (Massey and Espinosa 1997). It also explains why migration perpetuates itself, even when it is or has become 'illegal' (Espenshade 1995).

The concept of cumulative causation also refers to structural dimensions that affect household strategies, particularly in rural areas. Indeed, the existence of a migration flow leads to significant changes in the origin community's socio-economic structures. These changes have 'feedback mechanisms' that reinforce the factors leading to migration (Massey 1990). The way migrants tend to spend their remittances and savings can transform the organization of agrarian production and work in the region of origin (Reichert 1982). Because they have access to more resources, immigrants tend to buy more agricultural land in their region of origin (e.g. if they return). However, they farm this land less intensively than it used to be because they see the acquisition as a long-term investment. One outcome is reduced local food production, which raises its price. It also reduces opportunities for agricultural labour in the region of origin. Ultimately, as the cost of living increases and job opportunities decrease, more people emigrate, joining those who have already moved. The traditional organization of agrarian production can be transformed in other ways, but the effects are similar. Thus some (returned) migrants work the agricultural land they have acquired in their region of origin – but because they have more resources, they tend to do this using more advanced methods of production, which decreases the need for agricultural labour (Massey et al. 1987). Again, these tendencies reduce job opportunities in the region of origin and create more pressure for migration.

The concept of cumulative causation also refers to cultural and psycho-sociological dimensions, as the existence of a migration flow has cultural influences in the community of origin (Chavez 1998; Kandel and Massey 2002). Immigrants' stories about their experiences abroad often lead people in the community of origin to develop a romanticized valorization of migration. Also, the immediate family of migrants tend to become wealthier in comparison to other families, and they often buy goods intended to give the impression that they have 'made it' (Liang et al. 2008). The culture of migration can thus become quite central in this community, and migration can become a 'rite of passage' for younger members of the community (Massey 1999). Migration often exacerbates a sense of relative deprivation in the community of origin (Stark and Taylor 1989). As people hear stories about migrants' economic achievements, and as they see the material investments of those who are abroad (and/or their immediate family), they feel pressure to migrate in order to improve (or simply maintain) their own socio-economic status. Again, this process underpins a self-feeding mechanism: the more people migrate, the more a feeling of relative deprivation will arise among those who remain in the community of origin, leading ultimately to more people migrating.

Finally, although this aspect is less developed in the literature, the concept of cumulative causation also refers to macroeconomic factors that motivate immigration to a region that had hitherto mainly experienced emigration. Economic growth and the subsequent labour demand in a migrant-sending region leads to the development of an immigration inflow coming from poorer regions (often through active recruitment). This inflow tends to reinforce economic growth and thus increases labour demand, while at the same time decreasing growth and demand in the secondary origin. This is due to the fact that the individuals who migrate are generally highly productive: they are young, well endowed in social capital, and often ready to accept relatively bad working conditions (Greenwood et al. 1997). The (new) destination region thus gains a highly productive workforce, while the (new) sending region loses it. These increasing inequalities or imbalances can lead to further migration and, ultimately, to the development of a self-perpetuating and continually growing flow (Massey 1990).

Without referring explicitly to this concept, some political leaders and the media present a discourse that has affinities with the idea of cumulative causation. It is often argued that immigration brings more immigration and that immigration routes are organized through transnational social networks linking those who have already migrated with those who wish to do so. Since the mid-1970s, in a context of increasingly restrictive immigration policies, governments have tried to limit the self-perpetuating character of migration flows, in part via considerably reinforced immigration controls at the border as well as 'internal' enforcement. The effect has been to make immigration more risky for immigrants, increasing the level of migration-related capital necessary for successful migration. As is evident in the case of migrants from Fujian Province in China, however, these policies do not inhibit the diffusion and accumulation of this capital: the cumulative causation of migration continues to operate, even when immigration becomes 'illegal' and riskier (Liang et al. 2008).

Many countries have developed 'return programmes' to encourage migrants to move back to their country of origin. These programmes have had very limited effects; they certainly do not limit the self-perpetuating mechanisms of migration. Many governments try to fight against the cumulative causation of migration through policies that aim to limit changes in the socio-economic structures of immigrants' communities of origin. Thus, governments try to establish a linkage between aid/development policies and immigration controls. They often argue that immigration flows can be limited through policies catalysing the development of Southern countries, especially in rural areas. Empirical studies show however that, in fact, immigration is itself part of the development process (de Haas 2010).

See also: *Migrant networks; Chain migration*

KEY READINGS

Fussell, E. (2010) 'The cumulative causation of international migration in Latin America', *Annals of the American Academy of Political And Social Science: Continental Divides – International Migration in the Americas*, 630: 162–77.

Massey, D.S. (2010a) 'Social-structure, household strategies, and the cumulative causation of migration', *Population Index*, 56: 3–26.

Massey, D.S., Alarcón, R., Durand, J. and González, H. (1987) *Return to Aztlan: The Social Process of International Migration from Western Mexico*. Berkeley, CA: University of California Press.

12 Denizens

Definition: Immigrants who have resided in their 'destination' countries for long periods without becoming naturalized citizens but who nonetheless have substantial sets of rights.

Denizens lack citizenship but typically have secure rights of residence and cannot easily be deported. Key examples include American 'green card' holders, or those with 'indefinite leave to remain' in the UK. A more common dictionary definition of the word is simply 'inhabitants', but it now has a more developed conceptual meaning primarily as a result of the work of Tomas Hammar (1990), who observed the need for a way to describe the status of people who are not full members of the society in question but who are not exactly foreigners either. Denizens are people who have become members of and have rights in their adopted countries to a substantial extent – in other words they have gained a *degree* of citizenship – but they are not citizens in a formal status sense.

The combination of immigrants' long-term residence with lack of formal citizenship has significant implications for democratic countries. In democratic theory, the legitimacy of the state derives from the notion that the government expresses the will of the people. Mechanisms for expressing this will include the right to vote and to hold office (among other forms of political activity). These rights are sometimes imagined to be universal, though in practice there are always exceptions (e.g. children, prisoners/felons). Even so, there is indeed a historical trend towards universalization, with the progressive extension of political rights to women, the poor, particular minority groups, etc. – a trend which, however, has not included extension of national voting rights to immigrants who have not become naturalized citizens (i.e., denizens). (One can find hints of countertrends as well, e.g. in the US where measures ostensibly intended to prevent voter fraud are arguably better understood as attempts to discourage or inhibit voting by members of particular social groups.)

Denizens thus constitute a significant exception to the notion that democratic governments are (in the American expression) 'of the people, by the people…'. That phrase is indeterminate insofar as with large-scale immigration there is manifestly an ambiguity in the term 'the people'. In idealized understandings of modern nation-states, citizenship is to be congruent with membership of the nation – a point evident in the fact that 'citizenship' and 'nationality' are sometimes used interchangeably. To the extent that individuals are *not* (and do not become) members of the nation, then one might adopt the view that there is no problem when they are not included in mechanisms of democratic self-governance: they are not part of 'the people'. Few observers would worry about the lack of full political rights among people whose residence in another country is genuinely temporary, e.g. foreign students. But that perspective becomes less compelling the longer an individual lives in the country in question. In many instances (including those in which individuals were born in the 'destination'), periods of immigrants' residence are long enough to dispel any notion that these are temporary immigrants (e.g. guestworkers) who will someday return 'home'. When there are many people in this anomalous situation, it becomes a matter of concern not just for the individuals themselves but for the country as a whole: it raises questions about the quality of one's democracy and indeed about the legitimacy of the state.

The matter might resolve itself if most immigrants became naturalized citizens after a reasonable period of residence. Many immigration countries, however, continue to have large numbers of denizens. Two paths have led to this outcome. In some countries, requirements for naturalization are not prohibitive (at least for those having legal residence status) – but significant proportions of those who could become citizens do not choose to do so. In the USA in 2005, for example, only 59 per cent of those eligible for naturalization had become citizens (an increase from 48 per cent in 1995); among immigrants from Mexico, only 35 per cent of those eligible had become citizens, up from 20 per cent in 1995 (Passel 2007).

Why are some people content to remain non-citizens? One reason is that as permanent residents they already have most of the rights held by full citizens. Citizenship refers (in part) to the full set of civil, political and social rights held by members of democratic societies – and denizens hold most of those rights despite lacking citizenship in its formal status sense. They may express themselves freely, own property, travel without restriction, and even receive benefits under social welfare systems (though there are exceptions to that latter point, as in the USA under the 1996 reforms to welfare laws). In short, they are citizens to a significant extent. They lack only a subset of political rights – they cannot vote or hold office (though they can attempt to wield political influence in other ways). Some people do not care much about political participation, as when native citizens do not bother to vote, typically in double-digit percentages; a certain proportion of immigrants are no different in this respect. Their (relative) lack of citizenship is thus not a significant problem for them, though one might still make the case that it is a problem from the perspective of the society as a whole.

In other countries, the main reason many immigrants (and their children) do not become naturalized citizens is that the requirements for doing so are difficult or impossible to satisfy. These requirements express a point that operates at a deeper level: some immigrants cannot become citizens in a formal/status sense because they are not considered suitable as members of the nation. This point is particularly evident in countries where citizenship and nationality have strong ethnic dimensions, expressed in restrictive *jus sanguinis* citizenship laws: one is a citizen if one's parents are citizens. Until 1999, people lacking German ethnicity could become German citizens only with difficulty (if at all) even if they were born in Germany (i.e., to immigrant parents). The result was a large population of denizens, particularly of Turkish background – a group that included people who spoke only German, had never lived anywhere else, and who had no significant political allegiances outside of Germany. This population is now slowly diminishing following the introduction of more accessible provisions for naturalization, leading to more applications.

Political rights for denizens have evolved considerably particularly in Europe since the onset of mass immigration in the 1950s (Miller 1981). Early in this period, many countries had significant restrictions on immigrants' political activities, e.g. limiting their rights of expression and association; the passports of immigrants from the Baltic countries in Sweden were stamped with the words 'political activities are not allowed' (Hammar 1990). These restrictions were progressively eased, and in some instances governments adopted laws explicitly granting political rights, though retaining the discretion to impose limitations, e.g. on grounds of national security. In some countries governments created structures for consultation with foreign residents via immigrant associations, providing a means of representation designed to compensate for exclusion from regular political processes – though views expressed via this mechanism were not binding on those with authority to make and implement policy (Andersen 1990). By the mid-1980s, the Nordic countries and the Netherlands had extended to immigrants the right to vote and run for office in local/municipal elections after a minimum residence period – a significant step particularly in light of the fact that immigrants were (and are) highly concentrated in particular cities (Layton-Henry 1990). In most cases, however, these trends have stopped short of granting rights for participation in national elections to those who have not become naturalized citizens (one exception is New Zealand, where non-citizen immigrants can vote following three years of residence).

Denizens are excluded, then, from certain political rights associated with citizenship – to a greater extent in some countries than in others. Variation also characterizes inclusion/exclusion of denizens from the social rights of citizenship (Rosenhek 2000). In many countries settled immigrants are eligible for most if not all of the programmes and institutions that constitute the 'welfare state', e.g. unemployment insurance. This is particularly true for those with rights of permanent residence, but even illegal/undocumented immigrants can often access basic services (Joppke 1999a). A key reason for inclusion of immigrants – for not making formal citizenship a condition of eligibility – is the fact that immigrants and citizens alike pay the taxes that support these programmes. On the other hand, the welfare state does not operate according to a fiscal logic alone – it also reinforces (or is intended to reinforce) solidarity. That point raises the question: solidarity *among whom*? Some countries have adopted a more restrictive answer to that question, as when the USA in 1996 amended its welfare eligibility rules to exclude non-citizens from certain programmes, including core income support programmes (e.g. 'Temporary Assistance for Needy Families' and food stamps). Understanding the exclusion of non-citizens from welfare programmes which they nevertheless support with their taxes requires recalling that citizenship is not only a matter of rights; it is also about identity, a way of drawing the borders around 'us'. Solidarity is always bounded.

The concept of denizens is useful particularly insofar as it reminds us that citizenship is not an all-or-nothing status. Immigrants by definition begin (when they first arrive in the destination) as foreigners. But even foreigners have certain rights, and in most democratic countries one gains rights via residence, not only via formal naturalization. The extensive rights held by denizens add up to a significant degree of membership despite the absence of formal citizenship, and in this respect denizens have more in common with citizens than with foreigners. Even so, the right of permanent residence is an important precondition for this (unofficial) status, and immigrants in many categories do not achieve it (Castles and Davidson 2000). The discussion above highlights important inclusionary trends, and in some cases, e.g. Germany, the result has been a significant redefinition of the nation-state, an abandonment of an exclusively ethno-nationalist understanding of what it means to be German. But these trends are by no means universal or irreversible: some immigrants are effectively confined to a status best captured by the word 'margizens' (Martiniello 1994), though this concept as well denotes a (limited) degree of membership and rights as against complete exclusion.

See also: *Integration; Citizenship*

KEY READINGS

Cohen, R. (2006) *Migration and Its Enemies: Global Capital, Migrant Labour and the Nation-state*. Aldershot: Ashgate.

Hammar, T. (1990) *Democracy and the Nation State: Aliens, Denizens, and Citizens in a World of International Migration*. Aldershot: Avebury.

13 Deportation

Definition: The forcible expulsion of immigrants.

Most wealthy democratic countries devote significant resources trying to control immigration to their territory – allowing entry to some, excluding many, and trying to dissuade others from even attempting the trip. In many instances these efforts fail, as amply demonstrated by the presence of roughly 11 million undocumented immigrants in the USA. Governments sometimes then resort to the forcible removal of immigrants – a practice that has increased in recent years, though the number of deportations is arguably small relative to the number who could be deported. Key questions scholars have raised in relation to deportation include: why are so few people deported? Why are some people more likely to be deported than others? What is the broader significance of deportation in democratic countries?

States have a long history, extending well into the modern era, of expelling people from their territory in large numbers. An older example is the expulsion of Jews from England in 1290, and from Spain beginning in 1492. In the early modern period, a significant instance was the expulsion of the Huguenots (Protestant Christians) from France in the seventeenth century. Britain beginning in the nineteenth century used deportation as a criminal punishment, 'transporting' certain categories of criminals to Australia. Expulsions become much more numerous in the twentieth century with the consolidation of nation-states in Europe and the withdrawal of European powers from their African and Asian colonies (e.g. the 'population exchanges' of Greece/Turkey and India/Pakistan). The Nazi Holocaust certainly merits mention in this context, with forcible removal of Jews to concentration camps in neighbouring countries; in recent decades, one speaks of 'ethnic cleansing', as in Bosnia and Rwanda in the 1990s. Even so, at least in democratic countries deportation has become a much rarer practice, with the notable characteristic that it is now limited to 'aliens' (Walters 2002). One sometimes finds assertions regarding the increasing incidence of deportation, and in a limited sense those assertions are correct – but in a broader historical perspective the trend is decisively in the opposite direction.

Deportations from democratic countries in recent years have indeed increased (for UK numbers, see Bloch and Schuster 2005; for the US and Germany, Ellermann 2009). Key factors include the increase in flows of refugees and asylum seekers beginning in the 1970s, and more recent trends towards the securitization of migration, especially following the World Trade Center bombings in 2001 (Nyers 2003). Particularly in Europe, governments in the early 1970s generally abandoned guestworker recruitment, opting for more restrictive entry policies. Potential migrants typically found that asylum claims constituted their only hope of gaining entry – and receiving states took the view that many asylum seekers were in fact economic migrants and thus rejected their applications for refugee status. The result was a growing population of 'failed asylum seekers'. This is the category of immigrants that European states have attempted to deport in most instances; while undocumented immigrants of other types are often much more numerous, governments have an easier time locating asylum seekers and are more confident in knowing who they are, as they have attempted to gain secure status by submitting applications often containing genuine information (Gibney 2008).

Other types of 'illegal' immigrants are often harder to deport, even if they can be located: being 'undocumented', they are less 'legible' to governments and it is sometimes impossible to determine where to deport them *to* (Ellermann 2010).

Democratic states wishing to deport unwanted immigrants face a number of difficult constraints; again, numbers of actual deportations are much smaller than the numbers of people who could legally be deported and typically make only a small dent in the population of illegal immigrants. In some instances, immigrants are 'ordered' to leave, but many deportation orders are not actually enforced by the state (though some of course are). A key reason is that democratic states are subject to liberal norms: in most countries, the deportation process involves court hearings (at least if the individual files suit) and detention (i.e., imprisonment) under conditions that are expected to respect human rights. Deportation is therefore quite expensive (Gibney and Hansen 2003). On top of detention, the actual deportation act itself commonly requires chartering airplanes (many commercial airlines refuse to accept deportees on regular flights) to carry not only the deportees but also security staff in large quantities.

Deportation is also sometimes impeded by lack of cooperation from the country of origin. Some countries are reluctant to facilitate return of deportees (e.g. by issuing travel/identity documents) in part because they don't want to lose remittances; their citizens constitute more of an economic asset as residents of wealthy countries, and the individuals in question are often economically marginalized if they are returned as deportees. In addition, many deporting countries act unilaterally, without concern for the interests of origin countries, which sometimes are then even more inclined to obstruct deportation processes (Ellermann 2008). Even so, some countries are more effective than others in carrying out deportations: a helpful condition is the insulation from political pressures of those who carry out the actual work (Ellermann 2005, 2009). Governments have made significant institutional innovations designed to increase operational effectiveness of deportation efforts in recent years, particularly in reducing the time between apprehension and getting someone onto an airplane (reducing the need for detention and thus decreasing the involvement of the courts) (Gibney 2008). Non-democratic countries, on the other hand, are not constrained by liberal norms and are already quite effective in deporting unwanted immigrants (Ellermann 2005, 2010; Gibney 2008).

Given the great expense of deportation and its apparent ineffectiveness in reducing the size of the undocumented population (or even failed asylum seekers), one might ask: why bother with it at all? Gibney and Hansen (2003) answer that question by describing its function as a 'noble lie': non-trivial numbers of deportations (which in countries like the UK and Germany typically amount to tens of thousands annually, and roughly 400,000 in the US) enable governments to assert that they are 'doing something' about the 'problem' of illegal immigration, or at least to immunize themselves against allegations that they are doing nothing. Even if ineffective in broader terms, deportation is essential for rebutting the notion that a government has lost control of its borders (an accusation to which the UK Labour government felt particularly vulnerable in the 2000s, see Gibney 2008) or is even operating an open-admissions policy. That message might even have some influence on the choices of would-be migrants, reducing their incentives to attempt migration. In these respects deportation is primarily a symbolic act (Cohen 1997a), akin to the 'performative' nature of border technologies described by Andreas (2000) – though the deported individuals naturally experience it as rather more than symbolic.

The symbolic nature of deportation operates also at a broader 'theoretical' level. Deportation, like denial of entry, is a right of states, an exercise of their sovereignty. While the rise of human rights regimes means that even foreign individuals have rights that must be weighed against those of sovereign states, states are generally entitled as a matter of international law to determine which foreigners it considers undesirable – and to enforce those preferences, via deportation. Walters describes deportation as a 'technology of citizenship', a way of ensuring that people are 'allocat[ed] ... to their proper sovereigns' (2002: 282). In more prosaic terms, Robin Cohen summarizes the logic of deportation as: 'we know who we are by who we eject' (1997a: 354). Even so, some of the citizens in whose name deportation is carried out reject the exclusionary understanding of citizenship it embodies, campaigning against deportation of particular individuals and against the policy more generally (Anderson et al. 2011).

A significant feature of deportation processes in the US and Britain is that many of the operations involved have been 'outsourced' and amount to big business for private companies (Lahav 1998; Dow 2005). Private firms commonly operate detention centres and transport facilities, employing security staff authorized to use force. Considering the profits to be made in this line of business, Walters suggests that deportation amounts to 'human trafficking in reverse' (2002: 276). Private companies operate in this sphere with a logic different from that of governments: for a corporation such as Wackenhut, a bigger 'immigration crisis' represents a business opportunity (Dow 2005). A particular mode of anti-deportation activism has emerged in response, targeting companies whose brand is a matter of their public image: Lufthansa, for example, was dismayed by spoof ads inviting customers to fly 'deportation class' (Walters 2002). In many instances, however, the companies involved are not well known to the public; their transport vans and other facilities are unbranded and anonymous.

As a matter of law, deportation is not a punishment for crime (though conviction for other crimes by non-citizens can certainly lead to deportation). Instead it is considered an administrative action, the result of bureaucratic (or perhaps quasi-judicial) decisions that do not require the standards of evidence or legal representation necessary for criminal trials; government agencies seeking to deport people have very wide discretion, especially in the USA (Kanstroom 2007; Hing 2006). This discretion is troubling to many: deportation is a drastic act, relying ultimately on coercion and sometimes physical force (occasionally resulting in injury or even death). For migrants (even those with legal rights of residence), it is also more than the act itself – it is an ever-present possibility, a constant source of anxiety (Talavera et al. 2010).

Even more troubling is the fate of deportees once they arrive back in their country of origin. Fekete (2005) describes predictable consequences (e.g. persecution and killings) when asylum bureaucracies make incorrect determinations as to whether someone is a 'genuine' refugee. In her analyses of Salvadorans 'removed' from the USA, Coutin (2007, 2010) shows how justifications of deportation rest on a number of fictions about citizenship and nationality – mainly, the notion that 'illegal' immigrants genuinely belong in the country of origin (not in the destination) and that deportation is thus a restoration of the proper order. In reality, deportation is often experienced as a profound displacement, not only for the deported immigrants (who are sometimes treated as aliens also by their 'own' countries) but for the people with whom ties had been developed in the deporting country (Brotherton and Barrios 2011).

See also: *Undocumented (illegal) migration*

KEY READINGS

Coutin, S.B. (2007) *Nations of Emigrants: Shifting Boundaries of Citizenship in El Salvador and the United States*. Ithaca, NY: Cornell University Press.

Ellermann, A. (2009) *States Against Migrants: Deportation in Germany and the US*. Cambridge: Cambridge University Press.

Hing, B.O. (2006) *Deporting Our Souls: Values, Morality, and Immigration Policy*. Cambridge: Cambridge University Press.

Kanstroom, D. (2007) *Deportation Nation: Outsiders in American History*. Cambridge, MA: Harvard University Press.

14 Diaspora

Definition: A dispersed population across more than one territory having a durable and salient relationship (consisting of a set of claims, practices and/or loyalties) to a common origin, identity or homeland.

The term diaspora has become so popularized that it often stands in altogether for immigrants or ethnic groups. Thus, in research from the last two decades, the 'Chinese diaspora' has been virtually synonymous with 'Chinese immigrants', for instance. Indeed, the term diaspora is used in a variety of different ways and by many sorts of people (researchers, advocates, journalists, officials, development experts, etc.) who want to understand the presence and activities of immigrants and ethnic groups around the world. It has been used to designate ethnic or immigrant communities living in different countries as well as ethnic populations living in just one location, such as the 'Pakistani diaspora in England'. It has also referred to a geographically indistinct area where one finds particular groups, such as the 'Greeks of the diaspora'. It can refer to a subgroup of a larger diaspora, such as the Sephardic diaspora or the Hindu diaspora. It can refer to particular types of migration flows as well (e.g. trade diasporas of the Chinese, or slavery diasporas). One can live in a diaspora, belong to a diaspora, or even have a diasporic consciousness (see Vertovec 1999). The meanings of and references to diaspora have become so varied and wide that its definition and even its use as a concept have come into question for many scholars. Nevertheless, the concept captures some important intuitions about certain migrant groups and continues to play a key role in analysis of the way some people relate to a common origin, identity or homeland.

The historical image of a diaspora was that of the Jewish, Greek or Armenian diasporas (Safran 1991). The Jewish diaspora has been characterized by trauma and exile – initially via expulsion to Babylon and then to other parts of the world including Persia, Syria, Spain and northern Europe (and beyond). More recently, the Palestinian diaspora reflects a similar set of traumatic conditions as Palestinians have been expelled from and/or fled the new state of Israel since 1948 (Cohen 1996). The Armenian diaspora also involved enormous trauma because it originated in the displacement of those who survived massacre and genocide as the Ottoman Empire disintegrated at the beginning of the twentieth century. The African diaspora (or parts of it, anyway), another victim diaspora, stemmed from various modes of slavery, the most extensive of which was the transatlantic slave trade with the Americas, spanning more than three centuries beginning in the 1500s. The historical Greek diaspora also involved suffering, as Greeks in the colonies were separated from their mother cities as a result of Greek conquest of other ancient lands and peoples in the Near and Middle East, northern Africa and southern Europe (Baumann 2000).

Early definitions of diaspora mostly had these cases of victimhood or trauma in mind. Recognition of other types of cases, however, led to a buoyant re-conceptualization of the term beginning in the early 1990s. Ironically, many recent influential works on the subject have resisted defining the term, and there is still no real consensus on a definition. Scholars such as Robin Cohen have improved our understanding of diasporas by expanding and at the same time delimiting the term to reflect certain characteristics. In addition to victim diasporas, we can also distinguish labour diasporas, imperial diasporas, trade diasporas, and deterritorialized diasporas (Cohen 1997b). The British recruitment of indentured Indian labour in Caribbean countries (e.g. British Guiana and Trinidad and Tobago) in the 1800s after slavery was abolished created permanent settlements of Indians in those countries. By the 1970s, a substantial proportion had also begun migrating to destinations in the United States, primarily New York City. Imperial diasporas have also been extensive. The British Empire recruited Sikhs to its army, and those Sikhs joined others on voyages across Britain's imperial sites as part of Queen Victoria's diamond jubilee celebrations in 1897. When they reached western

Canada, many Sikhs stayed there, though some eventually crossed into the US after being run out of their homes by racist, nativist groups. In California, their reception was often not much better; nonetheless, many Sikhs made their home there for several generations. These two examples demonstrate the enormous historical variation that can exist within just one 'diasporic' group, the so-called Indian diaspora. By the same token, the notion of a single Indian diaspora makes little sense, as we can see in these examples.

Trade diasporas have also long been considered significant. The Chinese, Lebanese, Indians and Armenians, among many others, have all had significant trading and merchant groups in their populations that have spread across many parts of the world in pursuit of commercial activities. Deterritorialized diasporas have included examples such as Parsis, who originated in Persia and are believed to have migrated to India around the eighth century CE. Today, they still present a distinct ethnic and religious identity in Indian society, even though they have also been well integrated and suffer little discrimination. The Kurds offer a contemporary example of a deterritorialized diaspora with a presence in several countries including Iran, Iraq and Turkey. Many Kurds retain a collective identity that refers to their common origins if not a common homeland; some also sustain a desire for a new homeland or state.

Although all of these delineations of diaspora have been important, we still face the critical question of whom to count as part of the various diasporas. Answers to this question in the various definitions of the term range widely. Some observers are willing to include virtually everyone who can be claimed as part of a particular group or population, usually by virtue of ancestry. Thus, we think of the Chinese or Irish diasporas, in which everyone of Chinese or Irish ancestry living in any part of the world belongs. Such an all-inclusive definition seems too broad and of little analytical use, as it essentially equates diaspora with immigrant groups using national identity as a signifier. How then would we distinguish between different groups of Indians in the 'Indian diaspora' – for instance, those Sikhs who seek a separate homeland as against those Hindu Indians who claim that India is the homeland of Hindus only? Or, what is the difference between Chinese traders and Chinese labour migrants? Can they be considered to have a shared identity if only because their place of origin and nationality suggest it? And what of the Kurds who do not want a new homeland or state? Are they part of a Kurdish diaspora? Notwithstanding multiple axes of difference, such as class, gender, and so on, who counts?

In trying to answer that question, it helps to distinguish the term diaspora from other terms commonly used in migration studies and to reflect on the multiple ways in which diaspora is experienced, understood and constructed within a particular group (see Anthias 1998; Brah 1996; Kalra et al. 2005). For instance, diaspora has often been intertwined with the concept of transnationalism in discussions of immigrants. However, the terms can be distinguished by their scope, the kinds of actors they involve and the identity of those who constitute the 'diaspora' or 'transnational community'. First, transnationalism is a broader concept than diaspora (Faist 2010). Diaspora implies bounded communities, or communities in which the maintenance of boundaries is important, while transnationalism and transnational groups or 'communities' are in principle much broader in scope with more porous boundaries. Second, the membership of a diaspora is generally more limited to ethnic or religious groups that actively understand themselves as a community. Some researchers have also called for other forms of identity to be counted as intrinsic to the diaspora concept, as ethnic groups often contain multiple cleavages and experiences binding people together (see Anthias 1998; Brah 1996; Kalra et al. 2005). Third, diasporas suggest a relatively cohesive identity related to the experience of dispersal, especially in the case of traditional diasporas whose dispersal emerged from collective trauma, victimization or violence. The nation, country or state to which the diaspora group refers itself is an important actor (along with so-called diaspora organizations promoted by the state or by representatives of the diaspora), as is the host country (or countries) where the diaspora population is located (see Brah 1996; Dufoix 2008; Kalra et al. 2005). Transnationalism, in contrast, involves a much broader range of actors that may include all those we see in diasporas as well as all sorts of other organizations, e.g. businesses – but without necessarily involving a collective identity or purpose that binds those actors together. With transnationalism there may be multiple networks of individuals and organizations transcending international boundaries that operate separately and perceive themselves as separate from one another. They may also overlap but even so not maintain a collective character. Thus, the concept of migrant networks is more relevant to transnationalism than to diaspora; for the latter a collectivity is usually more apparent and is often a basis of mobilization. Diasporas also tend to persist across generations (Faist 2010); in comparison, transnationalism may refer to contemporary or historical migrations, which often exist separately or may be linked together.

Still, answers to the question of whom to count remain vague and sometimes unsatisfying. How do we know whether someone is part of a diaspora? The difficulty of answering that question has led some to claim that it is fruitless to define the term concretely, though most believe it should be preserved (Brubaker 2005; Dufoix 2008). Brubaker (2005) argues that diaspora should refer instead to a category of practice in which people make claims, form projects, mobilize for those projects, and appeal to loyalties to advance those claims or projects. In this way, diaspora is not simply about the dispersal of a population from its origins or even the maintenance of a collective identity. Diaspora, according to Brubaker, is much more like a stance, idiom or practice that people adopt in their claims and projects vis-à-vis their homeland, community of origin, or 'referent-origin' (to use Dufoix's term).

The term 'referent-origin' avoids the error of assuming that national identities are the primary collective identities diasporas link to or engage with (Dufoix 2008). Dufoix also avoids defining the term diaspora in his recent treatise, *Diasporas*. Like Brubaker, he understands diaspora more as an idiom or stance used in a project or set of claims. He also sharpens our understanding of diaspora by describing four ideal types that structure the experience of diaspora.

These are the centroperipheral, enclaved, atopic and antagonistic modes (Dufoix 2008). Though they surely sound abstract, the four modes of diaspora experience illustrate the different ways a group can relate to its referent-origin. In the centroperipheral mode, a national group in a host country is closely linked with the group's 'home' country through official institutions (e.g. cultural centres and embassies) and the voluntary associations of the overseas group. This is perhaps the most common notion of a diaspora. The enclaved mode refers to a local organization of a community within a host country, such as those often found in urban neighbourhoods. Here, shared identity is more important than nationality. The atopic mode is a mode of experience between states; it implies a presence and circulation in many places around the world rather than in particular host countries of (permanent) immigrants. One might think here of transnational entrepreneurs, such as the Chinese entrepreneurs Aihwa Ong (1999) describes, who regularly shuttle across many different sites as part of their everyday commercial pursuits. The atopic mode most closely resembles a network rather than a link to a specific territory. Finally, the antagonistic mode resembles what Dufoix refers to as an 'exile polity'. This is a political space formed by groups who mobilize in opposition to the current regime of their country of origin. This group wages its war from outside the country of origin that it seeks to liberate (or be liberated from).

These four modes of experience show that diasporas are structured around different forms of relationships: the relationship to an existing regime/country, the relationship to a referent-origin or community (as against the corresponding state), and the spatial relationship between individuals, groups and communities. Dufoix succeeds in foregrounding the political relationships of diasporas and shows that diasporas can orient themselves *against* current state regimes or national identities as well as belong to them. He also indicates that the spatial range of diaspora experience can exist as if on a continuum from the most local, territorialized level (the enclaved mode) to a distinctly non-territorial level (the atopic mode). Dufoix's reworking of the diaspora concept results in a concise and profound way to conceptualize the experience of diaspora, even if a robust definition still remains elusive.

See also: *Ethnicity and ethnic minorities; Migrant networks; Transnationalism*

KEY READINGS

Brubaker, R. (2005) 'The "diaspora" diaspora', *Ethnic and Racial Studies*, 28 (1): 1–19.

Cohen, R. (1997b) *Global Diasporas: An Introduction*. London: UCL Press.

Dufoix, S. (2008) *Diasporas*. Berkeley, CA: University of California Press.

Faist, T. (2010) 'Diaspora and transnationalism: what kind of dance partners?', in R. Bauböck and T. Faist (eds), *Diaspora and Transnationalism: Concepts, Theories and Methods*. Amsterdam: Amsterdam University Press, pp. 9–34.

Safran, W. (1991) 'Diasporas in modern societies: myths of homeland and return', *Diaspora*, 1 (1): 83–99.

15 Displacement and Internally Displaced Persons

Definition: Displacement involves the obligatory or forced movement or removal of individuals or populations from their usual residence to another place within their national territory. Internally Displaced Persons (IDPs) are such persons as recognized by the United Nations and international organizations (both governmental and non-governmental) even though IDPs do not have international status as such.

The number of internally displaced persons around the world has been rising fast. As of 2011, 26.4 million people around the world were internally displaced (far exceeding the 15.2 million refugees); the number of *newly* displaced people in that year was 20 per cent higher than in 2010 (UNHCR 2011). Colombia had the highest number of displaced persons in the world, with at least 3.9 million persons, followed by Iraq, Sudan, Congo and Somalia. The recent uprisings and revolutions in the Middle East and North Africa have also resulted in massive displacement in those countries (particularly in Syria). The ongoing wars and political conflicts there are the most obvious cause of displacement and, conventionally, wars and conflict have been considered the only or most important causes of displacement. Recent thinking, however, has begun to recognize a much broader array of causes for displacement, including environmental disaster and change (natural and human-made), development (such as the harnessing of natural resources by states and corporations), urbanization, and economic vulnerability and threat.

Although the concept of internal displacement has come to be widely understood and used in international discourse about migrants, refugees and asylum seekers, it has also become increasingly clear that the conditions of IDPs are highly complex and that there are broad grey areas between them and other types of migrants who have crossed international borders. Initial attempts to distinguish between refugees (who are protected by a United Nations legal mandate in the 1951 Refugee Convention) and internally displaced persons were evident in the UNHCR's 1992 definition of displacement, which referred to

> persons or groups who have been forced to flee their home suddenly or unexpectedly in large numbers, as a result of armed conflict, internal strife, systematic violations of human rights or natural or man-made disaster, and who are within the territory of their own country. (Mooney 2005: 10)

The 1992 definition, however, was perceived as being too narrow in not capturing displacements that were protracted rather than spontaneous and among persons who were obliged to leave their homes as well as those who may have fled quickly. Thus, in 1998 the *Guiding Principles on Internal Displacement* established the category of internally displaced persons as

> persons or groups of persons who have been forced or obliged to flee or to leave their home or places of habitual residence, in particular as a result of or in order to avoid the effects of armed conflict, situations of generalized violence, violations of human rights or natural or human-made disasters, and who have not crossed an internationally recognized State border. (Mooney 2005: 11)

This definition expanded the time frame in which persons may become displaced, and accounted for sudden border changes common to situations of war and conflict. These amendments also captured some of the complex realities of the internally displaced. Internally displaced persons may flee or be obliged to leave their homes not only because of sudden war and conflict in the area where they usually live, but also because of protracted conflicts in which threats to their lives or livelihoods may change over the course of conflict. The new *Guiding Principles* also stress that IDPs may be fleeing or have been forced to flee their usual place of residence, which acknowledges that many may no longer have their own homes or a permanent place to which they can return. This condition might be most common for urban residents who have been forcibly evicted from their usual place of residence.

Colombia has well-known and long-standing examples of such evictions. For some thirty years of 'development' in the area, residents of Chapinero Alto in Bogotá have been undergoing forced eviction, usually without warning, compensation or adequate relocation (Everett 1999). The expansion of the city of Bogotá as well as rehabilitation of neglected neighbourhoods has required additional infrastructure and housing, making areas like Chapinero Alto (with its prime location) a victim of 'development' needs. Forced evictions have occurred equally in rural areas like Huila to make room for projects such as the El Quimbo hydroelectric dam. Protest and demonstrations have accompanied these evictions, though to little effect. One interesting and unfortunate consequence of these contentious politics is that the discourse on dislocation and development has connected to the notion of sustainability, with many local governments claiming that poor people stand in the way of environmental preservation and sustainable development when they protest eviction.

Sudden border changes also create complex realities for IDPs or those about to be internally displaced. Borders are meant, in part, to signal belonging and protection as long as one is located within them; here lies one of the distinguishing characteristics of a displaced person as opposed to refugees and asylum seekers (often grouped with displaced persons). Sudden border changes can literally and quickly define whether one might become a refugee or asylum seeker or remain an IDP (whether recognized as such or not). In cases like this, such distinctions are not meaningful, a point that is not lost on many humanitarian workers. For instance, the head of a delegation of the International Committee of the Red Cross (ICRC) in Khartoum, Sudan, facetiously asked: 'Excuse me, are you an IDP, a refugee, or a migrant? Are you a victim of conflict or another situation of violence? Oh, you are a nomad. Are you migrating because of conflict or because it is your way of life?' (ICRC 2009). His questioning, typical of the kinds of distinctions humanitarian workers must make on a daily basis, underscores the limitations and fuzziness of many migration concepts compared with the overwhelmingly complex realities that make up people's lives. Of course, from a human rights perspective, it is exceedingly apparent that such distinctions are quite irrelevant. On the other hand, the conceptual distinctions, particularly between IDPs and refugees, signal what Francis Deng (who, along with Roberta Cohen, has probably done the most at the United Nations to expose the plight of internally displaced people and to develop normative practices within the international community for dealing with them; see Cohen and Deng 1998) refers to as the 'paradox of national protection' and the difficulties inherent in the principle of sovereignty in the international state system.

Thus, although the concept of internal displacement has many similarities with and is much broader than the concept of refugee, the distinction is one that depends entirely on the notion of state sovereignty and the political construction of the state system. The term internally displaced person or IDP does not carry any special legal status as does the term 'refugee'. Here we are confronted with the tension between state sovereignty and the international human rights regime. In principle, IDPs have not lost the protection of their own country and might not be of international concern as long as their needs can be met by their own governments. However, in most instances, this is manifestly not the case, and we would struggle to believe that governments of countries in which individuals and populations have been internally displaced will treat the displaced with the full range of citizenship rights that they should be afforded. Many governments are in fact the perpetrators of violence that results in displacement in the first place. On the other side of the coin: if IDPs are denied protection and aid by their own governments, which is more commonly the case, then they may indeed become objects of concern to the international community.

Although there is no international legal sponsor for IDPs (the UN has no legal mandate concerning IDPs) and no international legal framework for them (see Weiss 2003), some international organizations and non-governmental organizations (NGOs) have incorporated assistance to IDPs into their mission and mandate. Even so, for most organizations, such as the UNHCR and ICRC, their mandate focuses almost exclusively on displacement that results from war or protracted conflict, even if they also acknowledge the broader definition as articulated in the *Guiding Principles*. Global statistics on IDPs or displaced persons also tend to count only those who have been displaced as a result of violence or protracted conflict. Displacement owing to environmental disaster (whether natural and man-made) or development is more difficult to account for when so many organizations do not focus their attention and services on those affected persons.

Women, children and the elderly constitute the populations most affected by displacement, and many of the pressing issues related to displacement are specific to these populations (Mooney 2005). Forced from their homes and lacking in the most basic protections and resources, displacement endangers their ability to survive and to help their families survive. The losses of the displaced include not only material goods but also social networks composed of family, friends and community, not to mention cultural heritage and a sense of belonging. Under these circumstances, social relationships break down and the displaced are often forced to fend for themselves. When this happens, they also become vulnerable to violence and abuse by an array of others, including other civilians, even, sadly, humanitarian workers whose role is to help them. The constant need for shelter and food often creates such exploitative conditions for women and children that they sometimes resort to previously unimaginable acts to survive. High rates of prostitution and sexual exploitation are common and lead to severe problems with health, especially sexual health. Women and children are also vulnerable to trafficking for sex and forced labour. Children have been forcibly recruited from IDP camps to become soldiers in internal wars and conflicts (Achvarina and Reich 2006). Suicide rates in IDP camps are also higher than national averages, as are death rates in general from malnutrition, disease and despair.

Although IDPs in many ways are not (or should not be) distinguishable from refugees and asylum seekers, one nagging question more specific to IDPs than to others who are forcibly displaced is: When do IDPs stop being IDPs? Because the status of an IDP is not a legal one, there is no clear way to determine when and under what conditions that category no longer applies. Are they no longer displaced when they are able to return 'home' or to the place they lived before being displaced? Safe return is often not possible for most IDPs, not only because of protracted conflicts that may span generations but also because their 'homes' might no longer physically exist or might have become occupied by others. Do they stop being IDPs when they are relocated into sufficient, permanent housing? How should we consider the loss of their former homes, communities and cultural environments? Furthermore, who decides when IDPs stop being IDPs – governments, international agencies? Governments may hasten to declare that IDPs are no longer displaced in order to demonstrate that internal conflicts have ended. Or they may maintain IDPs in displacement camps and other difficult conditions for longer than necessary, out of continuing discrimination or oppression of certain populations. The plight of IDPs remains extraordinarily complex and difficult, most unfortunately for the internally displaced themselves.

See also: *Borders; Forced migration; Internal/domestic migration; Refugees and asylum seekers*

KEY READINGS

Cohen, R. and Deng, F.M. (1998) *Masses in Flight: The Global Crisis of Internal Displacement.* Washington, DC: The Brookings Institution.

Deng, F.M. (2006) 'Divided nations: the paradox of national protection', *Annals of the American Academy of Political and Social Science*, 603: 217–25.

ICRC (International Committee of the Red Cross) (2009) *Internal Displacement in Armed Conflict: Facing up to the Challenges*. Geneva: ICRC.
Mooney, E. (2005) 'The concept of internal displacement and the case for internally displaced persons as a category of concern', *Refugee Survey Quarterly*, 24 (3): 9–26.

16 Ethnic Enclaves and Ethnic Economies

Definition: Ethnic economies consist of businesses or sectors that are dominated by members of particular immigrant/ethnic groups. There are two main types: an ethnic ownership economy (with ethnic enclave economies as a variant or subtype) and an ethnic-controlled economy.

In most metropolitan areas, we have become accustomed to seeing certain ethnic or immigrant groups having a concentrated presence in specific neighbourhoods, running businesses (usually small ones) in certain industries, or holding particular types of jobs in large numbers. These are ethnic enclave economies, such as Chinatowns, Greektowns and Koreatowns, Little Italies and Indias, where entrepreneurs from specific ethnic or immigrant groups have established businesses catering to a mostly co-ethnic clientele and employing mostly co-ethnic family, friends and others in a geographically concentrated area. Ethnic enclave economies are a type of ethnic ownership economy. Ethnic ownership economies need not be physically dense or concentrated in the way that ethnic enclave economies are. However, like ethnic enclave economies, they include ethnic owners and their co-ethnic workers, though the clientele can include native-born people as well as co-ethnics. For example, the many Vietnamese nail salons we see in New York City or 'nail bars' in East London are part of an ethnic ownership economy made up of co-ethnic employers and employees – but they are not part of an ethnic enclave as they serve a largely non co-ethnic clientele.

Ethnic-controlled economies, the other main type of ethnic economy, can be more difficult to see, because, rather than having a significant ownership component, a particular industry can come to be dominated by ethnic or immigrant groups without their 'owning' it. Some ethnic groups, for instance, can be found in such large numbers in the public sector (which they obviously do not own) that they have significant influence over hiring, wages or the course of everyday business. For instance, Indian medical doctors in the USA and UK form an ethnic occupational niche that began with intensive recruitment of Indian medical personnel in the 1950s in the UK and the 1960s in the US. Today, Indian doctors in the US constitute about 4 per cent of all medical doctors; some own their own practices, but many work in public hospitals and large corporate-owned health care organizations (Poros 2011). In the UK, where the government operates most health care via the National Health Service (which recruited Indian doctors heavily), they also constitute a significant portion of doctors (Robinson and Carey 2000).

Ethnic ownership economies emerge from the activities of at least two kinds of ethnic entrepreneurs: middleman minorities and enclave entrepreneurs. Middleman minorities were identified in the early literature on ethnic economies in the pioneering work of Edna Bonacich (1973) but can be attributed to earlier work by Max Weber (2003 [1927]). Middleman minorities are distinctive in that they occupy an intermediate position between a dominant and subordinate ethnic group or between the elite and the masses of a society. Historically, traders, merchants and other intermediaries, such as rent collectors, brokers and moneylenders, occupied this middle ground and were often subject to inter-ethnic conflict because of their privileged position relative to the masses who were subordinated by the elite. Indian merchants and traders, for example, were middleman minorities in colonial East Africa and were privileged by British colonials against the native African populations. Their privileges were not only economic, but also political and social, for instance extending to the educational systems that segregated African, Indian and European children in schools (Gregory 1993).

Many contemporary examples of middleman minorities exist as well. Korean businessmen in blighted urban neighbourhoods, such as Harlem in New York (i.e., those parts of Harlem that haven't undergone gentrification), are middleman entrepreneurs occupying an intermediate position between the local African-American and Latino populations that dominate the area and the largely white elite in American society (see Min 2008). A well-known instance of inter-ethnic conflict occurred in the Los Angeles riots in 1992, when 2,000 Korean stores were ransacked, looted and destroyed as the more impoverished African-American population reacted to the acquittal of four white police officers who had beaten a black motorist (Rodney King). Koreans got caught in the middle of this class and race warfare; local hostilities between Korean shop-owners and African-American residents had been growing, in part over the death of an African-American woman who was shot and killed by a Korean storeowner. The LA riots are one of the most severe examples of such inter-ethnic conflict involving middleman minorities in recent history. But there are many examples of conflict and unrest between middleman minorities and the native populations in the US and other countries around the world; other instances include Chinese middlemen in Malaysia and (historically) Jewish middlemen in Europe.

Enclave entrepreneurs are different from middleman minorities in that they operate their businesses in geographically concentrated areas where other co-ethnics live and work. Ethnic enclaves are often 'institutionally complete' (Breton 1964) and provide the full range of products, services and institutions needed by a community. Visit almost any Chinatown and you will find Chinese restaurants, groceries, clothing, furniture, books, music, health care providers, schools, banks, accountants, lawyers, and real estate and insurance agents. These neighbourhoods can fulfil all of the needs of the ethnic population that lives there, and enclave entrepreneurs are central to these full-service communities.

Ethnic ownership economies can operate in formal, informal or illegal spheres of the broader economy. The formal sector of an ethnic ownership economy includes those businesses that produce or sell legal goods or services, pay taxes and are registered with and regulated by public authorities. The informal sector contains businesses that produce or sell legal goods or services, but they may not pay taxes or have the required licences. The illegal sector of the economy involves the production or sale of illegal goods or services, such as gambling or narcotics. Its participants obviously also seek to escape notice by legal authorities.

The formal, informal and illegal sectors of ethnic economies do not exist independently of each other. Self-employment and employment in ethnic ownership economies are understood to result from disadvantages in the dominant labour market and in resources. Immigrants or minorities who find themselves unemployed because of discrimination or other factors, such as a lack of language skills, might turn to self-employment as a solution. Some immigrants or minorities are also disadvantaged in their access to crucial resources, sometimes as a legacy of historical discrimination. They lack broad resources – such as financial capital, social connections and cultural skills – necessary to start one's own business. Those immigrants and minorities, who are doubly disadvantaged in the labour market and by lack of resources, often turn to the informal and illegal sectors of an ethnic ownership economy to make a living (Light and Gold 2000). Employment in ethnic businesses is often also seen as double-edged, in that it can provide needed employment to immigrants and minorities who are disadvantaged in the dominant labour market but also can involve exploitative labour practices and tenuous work conditions (especially in the informal and illegal sectors of the economy).

Although employment in the ethnic ownership economy is often portrayed as a solution to unemployment or underemployment, some ethnic businesses are connected to brain drain or brain circulation processes, and they sometimes involve people who do not readily appear to be experiencing disadvantages. Roughly one-third of businesses in Silicon Valley (California) are owned by Taiwanese and Indians, and these often employ highly skilled immigrants possessing many of the requisite resources to move into self-employment (Saxenian 1999). Many entrepreneurs in these groups have now expanded their businesses to Taiwan and India, becoming transnational entrepreneurs in a lucrative ethnic ownership economy.

The social ties or networks of immigrants and ethnic minorities are crucial for employment in the ethnic ownership and ethnic-controlled economies. Immigrants need social capital to become self-employed or employed in an ethnic economy. Social capital refers to one's ability to gain access to valued resources and benefits as a member of a social network (Portes 1998, 2000). It is the mechanism for obtaining loans from family, friends or other co-ethnics to start a business or for access to information about jobs. In ethnic ownership economies, social capital helps entrepreneurs to develop a customer or client base for their businesses. Social capital can be essential for creating additional human capital – the knowledge, skills and experience one needs to operate a business or to be employed in one. Social capital can help generate financial capital; an example is found in rotating credit associations, where members of a group (often of the same ethnicity) establish an association in which they pool capital and take turns loaning out money to each member of the group. As each member of the group contributes to the pool and receives and then pays back their loan, the pool becomes bigger, allowing for ventures on a larger scale than one could possibly accomplish as an individual investor or borrower. Rotating credit associations are a prime example of how social capital can facilitate entrepreneurship in an ethnic economy.

Immigrants have often been associated with urban regeneration and economic revitalization because of their high rates of entrepreneurship. Although there are exceptions, immigrants generally have a higher rate of entrepreneurship than natives in many cities in the US and Europe. One of the pressing questions about ethnic entrepreneurship and ethnic economies concerns the future of these businesses. Will the children of immigrants – the second generation – inherit and continue operating the businesses of their parents? Recent research in the US by Philip Kasinitz and his colleagues (2008) suggests that many in the second generation will diverge from the path of their parents as they pursue economic interests that are part of the more general economy. These second-generation children are, after all, more integrated into American society than their parents and can better navigate the broader range of opportunities open to them. In Europe, too, many children of immigrants might not take on their parents' businesses – though recent research also indicates that some immigrant children, for instance in the Netherlands, have moved into more non-traditional sectors such as the ICT (information communication technology) industry or FIRE (finance, insurance and real estate) (Baycan-Levent et al. 2008). For the second-generation children who do continue to experience labour market disadvantage, however, employment in ethnic ownership economies might turn out to be a much better solution to labour market disadvantage than it has been for their parents.

See also: *Brain drain/gain/circulation; Ethnicity and ethnic minorities; Social capital; Second generation; Transnationalism*

KEY READINGS

Bonacich, E. (1973) 'A theory of middleman minorities', *American Sociological Review*, 38 (5): 583–94.

Light, I.H. and Gold, S.J. (2000) *Ethnic Economies*. San Diego, CA: Academic Press.

Min, P.G. (2008) *Ethnic Solidarity for Economic Survival: Korean Greengrocers in New York City*. New York: Russell Sage Foundation.

Portes, A. (1998) 'Social capital: its origins and applications in modern sociology', *Annual Review of Sociology*, 24: 1–24.

Weber, M. (2003 [1927]) *General Economic History*. Mineola, NY: Dover Publications.

17 Ethnicity and Ethnic Minorities

> *Definition: Ethnicity is an identification based on presumed shared characteristics, such as common ancestry, physical resemblance, language, religion, nationality, territory or historical experience. Ethnic groups involve boundaries or groupings of people who are perceived by others or see themselves as sharing the same identity or culture.*

The term ethnicity derives from the Greek word *ethnos*, which can be translated as 'nation', 'people' or 'tribe'. It entered Latin in its adjectival form as *ethnicus*, meaning 'heathen' or 'pagan', thus referring to those who did not share the cultural attributes of the dominant group. The term *ethnic* entered the English language in the Middle Ages. It designated the 'others' – those who were neither Christians nor Jews, those 'who were not us' (Petersen 1981). Despite this ancient etymology, it is only recently that the term ethnicity started to be used in common language; it was added to the *Oxford English Dictionary* in 1972 (Ibrahim 2011). Today, in many Western societies, the word is often used to refer in a euphemistic way to non-white people as a whole. However, in the USA and the UK, 'ethnic' and 'ethnicity' also refer to the various ancestral or pre-migration backgrounds of whites, while non-whites are often described in terms of race. Also, interestingly, the term is more often used as an adjective (ethnic group, ethnic food, ethnic conflict, etc.) than as a noun. Ethnicity is thus an identification used to qualify a group, an activity or a phenomenon (music, food conflict, etc.) rather than to name it.

It is also relatively recently that ethnicity became a central concern in the social sciences. Max Weber proposed an initial definition of ethnicity in *Economy and Society* (1968 [1922]). In the 1920s and 1930s, many scholars belonging to the Chicago School investigated immigrants' integration in American cities via analyses that focused on ethnicity. It was only in the 1960s and 1970s that ethnicity emerged as a field of research in its own right, first in North America and then in Europe. This focus coincided with the resumption of mass migration, which had slowed considerably in the USA from 1924 until the mid-1960s. The 1924 Immigration Act used eugenicist justifications to severely restrict the entry of immigrants from unwanted origins, primarily southern and eastern Europe, such as Italians, Greeks and Jews, who at the time were considered separate races (e.g. 'Mediterraneans', 'Slavs', 'Hebrews', etc.) (Jacobson 1999). At best, that period's racist ideology, based largely on eugenics, suggested that immigrants and subsequent generations from those origins would need several decades to assimilate. The ultimate atrocity rooted in eugenics was, of course, the Nazi Holocaust. Thus, after World War II, scholars and international institutions began to challenge eugenicist ideas and racist ideologies more directly, and it became clear that more nuanced approaches to the issues of ethnic relations were needed. Thus, in 1950, UNESCO produced its famous statement on 'The Race Question', arguing that 'national, religious, geographic, linguistic and cultural groups do not necessarily coincide with racial groups', and concluding that 'it would be better when speaking of human races to drop the term "race" altogether and speak of "ethnic groups".'[1]

The increased prominence of ethnicity in the social sciences is connected to the observation that ethnicity was increasingly persistent as a strong form of identification – rather than disappearing through assimilation as some had expected (Glazer and Moynihan 1963). Indeed, ethnicity has become an increasingly significant category of identification across societies in recent decades because it has come to replace earlier notions of race in many ways – particularly since the 1980s and 1990s, as identification in terms of social class has become less salient. In this period, observers began using terms like 'ethnic conflicts' or 'ethnic mobilizations' to explain divisions and episodes of violence in industrialized countries (also in some developing ones). A great deal of research on ethnicity stems from the perception of a 'collapse of assimilationism' (Cornell and Hartman 2007) and tries to explain why ethnic identifications are resilient or even resurgent.

One of the many persistent debates about ethnicity since the end of World War II is between the primordialist and social constructionist perspectives (addressing both race and ethnicity). Primordialism emerged in the 1960s and viewed ethnicity as a 'basic group identity' (Isaacs 1975). Proponents of the primordialist perspective, such as Pierre van den Berghe, argued that ethnicity is essentially a biological or natural characteristic of peoples. Others associated with the perspective, such as Edward Shils and Clifford Geertz, argue that ethnic ties reflect an attachment that is deeply embedded in our minds and in social interactions; ethnicity is assumed to be a 'given' – something one is born with – and is perceived by the ethnic group itself to be primordial and essentially unchanging. Ethnic identification is therefore seen as natural and enduring (McKay 1982).

The primordialist approach has been rightly criticized because it fails to consider that the intensity and nature of ethnic identifications can change across time and contexts. New forms of ethnic identities can also emerge. This is quite obvious for example in the case of Latinos (or Hispanics) in the United States, an identity that brings together immigrants coming from a variety of different contexts (Oboler 1995; Padilla 1985). Other identities can fade and eventually disappear, or they can become 'symbolic ethnicities': 'A love for and pride in a tradition that can be felt without having to be incorporated in everyday behaviour' (Gans 1979: 205). This is, for example, the case of German immigrants' descendants in the USA (Kamphoefner 1987) and of Italian immigrants' descendants in France. Finally, ethnic identities that seem latent can gain salience and become stronger, such as in the case of Afrikaners in South Africa in the twentieth century (Thompson 1985). These shifts can sometimes happen rapidly, through a dynamic of 'identity cascade' (Laitin 1998).

To explore the shifting nature of ethnic boundaries, a second approach, known as 'instrumentalism', emerged in the 1960s and 1970s – drawing on assumptions rooted in the social constructionist perspective. According to authors such as

Glazer and Moynihan (1963), Avner Cohen (1974), and Patterson (1977), ethnic identity is a resource used by social groups to advance their own interests, in a context marked by competition for resources and power. Ethnicity thus 'is fundamentally a political phenomenon' (Cohen 1974: 97); it is a medium used for the defence and advancement of group interests, and it can be manipulated (and thus is not fixed, as imagined by the primordialists). Instrumentalists therefore emphasize the power relations leading to the creation and recreation of identities (Nagel, 1994) and look in particular at the circumstances that shape these dynamics. Thus, in a classic study, Roosens (1989) argued that the mobilizations of ethnic groups were related to the construction of the welfare state and race policies in the USA: 'ethnic groups emerged so strongly because ethnicity brought people strategic advantages' (Roosens 1989: 14). From a similar perspective, Waters (1999) showed that Black Caribbean immigrants living in the USA could adapt their identity depending on its strategic utility in different settings: they could emphasize a belief in a common ancestry with African-Americans in some circumstances but identify themselves as a culturally distinct group in other circumstances.

Today, most researchers agree that, as with any form of identification that defines a community, ethnicity and ethnic groups are indeed social and cultural constructions (Anderson 1983). Ethnicity is viewed as the result of social interaction dynamics, and ethnic identities are therefore flexible (Barth 1969; Nagel 1994). To illustrate this idea of flexibility, Handelman (1977) focuses on the organization of ethnicity and proposes a typology of ethnic 'incorporation'. He thus makes a distinction between ethnic categories, networks, associations and communities. More generally, constructed ethnicity is at the intersection of two key processes of identity: how people categorize themselves and how they are categorized by outsiders. It is therefore a process of classification, a 'cognition', rather than something that can be objectively identified: it 'is fundamentally not a thing *in* the world, but a perspective *on* the world' (Brubaker et al. 2004: 32). This process works in and through common-sense knowledge, symbols, schemas, public ceremonies, elite discourses, organizational routines and private interactions (Brubaker 2004).

State institutions commonly use ethnicity as a system of classification in ways that can be highly consequential for this process. For example, instruments like the census and the passport can make ethnic (and national) classifications seem natural (Nobles 2000; Noiriel 1998). Actions of private sector organizations and the media can have similar impacts: these institutions often present different ethnic groups as having distinct cultures or consumption habits, making ethnic differences seem natural (Hall 1996). Even so, the instrumentalist and constructionist perspectives show that ethnic groups are not homogeneous, and individuals have some room for manoeuvre. Even if ethnic classifications are often powerful, individuals can move from one ethnic identity to the other, frame their identity in different ways, and have multiple identities (Baumann 1996). In fact, talking about 'ethnic groups' can be misleading as it tends to reify categories that are not unitary and do not always have common purposes (Brubaker 2004). On the other hand, some individuals have less room for manoeuvre than others. Typically, individuals belonging to ethnic groups that are subjected to stereotypes and discrimination experience more obstacles in trying to 'shift' their ethnic identity, as outsiders will strongly identify them as members of it. Thus, although some political leaders argue that the societies we live in are 'post-racial' and that ethnicity is no longer a relevant factor when considering questions of inequality, studies show that visible ethnic minorities still experience individual and institutional discrimination in many ways, a clear indication that processes of ethnic identification are still significant (see Craig and O'Neill 2013 for the British case).

Although ethnic and racial boundaries sometimes overlap, ethnicity can and should be distinguished from race (especially as that latter term is currently used). As suggested in the definition, the concept of ethnicity is rooted in people's beliefs and not primarily in perceived physical differences. Even if physical resemblances can underpin a belief about a common ancestry, phenotypic characteristics do not usually contribute as much to the constitution of ethnic boundaries. Ethnic boundaries can also shift over time and their meanings can change more readily than with racial boundaries. Ethnicity implies a significant degree of subjectivity; what is important is what people believe they are, not what they appear to be. While race is also constructed rather than natural, it is more strongly connected to perceived phenotypes and thus its boundaries are less porous (leaving 'Ali G' to one side, it is more difficult for a white person to become black, and vice versa). Nevertheless, many researchers now agree that both ethnicity and race are dynamic processes that involve the creation of boundaries around groupings of people who are perceived as and/or see themselves as sharing the same identity or culture. Thus, as shown by Ware (2009), the notion of 'Englishness' is commonly connected to the racial boundary of 'whiteness'. These boundaries and groupings are constructed at multiple levels of interaction in societies, such as politically through census categories, and socially and culturally through institutions such as schools, the media, places of employment and worship, and families. Thus, ethnicity and ethnic groupings are constantly subject to negotiation, revision and definition by competing groups and interests.

See also: *Assimilation; Multiculturalism; Second generation*

NOTE

1 For some, this statement did little more than replace one term with the other – ethnicity for race – without much alteration in the ideology itself.

KEY READINGS

Barth, F. (ed.) (1969) *Ethnic Groups and Boundaries. The Social Organization of Culture Difference.* Bergen and London: Allen & Unwin.

Brubaker, R. (2004) *Ethnicity Without Groups*. Cambridge, MA: Harvard University Press.

Glazer, N. and Moynihan, D.P. (1963) *Beyond the Melting Pot; the Negroes, Puerto Ricans, Jews, Italians, and Irish of New York City*. Cambridge, MA: MIT Press.

Shils, E. (1957) 'Primordial, personal, sacred, and civil ties: some particular observations on the relationship of sociological research and theory', *British Journal of Sociology*, 8 (1): 130–45.

18 Family Migration and Reunification

Definition: Migration facilitated on the basis of family ties. These ties sometimes create rights to 'sponsor' the immigration of relatives, and they can make migration easier to accomplish in other ways as well.

In many analyses, migration is something *individuals* do. This assumption obscures a key feature of contemporary as well as historical migration: individuals are embedded in families (as well as other types of kinship networks), and family ties therefore shape the migration process in important ways. Migration on the basis of family ties is a topic at the core of migration studies: it might be tempting to think of such migration as secondary, a mere appendage to the migration of those whose decisions are rooted in economic motivations, but this view would be misleading in several ways. Most importantly, migration facilitated by family ties typically constitutes the single biggest category (if not the outright majority) of contemporary inflows (e.g. in Western Europe and North America). In the USA, well in excess of half of immigrant visas are allocated on the basis of family ties, and family migration has been dominant in much of Western Europe ever since the curtailment of labour migration recruitment in the early 1970s. These dimensions have given rise to certain worries among some population segments in destination countries (e.g. regarding immigrants as an alleged economic burden), though it is clear that at least some of these worries are unfounded.

Family ties form a key component of the networks that help turn migration into a self-sustaining phenomenon (Massey et al. 2003; Boyd 1989). To a certain extent, these ties operate independently of larger social and political forces, but they are also reinforced by such forces. Perhaps the most important of these is the growing body of international human rights instruments designed to reinforce an expectation of protections for families (e.g. the UN Declaration of Universal Human Rights, the Convention on the Rights of the Child). To a certain extent, this expectation amounts to a legal right: many types of immigrants – even some who lack citizenship in the destination country – can sponsor the immigration of certain types of family members. From a different angle, these legal provisions mean that some individuals have opportunities for migration regardless of whether they possess characteristics (e.g. skills, cultural attributes) that people in the destination country might consider desirable. In principle, immigrants (particularly those who become naturalized citizens) can then bring family members as additional immigrants, who might themselves then bring additional family members, etc.

As noted above, these provisions have fostered concerns in destination countries. Above all, they sometimes reinforce a perception that migration is 'out of control', as when governments fail to act on campaign promises to restrict migration in part because certain types of restrictions would contravene human rights commitments and cannot be adopted. Most citizens in most democratic countries cannot be prevented from marrying a person of their choice and then bringing the spouse to live in the destination country (though as discussed below this right often depends on meeting certain conditions, usually including at a minimum an expectation that the relationship is heterosexual). These concerns are then exacerbated by some basic facts about families (a complex sociological topic in its own right). The most significant of these is the fact that 'family' has a variety of meanings in different contexts: the modern nuclear family is sometimes thought of as 'natural' in many destination countries, but some immigrants come from cultural contexts where the notion of family extends to other types of kinship connections that do not seem 'genuine' to some. Another worry arises from the practice of arranged marriages: when two people marry in a mode that does not emphasize the romantic love that typifies Western relationships, some observers take the view that the relationship is not genuine and might amount to nothing more than an immigration scam.

Quite apart from whether these concerns are legitimate in a normative sense, considered empirically it becomes clear that they are exaggerated in significant ways. Despite the notion that international human rights instruments create a 'right' of family reunification, this right is limited (Lahav 1997; Perruchoud 1989). In many countries, naturalization is a minimum condition (the right to family reunification works out in many instances to be a right of citizens); when it is possible for non-citizen immigrants to bring their families, they often must at least have the right of permanent residence (thus in many settings foreign students and temporary workers cannot bring their families). In addition, destination states determine which kinship relations count as family, declining to recognize some relations that are significant for the (would-be) migrants themselves. More generally, human rights do not trump national sovereignty; national governments decide to adopt (or not) the various instruments (declarations, conventions, etc.) in question, and some of these have no force at all in most countries (e.g. the International Convention on the Protection of the Rights of All Migrant Workers and Members of Their Families, adopted by the UN but ratified by very few countries that receive migrants in any significant numbers). Even when ratified, these provisions typically amount to general recommendations rather than specific requirements, and their implementation is then a matter for each national government (Lahav 1997). National governments routinely impose conditions and restrictions, such that in practice family reunification can be difficult to accomplish, rather than easy, as some imagine.

This point is borne out in analyses of the immigration 'multiplier': as noted in the chapter on chain migration, Jasso and Rozensweig (1986) found that immigrants who arrived in the US on an employment-based visa brought (on average) 1.2 family members in the ten years subsequent to their arrival. The extent of chain migration itself (in the sense that legally sponsored family members then brought more family members) was even more limited: the equivalent figure for those who themselves arrived in a family category was 0.2. To understand why, we can revisit the restrictions noted just above – and we can also recall the more general proposition that (contrary to certain expectations) many people do not want to migrate to wealthy countries. In addition, some immigrants in wealthy countries do not want to bring family members to live with them – they prefer instead to send remittances to the country of origin, where that money will carry greater purchasing power (Kofman 2004).

Another concern sometimes arises in relation to the economic contribution of immigrants who enter by virtue of family connections. When immigrants have work permits and/or are recruited for specific jobs, the premise of allowing them to enter is the prospect that they can offer specific skills or other attributes for which there is demand. In cases of family reunification, on the other hand, one might worry that the immigrant does not have anything much to offer employers – and perhaps immigrants in this category will even end up being dependent on welfare payments. Jasso and Rozensweig (1995) demonstrate that such worries are similarly misplaced, particularly in an extended perspective: family-class immigrants to the US typically show upward occupational mobility in the years following their immigration (while employment-class immigrants typically show downward mobility). They also suggest that employment-class immigrants themselves might do a particularly good job of 'screening' family members and potential spouses for long-term occupational/economic success.

This chapter has so far discussed family reunification as a legal right enabling immigrants to sponsor their family members for immigration – but family reunification also takes place in an undocumented mode. As noted earlier, family ties are one of the key resources constituting migrant networks, and those resources sometimes enable migrants to enter without authorization, or to find work in the absence of an immigration status permitting this. In addition, recalling that many family members of migrants do not themselves become migrants, migration studies benefit from research on families that are not 'reunified', instead maintaining relations across international distances in a mode familiar from the transnationalism perspective (Baldassar 2007).

The term 'family *reunification*' might be read to imply that the family after migration/reunification is the same as the family prior to migration. Nancy Foner's work (e.g. 1997a) demonstrates that this impression is likely to be quite misleading. Although migrants continue to be influenced by pre-migration cultural and social forces, migration also contributes to changes in family forms and relations, in part via exposure to the cultural and social patterns of the destination country (see Dumon 1989). Foner found that Jamaican women in New York, for example, were less inclined to tolerate men's infidelities – because the women had more financial independence and had been influenced by American ideals of monogamy and 'family togetherness'. More generally, while the word family in many Western societies connotes the conventional nuclear family, in a sociological perspective the term refers more broadly to a type of social relation – and migration research shows that family relations themselves are typically changed in particular ways by the experience of migration, such that the word 'reunification' is imprecise.

Another misimpression sometimes arises in the notion that family reunification is mainly a matter of wives following husbands. In this picture, men (breadwinners) migrate for economic reasons and women migrate for family reasons (Kofman 2004). Unsurprisingly, this picture is decidedly incomplete and out of date: economic migration has long included women as the 'primary' migrants (see Ehrenreich and Hochschild 2003), with men sometimes following. Even so, migration is a gendered process and women often make different choices from men, for different reasons; a key finding in this regard is that marriage to a migrant husband in the USA makes Mexican women *less* likely to migrate to the US, relative to single/divorced women (Kanaiaupuni 2000). It is also worth recalling the fact that migration decisions are often made by households, not by individuals in isolation (Stark and Bloom 1985).

Family reunification is highly consequential for migrants and for destination countries in a number of key ways. Migrants who initially envision only a brief period abroad are particularly likely to revise that intention and become 'permanent' settlers if they are joined by family members (e.g. Piore 1979); the arrival of children (either as migrants themselves or as offspring born in the destination) makes settlement even more likely and raises a number of issues that would not arise in relation to strictly limited labour migration (e.g. education). The fact that ostensibly temporary migrations have been followed so frequently by family reunification reinforces an observation that has been ignored (by policy-makers, at least) almost as often as it has been repeated: many in destination countries have perceived migrants as mere economic factors, but in reality they are people embedded in complex social relations. Certain aspects of family-related migration have been under-researched, and one would anticipate increasing attention to migration among members of non-conventional family types, e.g. homosexual partners.

See also: *Chain migration; Migrant networks*

KEY READINGS

Boyd, M. (1989) 'Family and personal networks in international migration: recent developments and new agendas', *International Migration Review*, 23 (3): 638–70.

Kofman, E. (2004) 'Family-related migration: a critical review of European Studies', *Journal of Ethnic and Migration Studies*, 30 (2): 243–62.

Massey, D.S., Durand, J. and Malone, N.J. (2003) *Beyond Smoke and Mirrors: Mexican Immigration in an Era of Economic Integration*. New York: Russell Sage Foundation.

19 Forced Migration

> *Definition: Migration that results from some sort of compulsion or threat to well-being or survival, emerging in conditions ranging from violent conflict to severe economic hardship.*

Initially, the notion of forced migration might seem relatively straightforward, referring to instances of migration that are not chosen freely but are instead the consequence of compulsion. The difficulty, however, is in determining what to count as compulsion, and a significant amount of scholarly effort has been devoted in recent years to clarification – and extension – of the forced migration concept (see Castles 2003a). One result is that many migration scholars no longer believe that a conventional dichotomy between economic migrants and refugees is cogent or persuasive. 'Economic migration', rather than being entirely voluntary, is in many instances better understood as rooted in compulsion of various sorts – especially when the economic deprivation that constitutes its proximate cause is rooted in deeper socio-economic structures that are determined primarily by the decisions and activities of states, corporations and individuals elsewhere (e.g. in wealthier countries). A range of factors – perhaps including environmental difficulties (particularly global warming) and development initiatives – can make the notion of compulsion relevant beyond the obvious category of refugees fleeing persecution and violent political conflicts. Instead of a binary opposition between refugees and economic migrants, then, we can perceive a continuum wherein compulsion plays a greater role in some migration flows and a lesser role in others (Turton 2003; Richmond 1994).

The archetypical instance of forced migration is displacement or refugee flows arising from violent conflicts, persecution and/or deliberate expulsion. 'Migrants' are sometimes created at the point of a gun or a cluster-bomb, and such instances seem clear-cut given the obvious persecution that induces people to leave. Even so, an essential element of many refugees' situations often remains implicit (though not in Zolberg et al. 1989, on which the following point is based). In some cases, refugees could avoid persecution or expulsion by submitting to the demands of their persecutors, e.g. to convert to a different religion or to cease engaging in certain forms of political activity. The observation is both analytical and normative: modern notions of freedom of religion and conscience dictate that individuals should not have to change their religion or refrain from political activity, and persecution on these grounds is a grave violation of human rights. The point, then, is simply that the concept of forced migration is more complicated than it otherwise appears: some refugees are forced out in part because of their 'voluntary' insistence on exercising their human rights. Emphasizing this element of the analysis is useful insofar as it facilitates arguments favouring extension of the bases on which refugee claims should be recognized: for example, one should not have to refrain from expressing one's (homo)sexuality in order to avoid persecution, and individuals persecuted on this basis should have their asylum claims accepted.

Refugees are at one end of the 'forced vs. voluntary' continuum. It is more difficult to find a term that effectively captures the experience of migrants at the other end;[1] 'economic migration' is a term that arguably hides more than it reveals, particularly in its implication that such migration is entirely voluntary. Some people choose migration as a strategy for improving their lives in economic terms without facing a significant challenge to their prospects for survival. In other instances, however, individuals encounter a challenge significant enough to make the 'forced migration' concept at least potentially relevant. Bacon (2008) describes the situation of corn farmers in Oaxaca, whose livelihoods were threatened by adoption of the North American Free Trade Agreement (NAFTA), which eliminated Mexican corn subsidies and opened the market to competition from corn produced in the USA by large-scale mechanized and government-subsidized methods. These farmers, unable to get a sufficient price for their produce to enable them to feed themselves and their families, effectively had no option other than migration (though Bacon is perhaps less successful in making the case that they had no option other than migration *to the US*): their migration was forced in the sense that they faced a strong likelihood of death by starvation, equivalent in essential ways to the prospect of death at the hands of soldiers or a militia.

In some instances, however, it is more difficult to reach such a clear conclusion. Some migrants leave because of challenges that are significant but less severe: one faces a dramatic decline in one's standard of living, not death. Is migration in such instances forced? The answer one gives likely depends in part on one's more general attitude to migration, and in particular on the conditions under which a particular destination country can be deemed to have an obligation to admit prospective migrants. When it is possible to establish the kind of causal chain described for Oaxacan corn farmers as above, then when they succeed in gaining entry to the USA it is arguably reasonable to describe their migration as forced, even if they had another option, i.e., of 'merely' becoming impoverished (as against outright starvation). The argument, not always stated quite so nakedly, is that powerful forces in the US are responsible for their displacement, and so the US has an obligation to accept them as immigrants.

The central question here thus seems to be: how restricted or undesirable must one's options be to justify the conclusion that it is reasonable for someone to reject those options and choose migration? The words 'reject' and 'choose' imply agency, not compulsion – but if forced migration is to have any scope beyond instances where the alternative is death, then the conceptual determination depends heavily on this judgement of reasonableness. One might perceive an affinity here with the point made above about insisting on exercising one's human rights: perhaps people should not have to suffer dramatic declines in their standard of living as the price that goes with remaining in their community of origin. There is undoubtedly a difference insofar as economic compulsion often does not involve a persecuting agent – but the socio-economic processes leading to impoverishment are not always mysterious or ineluctable (and sometimes even have identifiable agents). Alternatively, some might take the view that impoverishment is sometimes inevitable and individuals should make the best of things where they are, rather than seeking to impose immigration on a country that doesn't want it.

In any event, decisions about applicability of this concept turn on this inescapably normative judgement – and it is surely better to make that judgement explicit than to leave it hidden. Again, when migration is described as forced, one implication is that destination countries ought to accept the migrants (as with refugees in a conventional sense). This is an essential point, in an historical context in which many destination countries are grudging in their acceptance even of conventional refugees (when they accept them at all).

In some instances the concept of forced migration is perhaps easier to invoke, even though it is not a matter of persecution or violent force as with conventional refugees. Large-scale migration from coastal regions of low-lying countries like Bangladesh will surely be 'forced' by rising sea levels; even before people drown, their crops will fail (for a broader treatment of climate change and migration, see No. 31 of *Forced Migration Review*, 2008). Nor is it difficult to perceive other instances of forced migration emerging already from global warming, as with drought-induced migration from Burkina Faso to Côte d'Ivoire (Sachs 2007); the contribution of this migration stream to subsequent civil war in Côte d'Ivoire with consequent refugee flows shows also that one forced migration flow can lead to another. All the same, global warming is by no means the sole explanation for these migration streams, and the argument that the migration is forced depends on the cogency of a number of claims that might be considered contentious – which again means that the concept of 'forced migration' itself is inescapably contentious. As with many concepts in migration studies, it can be used to construct narratives for discernible political purposes (see Hartmann 2009), and it is therefore worth asking: who advocates adoption of the concept, for which applications, on the basis of what interests?

Another type of migration that might be forced is migration with root causes in development projects such as dams, where migrants' homes and fields are inundated over a short timescale. But (as with the Oaxacan example above) in instances such as the Three Gorges Dam in China (e.g. Heming et al. 2001), it is less clear that migration *to another country* was forced in a deep sense. Individuals' options would have depended in part on alternative economic opportunities within China – and the high rate of economic growth in China during this period suggests that opportunities might have been available for many, though those forced to become migrants (at least internally) no doubt would have preferred being able to remain where they were instead. We are confronted again by the question: was it reasonable under the circumstances to reject all options apart from emigration?

Some migrants are, unambiguously, forced out – and in some cases the element of compulsion is obvious even though it is not a matter of violence or persecution. But further extension of the concept requires engagement with a basic tenet of sociology (or the social sciences more generally): people's lives are determined in part by structures and forces beyond their control. Individuals always face restrictions on their options, and these restrictions vary in place and over time. As restrictions increase, the plausibility of describing migration as forced arguably increases as well. But this aspect of the concept makes categorization in many instances a matter of debate, to an even greater extent than with other concepts in migration studies.

See also: *Displacement and internally displaced persons; Refugees and asylum seekers*

NOTE

1 Perhaps 'lifestyle migration' (Benson and O'Reilly 2009) would be appropriate, but this term captures only a small slice of what seems relevant at the other end of this continuum.

KEY READINGS

Bacon, D. (2008) *Illegal People: How Globalization Creates Migration and Criminalizes Immigrants.* Boston, MA: Beacon Press.

Castles, S. (2003a) 'Towards a sociology of forced migration and social transformation', *Sociology,* 37 (1): 13–34.

Zolberg, A.R., Suhrke, A. and Aguayo, S. (1989) *Escape from Violence: Conflict and the Refugee Crisis in the Developing World.* New York: Oxford University Press.

20 Gendered Migration

Definition: Patterns of migration – undertaken by men as well as women – that are shaped quite powerfully by gender, and in particular by deeply rooted understandings of gender roles.

A common perception about migration processes is that people migrate primarily for structural reasons related to the global and local economic systems (economic migration) or to the dangers and persecutions they face in their country of origin (forced migration). When migration is framed this way, the connection of migration processes to gender relations and roles is often overlooked, even in research by social scientists (Morokvasic 1984). The mainstream media also generally neglect or misrepresent gender when they deal with migration: the typical image of the migrant is that of a young man (Andall 1992). This view of migration as a non-gendered process or one driven exclusively by men is misleading insofar as it implies that women are absent or passive, or that women typically follow men in migration (Kofman et al. 2000). Women are actors in their own right in migration processes (even in instances of family reunification), and gender relations are a 'key constitutive element' in these processes (Hondagneu-Sotelo 2003: 9).

The abundant research literature on gender shows that the social and cultural construction of gender roles and characteristics fundamentally shapes people's opportunities and expectations. A focus on gendered migration thus suggests that men and women often migrate for different reasons and through different processes – though there can be overlap in their experiences as well (women can sometimes engage in patterns more commonly followed by men, and vice versa). Put simply, gender helps determine how emigration and immigration are organized. The reverse is true as well: migration can change gender relations. Although these connections are quite basic, it is only recently that scholars of migration have put gender considerations at the heart of migration studies (Mahler and Pessar 2006).

It does not take an elaborate theory of gender to notice that men and women can face different migration regimes, as when the laws and administrative practices that organize immigration make explicit distinctions between men and women. These distinctions create a 'gendered labour recruitment' (Repak 1994): European guestworkers programmes in the 1950s and 1960s, for example, specifically recruited men. The same was true of the Bracero programme, which recruited Mexican workers in the USA in the 1940s and 1950s (ending in 1964): it provided job opportunities for men and led to the establishment of migration flows almost exclusively involving men, at least initially (Hondagneu-Sotelo 1994). Industrialized countries for long periods wanted to prevent the arrival of whole families and the establishment of new communities, and even today some countries prohibit migrant workers being joined by their spouses (and in the mid-twentieth century that restriction fell mainly on women). These policies led to a strict division of tasks between men and women in immigrants' families: men became responsible for sending resources from the destination country to the country of origin, while women were responsible for maintaining the household in the country of origin. In the 1970s, when it became clear that most of the guestworkers who had arrived in earlier years would stay in Europe, governments passed family reunification laws to organize the immigration of women. In doing so, they reinforced a gender division: the immigration of women at that juncture was mainly dependent on the prior immigration of men. Moreover, in the 1970s, in most European countries, women joining their spouses did not have the right to work in the initial years after their entry (Kofman et al. 2000).

Although the laws regulating family reunification have tended to become more and more restrictive since the 1990s (Kofman et al. 2000; GISTI 2011, for France), it is still the primary migration path for women moving from developing to industrialized countries (Boyd and Pikkov 2005). For other modes, the migration of women has developed mainly in an informal way. In industrialized countries, women are often recruited through informal networks to work as nannies or housekeepers (Chang 2000; Repak 1995), and many of them live without residence permits and access to welfare programmes (Calavita 2006). In some Middle Eastern countries, on the other hand, the gendered recruitment of domestic workers coming from South and South-east Asia (the Philippines, in particular) is organized legally (Huang et al. 2005). A similar process can be observed in Southern Europe, especially in rapidly ageing countries such as Italy and Spain: in these countries, the annual immigration quota systems prioritize the recruitment of Filipina and Latin American women as domestic workers (Calavita 2006). In each case, it is evident that policy-makers (and employers) operate with entrenched understandings about gender, i.e., whether women or men are more suited to the work for which migration would be undertaken, and under what conditions and restrictions migration will be allowed.

In recent decades, labour migration among women has developed in sectors well beyond domestic work. Women migrate from developing to industrialized countries to work in a wide range of activities including (to name just a few) catering, tourism, manufacturing and agriculture. Moreover, with the development of sex-tourism and human trafficking, women also migrate (sometimes against their will) to work in the sex industry (Ehrenreich and Hochschild 2003). These gendered practices are shaped by pragmatic economic reasons as well as by cultural perceptions regarding roles of men and women in countries of destination (Piper 2006). Structural factors also help explain the specific migration patterns of women; the current labour migration of women is closely related to large-scale economic transformation in industrialized countries – in particular, the transition to a service economy, especially in large cities (Sassen-Koob 1984). In many cases, these trends lead to a loss of professional status: migrant women (whether professionally qualified or not) find it particularly difficult to enter the labour market, and work often in unskilled jobs or through self-employment (Kofman et al. 2000).

The notion of gendered migration also refers, at a more micro level, to immigrants' household strategies, and to key features of their kinship and social networks. Gendered patterns of migration emerge in the way family decisions are made about whether migration should happen, about which member(s) of the family should migrate, and about whether migration should be temporary or permanent (Pedraza 1991). As shown by Grasmuck and Pessar (1991) in research on migrants from the Dominican Republic, these family decisions depend heavily on power relations between men and women. The focus on household strategies thus indicates a relation between gendered patterns of migration and the sociocultural definition of men's and women's roles at the family level. Grasmuck and Pessar (1991) show that the emigration of men was generally approved as a way to increase the socio-economic status of a family. However, the emigration of unmarried women was often experienced as more problematic (despite its economic benefits) insofar as parents perceived it as a threat to the family's reputation. De Jong (2000) shows via analysis of migrants from rural areas in Thailand that the decision to migrate is often motivated by different reasons depending on gender: the presence of children or elderly dependents increased men's intentions to migrate because of the need for increased financial resources – but it reduced women's intentions to migrate by augmenting their responsibilities at home. With a focus more on culture, Dreby (2009) shows that perceptions about migration are also gendered. For many men migrating from rural Mexican areas to the USA, migration reinforces one's masculinity: it implies a sense of risk and sacrifice that is viewed by many as proof of one's manliness.

Gendered patterns of migration can differ depending on the prevailing gender relations in the countries of origin and on gendered recruitment policies in destination countries (Hondagneu-Sotelo and Cranford 1999). Thus, in the case of the rural communities in Mali (de Haan et al. 2002), Kenya, Lesotho and South Africa (Francis 2002), women's role in agricultural activities means that migration is more commonly undertaken by men; women are generally left behind and are then responsible for the land and the household. This system helps maintain a circular or seasonal migration. It is only recently that women coming from these countries have started to migrate in significant numbers, whether through family reunification or independently, mainly to work in the domestic labour sector. By contrast, in the case of rural communities in Malaysia (Ong 1987) or the Philippines (Hondagneu-Sotelo and Cranford 1999), women are traditionally considered to be more adapted to assembly work than men, and so they are more likely than men to migrate to the cities. Another example is migration from Central American countries to Washington DC in the 1960s and 1970s, which was predominantly a migration of women (Repak 1995). This can be explained by the development of informal recruitment networks which targeted women for work in the domestic or health care sectors.

Immigration processes are thus shaped in a variety of ways by gender relations. The reverse is also true: immigration affects gender relations between men and women, in particular at the household level. When men migrate, women often gain new roles: for example, as they gain greater responsibility for the household, they typically acquire greater control over the household budget and property. Their authority and social status can sometimes increase considerably, a point evident in some instances of migration from southern India (Zachariah et al. 2002). In some cases, women can withdraw from agricultural work because of the family's higher income (Grasmuck and Pessar 1991). On the other hand, they can also experience greater isolation (Afsar 2011). In other cases, after men leave, women can access a wider range of employment opportunities and so increase their autonomy (Hondagneu-Sotelo and Cranford 1999).

The migration of women as well (whether individually or with the whole family) can also lead to a renegotiation of gender relations. To the extent that one can generalize about outcomes of this sort: women often gain power via migration while men often lose some of their power vis-à-vis women (though of course there is no shortage of instances where the reverse is true). Several migration-related dynamics help account for this shift: migrant women's engagement in paid work is often necessary to a greater extent than in pre-migration circumstances, women often make concerted efforts to construct a social network in the country of destination, and they can gain a more active public role (Hondagneu-Sotelo 1994).

Some women originating in rural areas perceive migration as a way to escape unwanted social pressures in their immediate environment (Dreby 2009). This is especially the case for single mothers and for women who did not marry at a young age. However, in some instances, especially when job opportunities are scarce in the destination country, women's dependence on men can increase and they can experience more isolation (Wilkinson 1983). The renegotiation of gender relations can also lead to increased conflict within the family (Grasmuck and Pessar 1991). That point also helps explain why men and women often have different perceptions of the immigration process: men often perceive immigration as being temporary and cultivate an intention to return (someday ...), while women (especially those who gained emancipation via migration) are more likely to perceive return as less attractive (Pessar 1999). Even so, broad generalizations about migration and gender must be tempered by appreciation of variation and of the specific circumstances shaping people's lives: for example, Somali Muslim women can have very different experiences depending on whether they end up in France or in Canada (Bassel 2012).

KEY READINGS

Calavita, K. (2006) 'Gender, migration, and law: crossing borders and bridging disciplines', *International Migration Review*, 40: 104–32.

Grasmuck, S. and Pessar, P. (1991) *Between Two Islands: Dominican International Migration*. Berkeley, CA: University of California Press.

Hondagneu-Sotelo, P. and Cranford, C. (1999) 'Gender and migration', in J. Saltzman Chafetz (ed.), *Handbook of the Sociology of Gender*. New York: Kluwer, pp. 105–26.

Kofman, E., Phyzacklea, A., Raguram, P. and Sales, R. (2000) *Gender and International Migration in Europe. Employment, Welfare and Politics*. London: Routledge.

Pedraza, S. (1991) 'Women and migration – the social consequences of gender', *Annual Review of Sociology*, 17: 303–25.

21 Guestworkers

Definition: Immigrants whose entry and employment (typically via formal recruitment programmes) is allowed under the assumption that their presence will be temporary – an assumption that often turns out to be incorrect.

The term guestworkers is used to describe a form of labour migration where the workers in question are intended to live and work in the receiving country on a strictly temporary basis. This intention is held by the host country and, at least initially, by many of the workers themselves. But the assumption of a limited time frame has so often proven to be wrong in practice that the word itself is best considered a misnomer, as implied already in the title of Rosemary Rogers' book, *Guests Come to Stay* (1985). Guestworker migration is best understood, via the experience of many countries, as a form of migration that typically leads to permanent settlement under particularly unfavourable conditions, precisely because the permanent settlement of the migrants was unanticipated and generally considered undesirable. Guestworkers are also typically restricted at least initially to employment only by a specified employer (or limited to a particular type of work), a condition that enables employers to pay them less than the wage that would be set in a normal market (Amir 2002).

The US experience with guestworkers had early roots in the use of seasonal Chinese and Japanese workers in the late 1800s, but towards the end of World War I farm employers turned to Mexicans in the first instance of a Bracero programme (Martin 2009). This practice was repeated during World War II and was then expanded in the better-known Bracero programme lasting from 1942 to 1964 (Craig 1971), which saw more than 4.5 million admissions of Mexican workers for agricultural employment in the US and created deep roots for other modes of migration from Mexico (Massey et al. 1987). A parade of legislation in more recent decades has created new guestworker programmes, with workers being imported in the 'guest' mode for other economic sectors as well (Griffith 2006), including high-tech jobs such as computer programming (Espenshade 2001). Many of these latter workers find it relatively easy to convert their 'guest' status into permanent residence.

The use of foreign labour in Europe under temporary and otherwise restrictive conditions can be traced to the late 1800s; these earlier flows were driven by employers' actions more than by systematic government policy. Many workers were later expelled, and recruitment during the inter-war period happened only on a smaller scale (with the significant exception of Nazi Germany) (Hahamovitch 2003; Castles and Kosack 1985). Most – but by no means all – Western European countries used guestworkers in the post-war period, some beginning immediately after the war ended. The British government recruited workers from Poland and Italy under its European Voluntary Workers scheme, though most of its later immigration came in a different mode from South Asia and elsewhere in the Commonwealth (Kay and Miles 1992). France and the Netherlands recruited workers from elsewhere in Europe but also drew immigrants from their own colonies. West Germany again made extensive use of guestworkers, beginning in the late 1950s, bringing Turkish and Italian workers to address labour shortages in specific sectors such as automobile manufacture (Herbert 1990). As in the US, in most cases the official recruitment programmes were accompanied by inflows of workers in other modes, including use of tourist visas to gain entry followed by irregular employment (Castles et al. 1984).

By 1973, with the first OPEC oil crisis, there was widespread awareness in Europe that the alleged merits of guestworker migration depended on assumptions that were simply wrong in many cases (Miller and Martin 1982). Workers were initially given visas with limited validity, under a principle of 'rotation': it was considered important to send them home before they put down roots, and then to replace them with new workers. But some of the migrants put down roots more quickly than anticipated, and their employers discovered they had no reason to favour losing employees who knew their work, and then replace them with people who didn't. Governments then discovered that enforcing departures was more difficult and more costly than they had imagined (if they had considered it at all).

With the recession following the oil crisis, most wealthy countries no longer recruited guestworkers. But many existing workers stayed and became permanent immigrants (though many also left), eventually with the right of permanent residence (Rogers 1985). Having gained a degree of permanent status, some then exercised a widely accepted right of family reunification. As the majority of guestworkers had been men, family reunification typically meant bringing wives (and children), in some cases via arranged marriages subsequent to migration.

As noted at the outset, however, these 'new' permanent immigrants had not initially been conceived as such, and in some countries adjustment to their permanence has been very slow, and indeed remains unresolved in the present. Particularly in 'ethno-nationalist' countries such as Germany, which for many years followed a *jus sanguinis* model of citizenship (passed through familial descent), the idea that workers from elsewhere could become German was simply not plausible. Conditions for naturalization were very restrictive; large proportions of the second and even third generations continued to be excluded from German citizenship, despite speaking German as a first language and (at least for some) never even visiting their 'home' country (e.g. Turkey). Guestworker migration, then, was in the end a mechanism for creating a set of excluded ethnic minorities in countries that had been homogenous (at least in their imaginations) (Martin and Miller 1980).

As people in these groups became permanent residents with greater rights and a stronger sense of membership in the local setting, they typically became less willing to play the economic roles they had initially been recruited for: they came to shun low-status work and wanted employment security just as other local workers did (Piore 1979). Permanent settlement, then, helped to recreate some of the labour shortages that had initially led employers and policy-makers to recruit workers abroad, leading Martin and Miller to conclude (1980) that dependence on guestworkers had become self-sustaining (see 'cumulative causation').

Despite being the subject of an 'obituary' in the 1980s (Castles 1986), the guestworker idea continues to attract policy-makers in wealthy countries (Castles 2006; Martin 2009). Some politicians and others persist in believing that it will be possible to bring workers without bringing people (to paraphrase Max Frisch's [1967] well-worn aphorism). Israel in the mid-1990s imported large numbers (relative to the population) of workers from places such as

Romania, Thailand and the Philippines, despite the pleas of people who knew well what had happened in Europe and who feared that the consequences for Israel would be even more difficult (Bartram 2005). Germany in the 1990s resuscitated its own guestworker programmes (Martin 2004). And the American government in 2013 was contemplating a new guestworker programme, as part of a package of measures designed to address the very large population of undocumented immigrants.

In countries lacking a strong commitment to principles of democracy and human rights, guestworker programmes were not as dysfunctional in the ways described here (though they were surely more dysfunctional in others). Countries such as Singapore and Saudi Arabia have been more able and willing to enforce time restrictions and other limitations on workers' rights; some countries (e.g. Libya and Nigeria) have deported workers en masse. The guestworker dilemma is, to a certain extent, a problem specifically for democratic countries, though even in places like Kuwait the use of guestworkers has social and political dimensions and is not a solely economic phenomenon (Birks et al. 1986). Another notable recent trend is the 'feminization' of guestworker programmes, sometimes dubbed the 'Maid Trade' (e.g. Chin 1998).

The discussion above paints guestworker migration in a negative light, but some scholars see it differently. Whether guestworker migration is a good idea is a question that cannot be answered properly in the abstract; instead, it has to be considered in comparison to available alternatives. One alternative is that workers who might merely be 'guests' would be able to enter under more favourable conditions, perhaps even freely, right from the outset. But that alternative is not actually available in most destination countries, mainly for political reasons. Another alternative, then, is that instead of being admitted as guestworkers, prospective migrants might not be admitted to wealthy countries at all.

Having framed the question in those terms, some writers assert that it is ethically preferable (when considering the interests of immigrants, at any rate) to allow guestworker migration over not allowing immigration at all (Ruhs and Chang 2004). People might choose to accept the restricted rights associated with guestworker status, simply because the benefits associated with gaining extra income outweigh the costs of the restrictions on rights (in particular, prospects for settlement).

See also: *Denizens; Labour migration*

KEY READINGS

Castles, S. (2006) 'Guestworkers in Europe: a resurrection?', *International Migration Review*, 40: 741–66.

Martin, P.L. (2009) *Importing Poverty? Immigration and the Changing Face of Rural America*. New Haven, CT: Yale University Press.

Piore, M.J. (1979) *Birds of Passage: Migrant Labor and Industrial Societies*. Cambridge: Cambridge University Press.

22 Human Trafficking and Smuggling

Definition: Human trafficking and smuggling denote illicit (and usually profitable) activities that facilitate migration. The actions of traffickers typically include coercion and/or deception of migrants, while smugglers help undocumented (or 'illegal') migrants cross borders.

The concepts of human trafficking and human smuggling cover the activities of people and organizations who profit from assisting or coercing others in migration. Though closely related, there are important differences between the two concepts, and the point of treating them together in this chapter is to analyse those differences and thus to overcome some of the confusion apparent in the existing research.

'Human trafficking' conveys the sense that migrants are treated as objects by the traffickers for their own gain. In conventional terms trafficking involves coercing unsuspecting women and girls into prostitution: the traffickers woo them with promises of jobs as waitresses or models, but upon arrival they are forced to work instead as prostitutes, trapped by threats of violence (often carried out) and by demands that 'debts' incurred in the course of migration be repaid. Other instances of trafficking involve international adoptions, as well as other forms of work where the migrants are treated as slaves or otherwise severely exploited (Scarpa 2008).

'Human smuggling', on the other hand, describes those whose activities are limited to helping migrants gain illegal entry into the destination country. A typical example of smuggling consists of 'coyotes' who lead migrants ('pollos', chickens) through the desert to remote regions of Arizona along the Mexican border, or people who ferry migrants across the Mediterranean to Spain or Italy in overcrowded small boats. A key point of difference is that the migrants usually pay the smugglers in advance (rather than incurring debts to them) and then have no further interaction with them after the trip is completed (Lee 2007).

Trafficking has attracted enormous interest among governments and non-governmental organizations (such as the International Organization for Migration) in recent years – though the practice itself is ancient, a point evident in the biblical story of Joseph, sold by his brothers into slavery in Egypt. The United Nations in 2000 adopted a Convention Against Transnational Organized Crime, comprising a Protocol to Prevent, Suppress and Punish Trafficking in Persons, Especially Women and Children, and a Protocol against the Smuggling of Migrants – known collectively as the 'Palermo Protocols'. Other organizations such as the European Union have adopted their own measures. These agreements demonstrate the perception that trafficking and smuggling are a significant problem.

However, there are difficulties in determining exactly how significant they are. In part, these difficulties arise simply because the activities in question are illegal and the people involved make great efforts to hide them (Di Nicola 2007). This does not prevent various bodies from offering estimates (the US Department of Justice, for example, suggested in 2007 that 800,000 people are trafficked in an average year, see Scarpa 2008) – and these estimates sometimes then take on a life of their own, repeated as if entirely factual. Wong (2005) suggests that some organizations, particularly the International Organization for Migration, might offer inflated estimates because large numbers imply a compelling need for a response and thus justify their activities and budgets. In any event, while individual articles or reports sometimes convey a certain confidence in their findings, an analysis of the literature as a whole demonstrates significant limits of knowledge and data on this topic (Dowling et al. 2007).

A further complication emerges in the difficulty of distinguishing between the two types in both empirical and conceptual terms. One could argue that the conceptual distinction developed above is relatively straightforward; it turns primarily on whether the migrants in question are freely choosing to go on the basis of reliable information. If they are, then smuggling is the appropriate category, especially if the 'transaction' is completed upon arrival. If they are being deceived by false promises and then subsequently coerced and exploited via debts (which they might even not know they were incurring), then it is trafficking. Even so, the components of the distinction – 'exploitation', 'free choice', 'reliable information' – do not denote dichotomies (O'Connell Davidson 2005; Plant 2012): just how unreliable does the information have to be for one to conclude that a particular instance is properly described as involving deceit? Again, in many cases it is virtually impossible to know which category is appropriate because of the difficulties in doing empirical research, and an estimate of numbers of trafficked persons might be inaccurate insofar as some might arguably belong in the smuggled category, or vice versa.

In addition, not everyone would accept this way of marking the distinction. The fact that significant numbers of the migrants in question end up working in prostitution (or doing 'sex work') means that debates among feminist scholars and others about prostitution have spilled over into disputes about what constitutes trafficking (Outshoorn 2005; Scarpa 2008). From one perspective (abolitionism), it is unacceptable to assert that women could ever freely choose to engage in prostitution, and anyone whose migration includes the intention of working as a prostitute is therefore trafficked. This perspective is bolstered by the fact that the Palermo Protocols include 'abuse of vulnerability' as a form of coercion (Malpani 2009): at a minimum, women's restricted economic opportunities would constitute a form of vulnerability, and to the extent that smugglers profit from helping them enter prostitution, the smugglers are in reality traffickers.

Others, starting with a different perspective on prostitution, assert that many migrant women (similarly to many 'native' women) fully intend to engage in sex work and make that choice knowingly as the best among the options actually available to them (Agustín 2005). In this perspective, the trafficking discourse (and in particular its insistence on referring to 'victims') inappropriately casts women as passive objects and leads to 'solutions' that many of the migrants don't actually want, including deportation (see Parreñas 2011). Agustín emphasizes that the trafficking/anti-prostitution position fails to capture the specific problems faced by *migrant* sex workers: their main concern is not prostitution per se but their lack of legal status, which exacerbates their difficulties with pimps, creditors, customers, the police, etc. (see O'Connell Davidson 2006; Andrijasevic 2010; Dwyer et al. 2011). In some instances the prostitutes in question are children, such that these considerations might amount to irrelevant subtleties (see Ebbi and Das 2008) – though O'Connell Davidson (2005) asserts that even for children there is variation in experiences that is not captured by the black-and-white moral and legal categories of activists and governments. One would also want to avoid assuming that all sex workers are female and provide services to heterosexual men; trafficking can involve homosexuals and transgender people as well (Mai 2012).

Debates on trafficking vs. smuggling are coloured in related ways by differing perspectives on illegal immigration and the measures considered appropriate to combat it. Both categories refer to people whose presence is undesired ('officially', at least) by the destination country: those who are smuggled enter the country illegally, and those who are trafficked engage in illicit activities (e.g. prostitution, but extending to any form of undocumented work), even if they used legal means of entry. The difference is that in the trafficking discourse it is easier to conclude that the *migrants themselves* do not really want to be there – and so it is easier to justify deporting them.

Perhaps unsurprisingly, then, national governments, while certainly opposed to smuggling, are particularly drawn to the trafficking perspective and inclined to emphasize the dimensions of that problem; as is apparent in the discussion above, these terms do not have neutral definitions and uses, but on the contrary are highly politicized. A related tendency is to highlight the involvement of transnational criminal gangs in trafficking (e.g. Truong 2003; Vermeulen et al. 2010), likewise justifying an increased law-enforcement effort. Wong (2005) asserts that the real dimensions of this aspect are smaller than that portrayed by such reports. By contrast, Shelley (2007) argues that transnational gangs, faced with a sustained crackdown on the drug trade, have moved into the human trade where profits are high and the risks relatively low.

These two influences on trafficking/smuggling debates converge in a critique of existing state responses: even while speaking of 'victims' of trafficking, governments are typically more interested in deporting them as irregular migrants than in assisting them as genuine crime victims. The Palermo Protocols encourage signatories to make efforts to restore victims' human rights, but these provisions are non-binding and poorly defined, and some of the states that do honour them nonetheless require, as a condition for the protections offered, victims' cooperation in efforts to prosecute the traffickers (e.g. Malpani 2009).

Some research on trafficking/smuggling is less concerned with the moral and practical issues that feature prominently in the discussion above, providing instead an analysis framed more deliberately in economic and sociological terms.

Kyle and Siracusa (2005), for example, describe smuggling as 'migrant-exporting schemes', organized as businesses that provide services in a market and social setting determined by global forces such as International Monetary Fund 'structural adjustment' programmes and unfair trade regimes. These businesses help migrant-exporting countries earn much-needed hard currency, and so governments in these cases have little incentive to restrict activities that, from the point of view of destination countries, are simply illegal and wholly illegitimate. This work is a useful reminder that migration, typically the object of research and concern by scholars and politicians/voters in wealthy destination countries, often looks quite different from the perspective of people in poorer sending countries.

See also: *Forced migration; Undocumented (illegal) migration*

KEY READINGS

Andrijasevic, R. (2010) *Migration, Agency and Citizenship in Sex Trafficking*. Basingstoke: Palgrave.
O'Connell-Davidson, J. (2005) *Children in the Global Sex Trade*. Cambridge: Polity.
Scarpa, S. (2008) *Trafficking in Human Beings: Modern Slavery*. Oxford: Oxford University Press.
van Schendel, W. and Itty, A. (eds) (2001) *Illicit Flows and Criminal Things: States, Borders, and the Other Side of Globalization*. Bloomington, IN: Indiana University Press.

23 Integration

Definition: The process by which immigrants gain social membership and develop the ability to participate in key institutions in the destination country.

Broadly speaking, integration refers to changes that immigrants undergo after arrival in the destination country; in recent years it has been extended to indicate changes in the receiving society as well, thus integration as a two-way process. The phrase 'after arrival' points to a divide that characterizes much research on migration: many studies focus either on the determinants of migration (thus before arrival) or on the experiences of immigrants in the receiving society. Castles and Miller (2009) argue that this divide is artificial and make a case for research that engages with the migratory process as a whole. While this argument is persuasive, the ease of perceiving the field in terms of that dichotomy helps show that the concept of integration is very broad and is implicated in a number of other concepts covered in this book (e.g. multiculturalism, citizenship, ethnic enclaves).

To a greater degree than for many other migration-related concepts, 'integration' does not have a universally agreed meaning; indeed it is often used without being defined and is sometimes used (by different people) in ways that can fairly be described as mutually incompatible. At a minimum, one can perceive a degree of overlap between integration and assimilation; Bloemraad et al. (2008) identify the terms as alternatives (another is incorporation), which is not far from asserting that they are equivalent to each other.

The core meaning of integration has to do with increasing social membership for immigrants in the destination country. At least in an analytical sense, one can distinguish between integration and assimilation by noting that integration of immigrants can occur without their becoming highly similar to natives (assimilation), particularly in cultural terms. Entzinger (1990), for example, discusses integration in terms of achievement of equality/equal opportunities for immigrants without a requirement for cultural assimilation (see Brochmann 1996). That point is the motivating idea of 'multicultural integration' (e.g. Kymlicka and Norman 2000), wherein immigrants gain belonging/membership in part via increased acceptance of ethnic and cultural difference by natives (with changes not just in attitudes but in institutions as well). On the other hand, some destination countries have resisted multiculturalism, insisting (or attempting to insist) that immigrants adopt values and traits considered essential to a putative national 'way of life'; in practice, then, integration in some settings can be tantamount to assimilation – though one can still make the analytical distinction noted above.

If integration is 'increasing social membership for immigrants', then a number of dimensions and indicators are clearly important (see Ireland 2004). In the economic sphere, integration would mean that immigrants participate in the labour market on equal terms with natives, gaining jobs that reflect their qualifications and abilities (though the outcomes might not be equal in a comprehensive sense because some immigrants might start with higher or lower qualifications). Likewise in the political sphere, integration means participation (voting, campaigning, etc.) in ways that are similar or equivalent to participation patterns of natives (see Wright and Bloemraad 2012). What is at stake here is not simply absence of discrimination: lack of integration with regard to education might arise not from discrimination by teachers and other gatekeepers but from choices made by immigrant children and/or their parents, who might not have learned how to take advantage of opportunities genuinely on offer. In this sense, integration includes development of abilities to navigate key social institutions that might work quite differently from their counterparts in the country of origin. Language competence is usually a key capability for integration, though ambiguities about that point arise in destination countries that use more than one main language (perhaps as a consequence of earlier mass immigration). Gaining citizenship is often a milestone of integration: integration on various dimensions is sometimes a precondition for naturalization (e.g. with language tests), but naturalization can also be a mechanism for integration – a point evident in the way exclusion from formal citizenship often reinforces social exclusion more generally (Hansen 2003).

The idea so far, then, is that immigrants are 'integrated' when they do not experience exclusion arising from their status as immigrants. Some aspects of integration have fairly straightforward indicators (e.g. as with labour market and educational attainment). But integration also usually refers to development of a shared sense of belonging and identity. The issue here is whether immigrants come to feel that they are no longer mere foreigners but are in some meaningful sense American, British, Dutch, etc. – and (no less important) whether natives come to accept immigrants in that sense.

Reflection on that issue shows that certain common assumptions about immigrant integration operate at quite a deep level. As Joppke and Morawska (2003) argue, a key premise of much discussion about integration is that prior to the arrival of immigrants societies are themselves well integrated – cohesive, bounded, with natives enjoying a uniformly high level of belonging. In this frame, the arrival of immigrants is destabilizing, and to restore things to their proper state immigrants must *be integrated,* in particular via state policies and interventions (see Favell 2005). In reality, complex modern societies are marked by varying degrees of difference, fragmentation and conflict among existing members. Even on arrival, then, immigrants are already integrated to varying degrees on different indicators: some share high levels of education with certain types of natives, others experience exclusion and/or disadvantage, again in common with certain types of natives. The idea of immigrants' 'difference' from natives – another key premise of integration discussions – rests to a great extent on an illusory notion that natives are all essentially the same (see Banton 2001). While that notion might sometimes be true in relation to national identity (though in many cases a common national identity is manifestly absent even for natives), the 'content' of a society extends well beyond national identity to include dimensions where immigrants and natives are often not terribly different. We might then wonder: is integration in the sense of developing shared national identities important? How might one justify imposing that mode of integration on immigrants who do not want to become 'American', 'British', 'Dutch', etc.?

That question arises in part because normatively laden expectations of integration (particularly in its assimilationist connotation) are often rooted in ethnocentrism. Many natives in wealthy destination countries did not welcome the arrival of immigrants, and many now appear to hope that immigrants can 'disappear' as such by becoming 'like us', adopting 'our' traits and values. At least in Europe, however, one finds a set of concerns about integration that many would likely consider more legitimate. These concerns usually focus on the situation of some Muslims in liberal democracies. Many Muslim immigrants originate from non-liberal countries, and some (including some in the second and subsequent generations) adhere to a version of Islam that clashes in certain respects with some core liberal principles, e.g. on gender equality and the role of religion in public life. (We are emphatically not asserting that 'Islam is incompatible with liberal democracy'; in any event, similar concerns arise also with regard to some non-immigrant adherents to other religions, e.g. certain versions of Christianity in the USA.) As Joppke (e.g. 2012) notes, some paradoxes and dilemmas then arise. How can one respect freedom of religion and conscience while at the same time fostering (preferably without recourse to non-liberal means) adherence to other core liberal values? A key element of any reasonable approach, Joppke argues, is to address the socio-economic exclusion that feeds the adoption of more radical forms of Islam; that point is reinforced by noting that these issues are not nearly as intractable in the USA, where Muslims are both less disadvantaged and less radical. The European experience, on the other hand, helps demonstrate another core point about integration: it is often not a linear or unidirectional process (see 'segmented assimilation' in the chapter on assimilation).

Another major interest among migration scholars has been to discern or construct typologies of citizenship 'regimes' at the country level and to analyse their consequences for immigrant integration. A well-known example is that of Brubaker (1992a), who identified distinct patterns in France and Germany: France embodied a 'civic-territorial' model while Germany's regime is 'ethnocultural'. Castles and Miller (2009) extend this mode of analysis to cover a broader range of countries, in part by distinguishing multiculturalism as a third model particularly relevant to countries like the USA and Canada. Freeman (2004) argues that models and typologies of this sort overstate the degree of coherence that characterizes incorporation[1] policies and practices (see Bertossi 2011). Many policies and practices that affect the integration of immigrants were not adopted for that purpose and do not apply specifically to immigrants; in this respect they are arguably accidental rather than components of a self-conscious integration regime. An example is welfare benefits, where eligibility rules have been extended to include immigrants often not as a matter of policy but by courts applying legal principles in ways that sometimes contradicted policy-makers' intentions. In addition, in some countries one finds divergent or even contradictory elements in the various domains (state, market, welfare, culture) that constitute the more general incorporation process. At best, Freeman argues, one might be able to discern 'syndromes' (instead of regimes), though even then the classification decisions one makes are inevitably contestable. In another critique of 'national models', Joppke (2007) argues that there is broad convergence in liberal democratic countries towards a common mode of integration policies.

As with other migration topics, most research on integration focuses on the usual set of wealthy destination countries in North America and Western Europe. Many reviews of existing research do not discuss integration of immigrants in developing countries at all; only some of these reviews explicitly limit their scope in this respect (the others perhaps purport to be 'general'). One paper (Klugman and Medalho Pereira 2009) addresses integration in developing countries in a rudimentary way, identifying the extent to which immigrants have access to education and welfare state benefits. Sadiq (2009) shows how immigrants in countries such as India sometimes gain formal citizenship (or at least documents attesting to citizenship) by exploiting weaknesses in state bureaucracies; in that regard, integration by immigrants might be easier in countries with a less developed set of state institutions (one purpose of state institutions in wealthy/developed countries is, after all, to maintain boundaries and exclude immigrants). Again, however, there is very little research on this topic and confident assertions in this area would be premature.

Some migration scholars believe the entire integration research agenda is flawed (and a few even argue for its abandonment). As several contributors to this field note (e.g. Favell 2005), integration is usually identified as a matter of concern by politicians, and academic research in this area often seems to echo their concerns; some of this research is funded by governments and then predictably emphasizes issues that can be addressed by governments. At a minimum, integration questions can and should be addressed at levels both above the nation-state (transnationalism) and below it (e.g. integration into cities – Banton 2001; see Price and Benton-Short 2008).

If the concept of integration is taken at the broadest level to refer to what immigrants and destination societies experience after arrival, then rather than abandoning the concept one might embrace efforts to reshape it, in hopes of remedying the failings that are sometimes apparent in public discourse and policy on immigrants. To the extent that integration requires development of competencies regarding destination-country institutions (as noted above), then it is not obviously desirable to have critiques of government-centred integration research agendas turn into an argument for laissez-faire citizenship regimes (see Bloemraad 2006). In other words, governments can sometimes play a constructive role in the integration of immigrants, and it is surely useful to have research exploring how and why that happens in some instances but not in others. In addition, as Favell (1998) observes, integration has a more general meaning, engaging fundamental questions dating back at least to Hobbes about social order, i.e., how complex societies can reconcile differences and solve conflicts without violence. That question is an ongoing concern for any society – and immigration sometimes sharpens it by adding to social and cultural diversity, though that aspect of the issue perhaps emerges just as much (if not more) from some natives' distaste for diversity as from the arrival of the immigrants themselves.

See also: *Assimilation; Citizenship; Social cohesion*

NOTE

1 Note that Freeman might not accept this paragraph's premise, i.e., that 'incorporation' is equivalent to integration.

KEY READINGS

Bloemraad, I. (2006) *Becoming a Citizen: Incorporating Immigrants and Refugees in the United States and Canada*. Berkeley, CA: University of California Press.

Freeman, G.P. (2004) 'Immigrant incorporation in Western democracies', *International Migration Review*, 38: 945–69.

Joppke, C. and Morawska, E. (2003) 'Integrating immigrants in liberal nation-states: policies and practices', in C. Joppke and E. Morawska (eds), *Toward Assimilation and Citizenship: Immigrants in Liberal Nation-states*. Basingstoke: Palgrave Macmillan, pp. 1–36.

Portes, A. and Rumbaut, R. (1996) *Immigrant America: A Portrait*. Berkeley, CA: University of California Press.

24 Internal/ Domestic Migration

Definition: Migration from one area to another within the same country. In many countries internal migration (e.g. from one city to another) is quite common. In developing countries it consists mainly of movement from rural to urban areas.

In global terms, internal migration is quantitatively more significant than international migration (though it is difficult to be precise because there is no global estimate of internal migration). In 2000, the International Organization for Migration (IOM) estimated that 175 million people were international migrants (around 3 per cent of the global population). In the same period, in China and India roughly 400 million people were internal migrants (100 million in China and 300 million in India). In these two countries alone, then, the number of internal migrants was more than twice as large as the number of international migrants globally (King and Skeldon 2010). In India, as much as 30 per cent of the country's population were internal migrants in 2001. Internal migration represents 40 per cent of the urbanization process (the demographic growth of urban areas) in Asia, Africa and Latin America (Skeldon 2006). Even so, political leaders and the public at large tend to focus their attention on international migration, and thus ignore the significance of internal migration. This is also the case in the academic field of migration studies. These 'two migration traditions' (Skeldon 2006) are generally separate (analysed through different concepts and methods), and there is more attention on international migration. This tendency is present also in common language, where the term 'migration' usually refers to international migration, and the term 'migrant' then applies only to an individual who has crossed an international border.

By definition, internal migration does not entail crossing an international border. Unlike international migrants, then, internal migrants usually do not face legal obstacles that might impede their movement. They do not experience a change of jurisdiction, and they retain their citizenship and the rights attached to it (such as the right to vote, to work or to access health care). Internal migrants generally experience less difficulty in terms of cultural and linguistic adaptation than international migrants.

Even so, the differences between these two types of migrations are not absolute, and in some instances there are significant affinities. As with international migration, internal migration is sometimes regulated by laws and controls. This is true for China (Solinger 1999) and Vietnam (Dang et al. 1997): governments there attempt to control internal population movements and differentiate the rights of unskilled rural-to-urban migrants from those of native-born urbanites. Thus, Chinese migrants who move from rural to urban areas must officially declare their presence in the city and, like foreign workers, must obtain a labour permit. They also have to pay fees to get a temporary residence permit (Solinger 1999). Legal regulations that aimed to organize internal migrations were also implemented in South Africa under the apartheid regime and in Albania until the end of the 1980s (King and Skeldon 2010). In many countries, internal migrants also experience discrimination on the basis of perceived cultural or linguistic differences, as with Italians migrating from southern rural areas to northern urban areas in the 1950s and 1960s (Sonnino 1995) and with internal migrants in contemporary China (Solinger 1999).

On the other hand, some instances of international migration share characteristics more commonly associated with internal migration. This is especially true for people living close to a border, who sometimes find it easier and more advantageous to move across that border than to migrate to another region in their own country. Another type of similarity emerges for European Union citizens, who can move from one country to another without significant legal obstacles. In addition, international migrations can become internal migrations, and vice versa: borders sometimes shift over time, especially in zones in which conflicts are frequent – and so those who migrated into what was once merely a different region can thus suddenly become international migrants (Adepoju 1998).

Internal migration is often related to long-term socio-economic changes within a country. In Europe, the process of industrialization in the nineteenth century stimulated internal migrations through the rapid increase of employment opportunities in cities. This process of urbanization catalysed further internal migrations as employment in the agricultural sector declined and cities generally became more attractive places to live. In contemporary societies, internal migrations (like international migrations) are often related to inter-regional socio-economic inequalities. Thus, regional economic inequalities are the primary explanation for the significant migration flow from southern to northern Italy in the 1950s and 1960s (Bonifazi and Heins 2000). Moreover, internal migration can produce its own dynamic of cumulative causation (a term more often connected to international migration). Social networks linking rural and urban areas often lead to the self-perpetuation of a migration flow over time: they provide potential migrants with migration-related social capital that facilitates their move (though typically internal migration requires less capital) (Davis et al. 2002).

Internal migration and international migration might amount either to competing or complementary strategies/choices. Thomas (1954) argued that migrants move to destinations where jobs are known to be available, preferring international migration if jobs are more plentiful abroad (and vice versa). But internal migration can be an initial step that subsequently leads to international migration: migrants from rural areas sometimes move to urban areas in their own country to accumulate money and work experience in the industrial or service sectors – and then use these resources to embark on migration to another country (Cornelius

1992). This sequence might even have multiple steps: migrants can move to different cities within their own country before moving to another country (Lozano-Ascencio et al. 1999), or they can move to the zone close to a border before subsequently crossing it (Cornelius and Martin 1993). Even when migrants do not initially plan to move to another country, the same process can be observed. Migrants sometimes move from a rural to an urban area in their own country but then lose their employment because of structural changes. They might then be reluctant to return to their region of origin and instead choose to migrate to another country in search of new opportunities.

In his well-known model of the 'mobility transition', Zelinsky (1971, 1983) offers an explanation for the evolution of internal and international migrations over time through a focus on development. He distinguishes different development phases and shows that rural-to-urban internal migration can be observed mainly in 'early transitional societies'. In more advanced societies, internal migrations are essentially inter- and intra-urban. He shows moreover that internal rural-to-urban migration is progressively replaced by international immigration of unskilled workers from developing countries. Empirical studies indicate that inter- and intra-urban migrations are an increasing part of internal migrations in industrialized countries since the 1970s. Thus, the results of the 2000 census in the United States showed that residents of urban areas are on average more mobile than those living in suburban or rural areas (Schachter et al. 2003).

Since the mid-1970s, this phenomenon has been coupled with an increase in internal migration from urban areas to suburban and rural areas (Beale 1977; Halliday and Coombes 1995). This process of 'counter-urbanization' is mainly taking place in developed countries and is explained by the movement of middle- and upper-class social groups who perceive rural areas as having lower costs of living and a better quality of life. There is a correlation between the size of the urban area and the degree of counter-urbanization: the larger the city, the more intense the urban-to-rural migration flow will be (Fielding 1982). Thus, in Italy, the large northern cities that were major poles of attraction in the 1950s and 1960s became areas with significant net out-migration in the 1980s (Bonifazi and Heins 2000). In the USA, counter-urbanization is selective, relating mainly to the migration of members of the white middle and upper classes (Barcus 2004). It might therefore lead to what Frey (1996: 760) describes as a 'demographic balkanization', i.e., the 'spatial segmentation of population by race-ethnicity, class, and age across broad regions, states, and metropolitan areas'.

See also: *Borders*

KEY READINGS

Skeldon, R. (2006) 'Interlinkages between internal and international migration and development in the Asian region', *Population Space and Place*, 12 (1): 15–30.

Solinger, D.J. (1999) 'Citizenship issues in China's internal migration: comparisons with Germany and Japan', *Political Science Quarterly*, 114 (3): 455–78.

Zelinsky, W. (1971) 'The hypothesis of the mobility transition', *Geographical Review*, 61 (2): 219–49.

25 Labour Migration

> *Definition: Migration motivated mainly by the prospect of employment in another country.*

The concept of labour migration is reasonably straightforward (at least in comparison to some other migration concepts): many people probably have a default understanding of international migration in which most migrants are motivated by the prospect of improving their economic situation by working in another country (often a wealthier one). If anything, there is a need for appreciation of the significant extent to which migration consists of *other* modes (e.g. family reunification, refugees, retiree/lifestyle migration). Even so, labour migration (a related term is economic migration) is a key type, and there is a great deal of complexity in the migration streams that can be described using this concept.

In conventional terms, labour migration consists of movement of workers from poorer countries to wealthier countries, mainly to do low-skilled, low-wage jobs that natives in wealthy countries do not want. Guestworker programmes are a specific instance of this type, but labour migration can also be permanent (i.e., envisioned as such at the outset, by the migrants and by employers and/or the state in the destination country); it might also be temporary but without the restrictions that characterize guestworker programmes (thus the migrants return by choice, whatever their original intentions). Labour migrants might arrive in the destination country with a work-related visa but can also enter in an undocumented (illegal) mode (Marfleet and Blustein 2011).

Michael Piore's (1979) analysis of migrant labour captures key dynamics of this form of migration. One essential consideration is status: citizens are reluctant to accept jobs at the bottom of the occupational status hierarchy, even at relatively favourable wages. Particularly in the secondary labour market, marked by unstable demand rooted in the business cycle, workers are difficult to find in the local population also because of their strong preference for employment stability. On both counts, migrant workers appeared (indeed, continue to appear, at least for policy-makers unfamiliar with history) to be an ideal solution. Being foreign, they are less concerned about their place in a local status hierarchy and are willing to accept jobs they would have considered inappropriate in their home countries, particularly at wages high in comparison to what was available to them there. Similarly, the lack of employment security does not matter as much to them given that their intention is typically to accumulate some savings and return 'home'. On the other hand, these perceptions and preferences can change over time (many migrant workers accumulate savings less quickly than they predicted), and they can become similar to native workers in ways that make them less suitable for the jobs they initially held.

In a conventional understanding, the jobs held by labour migrants are jobs typically held by men (e.g. factories and agriculture), while women would migrate primarily in a family reunification mode after their husbands had established themselves economically in the destination. That image was always inaccurate to an extent (see the separate chapter on gendered migration), and it has become increasingly outmoded in recent decades as labour migration streams have shifted and become more diverse. Women are quite often primary migrants, working in a wide range of economic sectors – but there has also been significant growth in employment of migrant women as domestic workers (e.g. cleaning house, caring for children and elderly people). Prominent examples of these migration flows include the employment of Filipina and Indonesian women as maids in Hong Kong and Saudi Arabia, and Filipina and Mexican women in a wider range of jobs in the USA (Constable 2007; Ehrenreich and Hochschild 2003; Parreñas 2001). One might consider migration of sex workers as a form of labour migration, even if this involves an unconventional notion of work. Workers are also increasingly migrating among relatively poor countries, not just from poor to wealthy ones (Ratha and Shaw 2007). Another divergence from the usual depiction of labour migration emerges in the increasing use of highly skilled migrant workers for technical and professional work (Espenshade 2001).

Policy-makers in destination countries have in recent years been trying to manage labour migration flows in ways designed to reduce the low-skilled component, in the face of rising unemployment (and welfare dependency) particularly among natives with limited education and skills. Labour migration policies in many countries have recently been focused on bringing highly skilled workers – not just in a general way but instead targeted at specific occupational needs, with emphasis on altering policy (e.g. quotas) rapidly in response to changes in needs (Martin et al. 2006; Menz and Caviedes 2010). Even so, some countries struggle to manage labour migration in these ways, particularly when it involves undocumented workers, and many labour migration streams continue to comprise considerable proportions of low-skilled workers (especially in the USA).

That point raises a question that arises quite frequently in migration studies: what sort of data is it possible to have on labour migration? Answering that question is difficult not only in relation to undocumented migrants but for the concept of labour migration quite generally (Salt et al. 2005). Some migrants fit into more than one type. The (rapidly increasing) flows of students, for example, consist to a certain extent of labour migration: many students are employed part-time (their residence permits often permit this). In addition, some people use student visas purely as a cover to gain entry for employment that would otherwise be prohibited to them; the institutions in which they are registered might be bogus or of dubious quality, and the 'students' spend most of their time working (Liu-Farrer 2011). Other categories can have similar ambiguities: people who enter for the purpose of family reunification often end up employed, as do many refugees and asylum seekers (though in the case of asylum seekers work is often prohibited and thus illegal when actually attained). All of these points would bear consideration when using data constructed on the basis of official statuses (e.g. as evident in visa types).

The understanding some people have of labour/economic migration is rooted in a common-sense economic perspective that has certain shortcomings (even if it is reinforced by the conventional neoclassical assumptions routinely employed by many economists). Migration is usually seen as a choice made by an individual whose main goal is to raise their income (or maximize their utility). An important corrective emerges in the 'new economics of labour migration' (Stark and Bloom 1985, Stark 1991). In this more realistic view, migration is typically a strategy considered by households, not individuals acting alone, and their goals include diversification of risk, not just greater income. In many poorer countries, certain markets are underdeveloped or even entirely missing: in particular, it can be difficult or impossible for people to get credit and insurance. The risks that arise for people's well-being and even survival can be mitigated if a household member leaves to work in another country: in the event of drought and crop failure, for example, remittances from someone employed in another country can function as an essential substitute for crop insurance. Remittances can also substitute for bank loans, i.e., when there are no banks to make loans. Again, in this perspective labour migration is often not a matter of individuals' desire for the higher wages available in wealthier countries: many people engage in labour migration not out of aspiration or avarice but out of necessity (whether real or perceived).

There are other respects in which a corrective to individualistic assumptions about labour migration is required. The choices of individuals and/or households are embedded in structures operating at a number of levels (e.g. regional, national, global). It is obvious enough that people cannot just choose to engage in labour migration: restrictionist government policies might simply thwart that option. But structures can also facilitate or even compel migration – perhaps more for certain types of people than for others. In a world-systems perspective (e.g. Sassen 1988), the incorporation of peripheral areas into the global economic system sometimes disrupts people's survival strategies, while also creating 'bridges' to particular destination countries. In addition, differently situated migrants find themselves in a wide variety of positions in the destination: while some people (such as daily cross-border commuters, e.g. living in France but commuting each day into Geneva or Basel) enjoy situations not terribly different from native workers, others encounter conditions that seem antiquated or even antithetical to pervasive understandings of capitalist societies. Robin Cohen (1987) argues that analysis of labour migration reveals a picture of capitalist economies fundamentally at variance with a classic Marxist understanding: instead of being characterized by 'free' labour, capitalism (particularly as practised in the most 'advanced' countries) requires significant quantities of unfree labour, supplied mainly by migrants, many of whom are constrained in ways that are not easily reconciled with standard market theory. Again, labour migration is sometimes not purely a matter of choice, and it often does not have the consequences that the migrants themselves anticipate.

As with other issues relating to migration, many people are interested mainly in what labour migration means for destination countries (e.g. Castles 2010). It is clear, however, that labour migration can have very significant consequences for countries of origin. One particular concern, arising mainly for the emigration of skilled workers, is the brain drain. For sectors such as health care, for example, some countries find that educational investment in their own citizens does not produce a good return: the beneficiaries are (in addition to the migrants themselves) mainly the wealthy countries that succeed in attracting workers by paying wages the origin countries cannot match. Martin et al. (2006) suggest compensating origin countries for their losses, in part by enabling origin-country taxation of emigrants' earnings in destination countries. On the other hand, labour migration (whether of skilled or unskilled workers) might enhance development prospects for origin countries via emigrants' remittances and return migration, though there can be substantial regional variation in this regard (Verduzco and Unger 1998). In addition, it is no longer possible to make a clear distinction between destination countries and sending countries, as many countries now fall into both categories (e.g. Thailand, on which Martin et al. 2006).

See also: *Guestworkers; Brain drain/gain/circulation*

KEY READINGS

Martin, P.L., Abella, M.I. and Kuptsch, C. (2006) *Managing Labor Migration in the Twenty-first Century*. New Haven, CT: Yale University Press.

Parreñas, R.S. (2001) *Servants of Globalization: Women, Migration, and Domestic Work*. Stanford, CA: Stanford University Press.

Piore, M.J. (1979) *Birds of Passage: Migrant Labor and Industrial Societies*. Cambridge: Cambridge University Press.

Sassen, S. (1988) *The Mobility of Labor and Capital: A Study in International Investment and Labor Flow*. Cambridge: Cambridge University Press.

Stark, O. (1991) *The Migration of Labor*. Oxford: Basil Blackwell.

26 Migrant Networks

Definition: Social networks are sets of relationships that are open in principle and are composed of different kinds of social ties. Migrant networks involve social ties that take shape via the distinctive experiences of migration; these networks usually persist across international boundaries.

Everyone has social networks. We are all connected in various ways to family members, friends, neighbours, community members, schoolmates, teachers, colleagues, employers, co-religionists, and even bureaucrats and government officials. Migrants are no different in this respect – they have social networks too. However, migrants' networks are usually different from those of native-born persons in some important ways and thus have different life consequences.

A social network is made up of individuals or organizations, often called 'nodes', which are tied together by different sorts of relationships based on friendship, common interests, values/beliefs, economic exchange, and/or influence. An individual can think of him- or herself as a node having ties to kin, neighbours, community members, schoolmates, colleagues and employers, not to mention religious, political, educational and state institutions. A social network, then, is a kind of social structure made up of nodes and ties. Individuals have social networks in that they are part of a social structure made up of different kinds of relationships – but institutions such as families, communities, organizations, cities and states can also constitute a social network in which people are connected by common interests, economic exchange, influence, animosity, and so on. Networks are different from groups or communities in that they do not have closed or visible boundaries. They are, in principle, open configurations of relationships that can encompass groups and communities, among other social formations.

Migration researchers such as Douglas Massey and his colleagues (1998) have typically defined migrant networks as interpersonal ties linking kin, friends and community members in their places of origin and destination. Several other migration specialists have shown that other kinds of social ties also exist for migrants. For instance, many migrants have organizational ties to institutions and organizations that help them to migrate, get jobs or adjust to a new society in other ways (Poros 2011; Portes 1995). These might be universities, alumni associations, diaspora organizations, refugee community organizations, state agencies, non-governmental organizations, private employment agencies, corporations, religious organizations, cultural institutions, and so on. Some ties reflect even more complex relationships, such as those of transnational entrepreneurs, whose ties can combine interpersonal and organizational relations as in family firms (Ong 1999; Poros 2011). These interpersonal and organizational ties represent only the most general ways that migration researchers have described migrant networks. Research on migrant networks is still limited, especially considering how significantly networks have been shown to affect various aspects of migrants' lives, for instance migrating to a particular destination, finding a job and housing, opening a business, participating in the development of one's home country and accessing health care.

Migrants as individuals are nodes in a network and in many respects have the same sorts of ties that native-born persons do – to organizations and other individuals, whether they are co-ethnic, native or non-native. However, the kinds of ties that migrants have are very much conditioned by the experience of migration and the processes they go through as migrants, not only to move across international borders, but also to find employment, settle into a new city, town or neighbourhood, and access everyday resources in their new place of residence. Thus, migrant networks can look quite different from native networks depending on how a person migrates, their pre-migration ties in their homelands and in their destination country (or countries), the length of time they spend in each of those places, and so on.

The most distinctive feature of migrants' social ties is that they exist across two or more countries. These ties can facilitate migration by connecting potential immigrants to opportunities for work and residence in another country where those ties exist. Thus, immigrants typically have a more limited or specific set of ties to organizations than native-born persons do. Immigrants' lack of citizenship may also limit their access to native institutions and organizations, most obviously to political institutions, but also to opportunities for schooling, housing and aid. This limitation, of course, varies greatly across different countries depending on the reception of immigrants and their institutional accommodation by states and governments, including the ability to become naturalized citizens.

A key consequence of the existence of migrant networks is that migration flows around the world are very selective. We can see this in the fact that roughly half of all movements across international borders take place between developing countries. People do not simply look around the world and abstractly decide where they might like to pick up and move to. Migration can be very risky – and most potential immigrants (including refugees and asylum seekers) seek to minimize their risks when they move, and therefore consider places where they know other individuals or organizations that can help them. Thus, social networks provide the kinds of connections needed to make migration possible. These social structures connect potential migrants in origin areas with migrants in destination areas. They may also connect potential migrants with institutions or organizations that are looking to recruit them or join them with their origin communities. Often, these organizations are in destination areas, such as refugee community organizations that facilitate the adjustment of refugees usually originating in the same ethnic or national communities (Griffiths et al. 2005). However, the relevant organizations might also exist in places of origin, facilitating migration flows from the home towns and countries of potential immigrants.

Simply being a part of a social network is usually not enough to make migration a reality. One must have social capital – the actual or potential resources linked to a migrant's social ties (Bourdieu 1986; Portes 1998, 2000). For instance, agricultural workers from Morocco sometimes rely on social ties with family and friends to migrate and work for the same employer on farms in southern Spain (Calavita 2005). High-tech workers from India might be recruited by employment agencies or by what Xiang Biao (2006) calls 'bodyshoppers' to work in IT firms, as they do in Australia and the USA. Traders from the Middle East may access foreign markets to expand their businesses by migrating to Venezuela or Brazil with the help of business contacts (Romero 2010). People join their parents, siblings or children, attempting to reunite their families (as happens in almost every migrant destination in the world).

The social capital embedded in migrant networks is often crucial for accomplishing migration, regardless of (though not instead of) specific country policies and restrictions. Necessary resources (such as information, money and aid) must also be *exchanged* via these ties to make migration happen. The relations inherent in the social capital of migrants constitute the mechanism by which such resources are distributed. As such, a social network by no means offers equal opportunities and resources to all of its members. Many studies have shown that transactions within migrant network ties often include tensions, conflict, resistance and capitulation emerging from wrongdoing or broken promises (e.g. Menjívar 2000; Poros 2011; Portes and Sensenbrenner 1995).

The economic incorporation of immigrants provides a good example of how migrant networks can be beneficial or harmful (Waldinger and Lichter 2003). Many immigrants use their social networks to find employment. The prominence of ethnic economies (see Light and Gold 2000) – particularly, ethnic enclave economies, usually most visible in cities, such as Chinatowns and Koreatowns, or Little Italies and Indias – attests to the way immigrants have used their social networks and co-ethnic social capital to find employment in businesses that primarily serve their co-ethnic communities. The businesses located in these enclaves rely on family (often unpaid) and co-ethnic labour to survive, sometimes setting up conditions for exploitation and conflict. Thus, inequalities can persist within immigrant or co-ethnic social ties.

A broader lens on ethnic economies reveals some of the global dimensions of networks and their connection to the economic incorporation of immigrants. Diaspora entrepreneurship, a subject of much recent attention (e.g. Newland and Tanaka 2010), refers to the development of businesses by immigrants who are in a position to take advantage of diaspora policies and organizations in countries that are attempting to promote entrepreneurship by their nationals living abroad. This kind of economic development relies much more on organizational ties with governments, institutions and agencies involved in its promotion. Its effects are much more global or transnational, in contrast to the more commonly cited local effects of an ethnic economy. Diaspora entrepreneurs can serve as a bridge connecting organizational ties in their home countries to those living in their countries of immigration. A variety of organizations (such as the Mexican Talent Network, the South African diaspora network, GlobalScot, Armenia 2020, Ethiopia Commodity Exchange and Fundación Chile) have promoted networking, mentoring, training, investment and venture capital initiatives to enhance development in the origin countries via connections with immigrants living in a diaspora. These organizational ties appear to hold potential for catalysing economic and social development on a much greater scale, in contrast to the effects of small- and medium-sized businesses that serve mostly local or regional ethnic economies.

Remittance economies, too, result from migration and the financial support immigrants provide via interpersonal ties within their networks. Remittance economies are constituted largely by financial exchange between migrants and their family members, friends and community. Two of the largest remittance economies, India and China, together received just over one-third of worldwide remittances in 2009 at US$55 billion and US$51 billion respectively (World Bank 2011).

A transnational mode of migration facilitates the transfer of remittances and development in immigrants' countries of origin. Transnational social networks are composed of people who live 'dual lives', e.g. speaking more than one language, having homes in two or more countries, and making a living through regular contact across borders (Portes et al. 1999). Transnational activities can be economic, political and social (e.g. import–export businesses, elite business activities, political campaigning among expatriates, or developing schools in one's home village). And they depend on both interpersonal and organizational types of ties. For instance, Jain Indian diamond dealers have far-flung diasporas across places such as Antwerp, Hong Kong, Bombay and New York, where they produce and trade diamonds for their markets. Or, as an example of political transnationalism, the US intervention against Spain during the Spanish-American War in 1898 was rooted to a significant extent in a campaign by Cuba's Revolutionary Party targeting exiles in New York City. Transnational managerial elites who shuttle back and forth between global cities as intra-company transferees have also become more prominent in recent years. Perhaps more commonly, we hear of ordinary immigrants who make continual trips back and forth to their homelands for social purposes, such as religious pilgrimages or to help build infrastructural projects. All of these transnational activities rely fundamentally on migrants' networks and the exchange of goods and resources within their social ties.

Finally, another area in which we see the influence of social networks on immigrants' lives is on their health. Migration researchers in the USA have found that, paradoxically, as immigrants acculturate to American society their health often deteriorates, with increasing rates of obesity, mortality and other physical and mental health problems (Rumbaut 1999). Migrant networks can protect immigrants' health by promoting greater access to health care, sometimes in immigrants' countries of origin where they may return for such services. Networks can also protect immigrants' health by encouraging traditional nutritional habits rather than the adoption of less healthy American ones. They can provide support for immigrants needing health care and food security. Of course, migrant networks also interact with other factors that affect the health of immigrants, such as educational achievement and occupational status.

Social networks have significant effects on many aspects of the migration process and on migrants' lives. Interpersonal and organizational social ties affect who migrates and to which destinations. They influence the kinds of employment migrants obtain in their host countries. They can foster development in sending countries and create large remittance economies. They are the conduits of transnationalism. They can assist refugees in a new society. And, they can protect immigrants' health. Although migrant networks clearly have benefits, they can also create disadvantages for immigrants by limiting their access to co-ethnic resources or facilitating their exploitation. Nevertheless, migrant networks are a key component of immigrants' lives, typically used on a daily basis to secure goods and resources.

See also: *Diaspora; Ethnic enclaves and ethnic economies; Remittances; Selectivity; Social capital; Transnationalism*

KEY READINGS

Massey, D.S., Arango, J., Hugo, G., Kouaouci, A., Pellegrino, A. and Taylor, J.E. (1998) *Worlds in Motion: Understanding International Migration at the End of the Millennium*. Oxford: Clarendon Press.

Poros, M.V. (2011) *Modern Migrations: Gujarati Indian Networks in New York and London*. Stanford, CA: Stanford University Press.

Portes, A. (1995) 'Economic sociology and the sociology of immigration: a conceptual overview', in A. Portes (ed.), *The Economic Sociology of Immigration: Essays on Networks, Ethnicity and Entrepreneurship*. New York: Russell Sage Foundation, pp. 1–41.

Portes, A. (1998) 'Social capital: its origins and applications in modern sociology', *Annual Review of Sociology*, 24: 1–24.

Waldinger, R. and Lichter, M. (2003) *How the Other Half Works: Immigration and the Social Organization of Labor*. Berkeley, CA: University of California Press.

27 Migration Stocks and Flows

Definition: 'Stocks' and 'flows' are basic demographic concepts used to analyse and understand migration processes in a country or region. Migration stocks are the numbers of migrants living in a country or region at a given point in time. Migration flows are the number of migrants entering or leaving a country or region during a specific period of time.

The concepts of migration stocks and flows emerged when nation-states started to measure and analyse the features of the population living in their territories. They are closely related to methods of identifying individuals (e.g. passports, residence permits and border controls) and statistical instruments (the census and the population registers) that emerged in European and North American countries in the eighteenth and nineteenth centuries. As modern nation-states were constructed, these tools were used by governments to specify who could benefit from welfare and who had to pay taxes. In the context of nineteenth-century European wars, these instruments were also designed to keep foreigners under surveillance (Noiriel 1998; Torpey 2000). More generally, the emergence of migration stocks and flows as concepts is related to the construction of the 'national' as a category of identification by states, who aimed to distinguish citizens from foreigners. France was one of the first European countries to use data of this sort to make an 'inventory' of foreigners living in its territory. The first official measurements of an immigrant stock included the 1851 census (Silberman 1992), which estimated that immigrants were 1 per cent of the population living in the French territory. In the USA, the 1850 census established that 9.7 per cent of the population living in the territory were immigrants (Thernstrom 1992).

Today, the measurement of immigration stocks and flows is also used to observe trends in the composition and growth (or decline) of the population living in a country. These statistics also relate to more general political and ideological issues. Massey argues that the measurement of migration is related to issues of 'identity, citizenship, belonging, and entitlement' and that 'an international move is much more than a demographic fact, therefore; it is a social, economic, and political event with strong and often competing interests in how it is defined and measured' (2010b: 126). Figures on migration stocks and flows are used to define general orientations in policies related to immigration and citizenship. These indicators can also influence the orientation of foreign policies (as when one country experiences significant immigration inflows from another) or affirmative action policies in the countries that implement them. As observed by scholars drawing on the concept of cumulative causation, the directions and strength of migration flows connect to the features of migration stocks. The existence of a significant migration stock originating in a specific region usually leads to the self-perpetuation of the flow that produced it. Figures on migration stocks are thus used to estimate the characteristics of future migration flows in a country, and so to analyse the evolution of its population in the long term.

The measurement of migration stocks and flows depends on definitions of migration, because those definitions determine who can be counted as a migrant. The task of definition raises many difficulties for demographers and others who 'measure' migration. For example, how do we distinguish immigrants from tourists? How do we distinguish immigrants from border workers (those living in a country and crossing the border every day to work in another country)? Should we count foreign-born naturalized citizens as immigrants? Definitions of 'migrants' can vary across countries and over time. The majority of countries in the Organization for Economic Cooperation and Development (OECD – a 'club' of the world's wealthiest countries) define the immigrant population by country of origin/birth (e.g. Australia, Canada, the Netherlands, the United Kingdom and the United States); others use citizenship or nationality as the key criterion (e.g. France, Germany, Japan and Spain). These differences have major implications for measuring immigration. For example, in the first set of countries figures on migrant stocks include immigrants who have become citizens, while in the second group migration statistics do not include naturalized citizens. Depending on legislation regarding citizenship and naturalization, the second group can also include children and grandchildren of immigrants in the migration stock, i.e., if it is difficult for them to gain citizenship/nationality. Again, these approaches can change: in Germany until the end of the 1990s, most descendants of immigrants did not have German nationality (even if born in Germany) and were therefore immigrants – but acquiring German nationality subsequently became significantly easier, with direct implications for the evolution of data on immigrants.

A deeper analysis of migration stocks and flows requires distinguishing between different categories of migrants: migrant workers, refugees, international students and long-term vs. short-term migrants. Again, there are challenges here for demographers. For example, how can we distinguish a migrant worker from a migrant student when an individual works part-time and/or wishes to remain and work in the country after completing their studies? What is the duration of stay that distinguishes a long-term migrant from a short-term migrant? Here as well, definitions of these categories can vary across countries and over time. For example, since the end of the 1980s, most European countries have changed their definition of 'refugees' and established a set of new criteria for granting this status. Consequently, an increasing number of asylum seekers could not enter the territory of these countries as refugees, and this specific migration flow has decreased in relative terms (Legoux 2012). These difficulties also apply to researchers who wish to compare migration flows in different countries, a point apparent in a discussion of how to define 'foreign workers' (Bartram 2012).

International organizations such as the United Nations, the European Union and the OECD have made considerable efforts to harmonize definitions of migration stocks and flows across countries. In 1976, the UN Statistics Division published *Recommendations on Statistics of International Migration* (revised in 1998) and provided some basic definitions that can serve as references. It is thus recommended to define a migrant on the basis of country of residence rather than of citizenship: 'an international migrant is defined as any person who changes his or her country of usual residence' (United Nations 1998: 84). From this perspective, the migration stock is defined as

> the set of persons who have ever changed their country of usual residence, that is to say, persons who have spent at least one year of their lives in a country other than the one in which they lived at the time the data are gathered. (United Nations 1998: 18)

For defining migration flows, it is recommended to distinguish long-term migrants ('a person moving out of his usual country of residence for a period of at least twelve months') from short-term migrants ('a person moving out of his usual country of residence for a period of at least three months but less than twelve months'). Based on these definitions, the UN calculated that the international migration stock in the world was 155,518,065 in 1990, and 195,245,404 in 2005 (2.9 and 3.1 per cent of the global population, respectively) (United Nations 2009). Migration stocks have increased significantly in Europe and North America since 1990: migrants were 6.9 per cent of the European population in 1990 and 8.8 per cent in 2005; they were 9.8 per cent of the North American population in 1990 and 13.6 per cent in 2005 (United Nations 2009).

Challenges of defining migration stocks and flows are coupled with difficulties of data collection. For example, in many countries, data on inflows are collected at the border, when a migrant enters the country. However, these data reflect the declared intention to stay and not necessarily the actual stay in a country. For example, an immigrant can state an intention to enter the country as a student but then look for a job and even abandon their studies completely. Also, a migrant can enter the country as a tourist or short-term migrant and then decide to remain in the country after the legal period of stay has expired. These difficulties also relate to the data collected within the country. In particular, although some estimates exist (e.g. the Clandestino project), it is usually very difficult to know with any real precision the number of undocumented migrants living in a country.

Definitions of migration stocks and flows can also vary significantly beyond the contributions of researchers and government agencies. When the mass media, political leaders and various social groups discuss migration, definitions are typically quite vague. The media in the UK often use the terms 'migrants', 'ethnic minorities' or 'asylum seekers' in an interchangeable way (Baker et al. 2008). Also, public discourse tends to focus on certain categories of migrants: asylum seekers, low-skilled workers and undocumented migrants tend to 'count' more than other types of migrants such as students or high-skilled workers (Anderson and Blinder 2011). It is also interesting to note that people who move from an industrialized country are often referred to as 'expatriates' rather than 'migrants' – but this term is never used when referring to people who immigrate from a poorer country. Public surveys may add to this confusion: some surveys do not present a definition of the term migrant, while others refer to a vague and sometimes even incorrect definition (Anderson and Blinder 2011).

See also: *Migration networks Undocumented (illegal) migration*

KEY READINGS

Massey, D.S. (2010b) 'Immigration statistics for the twenty-first century', *Annals of the American Academy of Political and Social Science*, 631: 124–40.

Pedersen, P.J., Pytlikova, M. and Smith, N. (2008) 'Selection and network effects –migration flows into OECD countries 1990–2000', *European Economic Review*, 52 (7): 1160–86.

Silberman, R. (1992) 'French immigration statistics', in D.L. Horowitz, and G. Noiriel (eds), *Immigrants in Two Democracies: French and American Experiences*. New York: New York University Press, pp. 112–23.

United Nations Population Division (2009) *Trends in International Migrant Stocks*. New York: United Nations.

28 Multiculturalism

Definition: An 'orientation' to immigration that embraces difference and diversity; it is in certain respects the opposite of an expectation that immigrants should and will assimilate.

All countries that receive any significant number of immigrants are multicultural (though many had a significant degree of cultural variety even before the onset of mass immigration). But multicultural*ism* is not merely a recognition of this empirical fact; it is an 'orientation' and an ideology, a particular way of identifying how immigrants integrate in the destination country, and how they are expected to integrate. In countries where a multiculturalist approach prevails, there is no expectation that immigrants will abandon their 'origin' culture and become culturally identical to natives of the destination society. In some instances one also finds active institutional support (particularly in educational institutions) for maintaining certain elements of immigrants' culture. A key feature of the multiculturalism concept is its legitimation of group-level identities, as against the classical liberal emphasis on equality of individuals; ethnic identities of immigrant origin are sustained at an intermediate level between individuals and the nation, and, instead of disappearing into the melting pot, immigrant groups now help make up a 'mosaic' or 'salad bowl'.

In an earlier era, immigrants commonly encountered strong expectations of assimilation. This demand had two ideological foundations. One can only be described as ethnocentrism – the belief (or presumption) that the destination country's culture was superior to that of the immigrants' country of origin. This attitude of superiority is sometimes framed in relation to 'Western' culture, and indeed immigrants from non-Western (and particularly non-white) countries commonly faced attitudes that were not merely ethnocentric but openly racist. But immigrants moving from one Western country to another often met with disdain rooted in ethnocentrism as well, e.g. Irish immigrants in the UK, or Italians in the USA. A second foundation for the expectation of assimilation is arguably more neutral (which is not to suggest that it is justified or desirable): some want to be surrounded by people who are culturally similar to them (i.e., without necessarily implying that those who are different are thereby inferior). While it is often unclear why certain aspects of identity and culture become salient for being 'different', immigrants can easily be assigned a role that highlights or builds on perceived differences, especially when cultural homogeneity has been identified as desirable.

A desire for cultural homogeneity has been supplanted in many contexts by a belief that diversity is more advantageous and appropriate. To an extent, this shift resulted from the refusal of immigrants to accept any longer the subordinate position that assimilationist approaches had assigned to them. In the USA, the Civil Rights Movement of the 1960s, in delegitimizing racism and encouraging the participation of African-Americans in a variety of political processes, empowered other minority groups to assert their own claims and resist demands for assimilation – particularly when those demands appeared to be rooted in ethnocentrism. Immigrant/minority-group assertiveness and discourses of anti-racism emerged in other countries as well, and in some countries, such as Canada and Australia (and perhaps the UK, though to a lesser extent), multiculturalism was embraced at the highest levels of government, as 'official policy' (Kivisto 2002).

Contemporary multiculturalism thus finds expression in a set of attitudes and policies designed to sustain diversity, and the differences between immigrants and natives are often celebrated rather than reviled. Kivisto (2012) identifies five types of claims that policies address: exemption, accommodation, preservation, redress and inclusion. Policies commonly pursued under these logics include bilingual education for children especially in early years; efforts to prevent harassment and stereotyping in the media, employment, schools and public services; and affirmative action to increase representation of immigrant groups in political and educational institutions as well as some employment sectors (Kymlicka 2001a). In the UK multiculturalism has extended to the creation of state-supported minority religious schools, building on the precedent of Christian and Jewish schools to establish Muslim and Hindu schools as well. There are also measures intended to grant public recognition, as when political elites participate conspicuously in holiday celebrations of minority groups, e.g. Diwali, and certain regulations are sometimes varied for minority groups, in relation to dress codes or weekly/holiday schedules.

Sometimes multiculturalism is presented as a radical departure from past practices, and some observers (as well as some activists and politicians) frame multiculturalism as a path towards 'separatism' and national disintegration. A lament by Schlesinger is typical of this mode of critique: 'The cult of ethnicity exaggerates differences, intensifies resentments and antagonisms, drives ever deeper the awful wedges between races and nationalities' (1992: 102). In giving salience to differences, multiculturalism is said to undermine a shared American identity – perhaps endangering prospects for democratic governance (if not portending schism or secession, as once seemed possible for Canada). Some commentators in Europe worry particularly about Muslim immigrants, who are said to be insufficiently committed to democratic values while harbouring 'dual loyalties' (with Islam predominant as a hyper-identity); insofar as European countries have failed to insist on assimilation to 'European values', Caldwell asserts that 'multiculturalism became almost … a self-directed xenophobia' (2009: 86) that might facilitate Muslim ascendancy in Europe.

Kymlicka (e.g. 2001a) argues these worries are misplaced, and that portrayals of multiculturalism as separatism are a misrepresentation of what multiculturalism advocates want and of what actually takes place. Multiculturalism is best understood as a way of promoting integration, on 'fairer terms'; it is thus the opposite of separatism. Measures such as bilingual education and affirmative action seek to facilitate immigrants' participation in core social institutions, rather than to exclude them – in recognition of the likelihood that stringent assimilationist demands can result in marginalization rather than inclusion. Multiculturalist policies do not replace or challenge the core institutions and policies that provide the foundation for integration, and they fall well short of meeting the conditions that would enable 'minority nationalism'. Tariq Modood (2005) makes similar arguments about Europe, where Muslims in the UK, for example, seek to be 'British Muslims' while working for a redefinition of British identity that can transcend its historical white Christian English core to embrace Muslims as well.

The 'separatism' critique comes primarily from the political right – but there is a similar critique from the political left, where some observers are uncomfortable with the emphasis given to identity/culture as against other bases of solidarity. Multiculturalist discourses, which typically self-identify as 'progressive', address (and perhaps reinforce) a need for 'recognition', which in the contemporary period amounts to validation of difference in the public sphere (C. Taylor 1992). In older progressive (i.e., leftist) traditions, the main goal is redistribution of economic and political power. Some in the 'old left' worry that the demand for recognition results in a fragmentation of class solidarity, undermining prospects for addressing the economic deprivation of immigrants and minority groups (Gitlin 1995; Barry 2001). A similar argument is constructed in relation to gender: Okin (1999) finds a significant tension between multiculturalism and the liberal feminism that has brought impressive gains to women in many Western countries. That tension highlights the question: who gets to define the culture of particular groups and speak on their behalf? When immigrants come from strongly patriarchal societies, multiculturalist integration in destination countries might (so the argument goes) perpetuate male privilege and the oppression of women.

Research on multiculturalism commonly takes ethnic groups as key units of analysis, with group identities and affiliations determined automatically by country of origin (thus 'Pakistanis in the UK'). While convenient for scholars and policy-makers, this practice might not do justice to immigrant experience: Pakistanis in the UK are by no means a homogeneous group. Vertovec (2007b) describes the emergence of 'super-diversity': in addition to country of origin, formation of immigrant identity draws on legal status, mode of entry, human capital and locality, among other factors. Context matters as well: multiculturalism in the UK is different from multiculturalism in the USA (Joppke and Lukes 1999) and also shows internal variation, with, for example, a distinctive mode in New York (Foner 2007).

In recent years there has been a backlash against multiculturalism, and in some places a partial retreat (though it was always contentious to a degree, see Vertovec and Wessendorf 2010). In part this trend comes as a response to the World Trade Center bombings in the USA and riots in several northern British cities in 2001. A variety of public figures in the UK (including, in 2011, the Conservative prime minister, David Cameron) have pronounced multiculturalism a failure; the previous Labour government, as well, promoted a discourse of 'social cohesion' designed to reinforce 'shared values' – though this was arguably a matter of minority groups 'sharing' the values of the majority/white population rather than vice versa (Schuster and Solomos 2004). To gain permanent residence, immigrants in the UK now have to pass a test to ensure they have sufficient familiarity with 'Life in the UK' (as well as facility in English). In theory, immigrants who take the test will have had exposure to 'British values' sufficient to convince them of their worth; in reality, this requirement was a means for the Labour Party to capture votes by outflanking parties further to the right, attempting to assuage fears among the white working class (Kundnani 2007).

The diversity genie is surely out of the bottle, and state-imposed assimilationist measures might simply alienate certain immigrant groups without actually achieving any greater degree of assimilation. The word multiculturalism is currently out of favour in some circles, but at least in English-speaking countries the practices and attitudes it has fostered are largely taken for granted, though again they can at times also be contentious (Vertovec and Wessendorf 2010; Kivisto 2012). A degree of assimilation is also typical: immigrants do not enter a condition of stasis, and they are inevitably affected by their new context. But the extent to which people and institutions can *impose* a comprehensive one-way process of assimilation on immigrants is now greatly reduced (e.g. Reitz 2009).

See also: *Assimilation; Integration; Social cohesion*

KEY READINGS

Barry, B. (2001) *Culture and Equality: An Egalitarian Critique of Multiculturalism*. Cambridge, MA: Harvard University Press.

Kivisto, P. (2002) *Multiculturalism in a Global Society*. New York: Wiley-Blackwell.

Kymlicka, W. (2001a) *Politics in the Vernacular: Nationalism, Multiculturalism and Citizenship*. Oxford: Oxford University Press.

Kymlicka, W. (2012) *Multiculturalism: Success, Failure, and the Future*. Washington, DC: Migration Policy Institute.

Taylor, C. (1992) *Multiculturalism and the Politics of Recognition: An Essay*. Princeton, NJ: Princeton University Press.

Vertovec, S. (2007b) 'Superdiversity and its implications', *Ethnic and Racial Studies*, 30: 1024–54.

29 Refugees and Asylum Seekers

Definition: Refugees and asylum seekers are migrants who have left their countries and request international protection on account of persecution, war or other factors that put their lives or security at risk.

Refugees and asylum seekers engage in migration as a consequence of a significant disruption in their current situation, such as war or persecution. A common perception is that refugees engage in 'forced migration', while other types of migrants have made a choice reasonably described as voluntary; that distinction is sometimes difficult to apply in practice (as discussed in a separate chapter on forced migration), though it is certainly true that many or even most refugees have encountered violence or at least faced the threat of it. Refugees can be 'recognized' for having met (in the determination of an authority of some sort) the criteria specified in various international agreements – or they can be 'unrecognized' even though their situation resembles that of recognized refugees. Asylum seekers are by definition not (yet) recognized as refugees, having arrived in another country asking to enter and remain on the basis of needing protection from threats they would face if returned to their country of origin (Gibney 2004). The concept of refugees can also extend to 'internally displaced persons' (IDPs), forced to move within their own country, though some observers prefer to reserve the term refugee for those who have gone to another country to seek protection from a different state (Hathaway 2007).

Refugees and asylum seekers have become a major political issue in some wealthy countries in recent decades, giving the impression that the numbers arriving in those countries have increased greatly. Numbers of refugees on a global scale have indeed increased greatly – but the vast majority flee to poorer countries, not to the wealthy ones: the biggest numbers are found in Pakistan (1.7 million, not including IDPs) and Iran (1.1 million), not the USA (331,000) or the UK (281,000). Among wealthy countries, the most significant destination is Germany (633,000).[1] If one includes IDPs and other categories that contribute to the UN High Commissioner on Refugees' 'total population of concern', countries where numbers are very large also include Colombia, Iraq, Democratic Republic of the Congo, Somalia, Syria, Sudan and Thailand (all above one million). The countries currently 'producing' the largest numbers of refugees (recognized and unrecognized) are Afghanistan, Iraq, Somalia, Democratic Republic of the Congo and Myanmar (UNHCR 2010) and, more recently, Syria. The majority of refugees are in protracted refugee situations, where displacement persists for many years, even many decades (Loescher 2005). As with any discussion of numbers, much depends on definitions and the means of collecting data; for refugees a particular concern is the tendency to focus on 'official' categories (see below) and to count those who are easy to count. That latter point pertains especially to the focus on people in camps; there is much less attention to 'self-settled' refugees who successfully blend in with the native population (Bakewell 2008).

With a sufficiently expansive definition of the word 'political' and an appreciation of the aphorism 'war is politics by other means', one can see refugee movements as rooted in political conflicts of particular kinds (Marrus 2002), in contrast to the economic factors commonly motivating other types of migrants (though there are of course risks in reducing complex situations to these ostensibly simple categories and oppositions). In 'developing' countries, where most refugees now originate, refugee migration typically emerges in conflicts rooted in the failed or incomplete consolidation of nation-states, in a global context where such states are the norm (Zolberg et al. 1989). The geographic boundaries of many present-day countries in Africa, for example, were formed via nineteenth-century European competition for colonies and do not correspond to the geographic distribution of peoples/tribes/etc. that had any real prospect of or desire for becoming nations. Some of these countries have limited scope for the peaceful democratic resolution of conflict, and violent conflict sometimes includes deliberate efforts to expel civilian populations, as part of a nation-building project rooted in a desire for national homogeneity or dominance. This dynamic was apparent also in the Balkans (former Yugoslavia) in the 1990s as well as a number of older conflicts in Asia and the Middle East (e.g. Palestinians, India/Pakistan).

During the cold war, refugee flows came also from instances of Western vs. communist conflicts that were not always so 'cold', as in Vietnam and Cuba, where national unity was not the issue; instead, the refugee-producing conflicts were better described as ideological in a more 'pure' sense. In earlier centuries refugee flows emerged from conflicts that were ostensibly religious (as with Huguenots fleeing from France) – but these were nonetheless political, in an age when the basis for political unity had more to do with religion than with national identity (Zolberg et al. 1989).

Refugee flows, then, are typically rooted in political conflicts in the region of origin – and the recognition (or denial) of refugee claims is also significantly affected by political factors in the various destination countries. Recognition of refugee claims in most countries is governed at a minimum by the 1951 Geneva Convention on the Status of Refugees (as extended by the 1967 Bellagio Protocol to apply beyond Europe), which refers to persons needing protection for having a 'well-founded fear of persecution by reason of … race, religion, nationality or political opinion'. But whether individuals' claims are recognized often depends on political factors affecting individual countries' implementation of the Convention – as is evident in the way the USA was content to grant recognition to refugees fleeing communist Cuba but quite reluctant to grant recognition to those fleeing Haiti, El Salvador and Guatemala (particularly given US support for their anti-communist regimes). This political dynamic is also apparent in changes over time: claims in the UK by Chileans fleeing the Pinochet regime after 1973 were rejected prior to the Labour victory in 1974 – and they were then typically rejected again after the 1979 victory of Margaret Thatcher, whose Conservative government considered Pinochet an important ally despite his regime's persecution of political opponents (Joly et al. 1992; Joly 1996). Dynamics like these help underscore the importance of the notion of 'unrecognized refugees', i.e., those in 'refugee-like situations' that do not meet the narrow definition of the Geneva Convention.

Politicization is also apparent in the administration of claims made by asylum seekers, which as noted above has become a major political issue in some countries despite low numbers (22,000 new claims in the UK in 2010, down from more than 30,000 in previous years; 55,000 in the USA) (UNHCR 2011). Some politicians, reflecting their perceptions of voter concern, worry that many asylum seekers use asylum claims to facilitate migration motivated not by violence or persecution but by economic factors (in a context of more restrictive entry regimes in most wealthy countries since the 1970s). Such countries set high barriers to successful asylum claims (on top of efforts to prevent arrival, so that claims cannot be lodged, see Castles 2003a), presupposing that many claimants will invent false tales of abuse and victimization. Unsurprisingly, most regimes intent on persecuting or expelling their own citizens do not provide them with the kind of documentary evidence preferred by modern rational bureaucracies, and decisions often turn on tribunals' judgements concerning the credibility of claimants' testimony. A non-trivial percentage of wrong outcomes is inevitable.

Some asylum seekers become (successful) refugees; others are commonly described as 'failed asylum seekers' when their claims are rejected but they nonetheless remain in the destination country – and with no right to hold legitimate jobs many become destitute (O'Neill 2010). Rejected claims can thus lead to a type of 'illegal' or 'undocumented' immigration – and indeed some governments take the view that 'illegal immigrants' is what they always were (Marfleet 2006). On the other hand, it is often impractical or even illegal to deport people to certain countries; some are given 'exceptional leave to remain' (i.e., in the UK, with equivalents elsewhere), while others remain in an undetermined or liminal condition. Those whose claims succeed are undoubtedly more fortunate, but legal recognition (even when accompanied by the various rights specified in the Geneva Convention) is no guarantee that destination countries will offer support that answers the specific needs distinguishing their situation from that of other types of immigrants (Joly 1996).

Refugees by definition need protection, and the need is typically urgent. In recent decades, however, there has been increasing interest in the notion of addressing root causes, so that refugees can return to their country of origin (or perhaps avoid being forced out in the first place) (e.g. Zetter 1988; Zolberg et al. 1989). Insofar as refugees are different from other types of migrants in that they are forced out and do not actively embrace migration (though this as well is a distinction that is difficult to sustain in many instances), permanent resettlement in the destination country perhaps amounts to an admission of failure with respect to some refugees' genuine preferences; others, however, embrace the destination country as their 'home' (Sales 2007; Bloch 2002). The dilemma is especially evident in the experience of many Palestinian refugees, particularly those in other Arab countries, where decades of displacement have not resulted in the kind of 'normalization' that one would usually encounter for other types of migrants and their descendants (e.g. Hanafi and Long 2010; Knudsen 2009). More generally it is difficult to perceive anything more than limited success of efforts to address root causes (Loescher 2001).

It seems highly likely that refugee flows will remain undiminished or even increase in the medium and long term. As described above, refugee situations typically arise from conflicts characteristic of poorly functioning nation-states. There is no shortage of such conflicts, and the potential for additional ones to emerge seems quite significant. In addition to ongoing conflicts in the Middle East and the Great Lakes region of Africa, there are a number of countries in which a prevailing relative calm is the result of repression of poorly integrated national minorities rather than a genuinely democratic mode of politics. Any weakening of repressive regimes could embolden secessionist movements that might in turn provoke violent backlashes, with predictable consequences for refugee flows – as with Chechnya in the 1990s following dissolution of the USSR, and Abkhazia (de facto seceding from

Georgia) in more recent years. One can also perceive an expansion of the basis for claims, e.g. sexuality, as with a successful claim in the US in 2005 by a Mexican man who had been persecuted for his homosexuality.

See also: *Forced migration; Displacement and internally displaced persons*

NOTE

1 Numbers pertain to the end of 2009, and include people in 'refugee-like situations' (especially significant for Pakistan), and for the USA, UK and Germany include asylum seekers: 63,800, 11,900 and 39,000, respectively.

KEY READINGS

Bakewell, O. (2008) 'Research beyond the categories: the importance of policy irrelevant research into forced migration', *Journal of Refugee Studies*, 21: 432–53.
Gibney, M.J. (2004) *The Ethics and Politics of Asylum: Liberal Democracy and the Response to Refugees*. Cambridge: Cambridge University Press.
O'Neill, M. (2010) *Asylum, Migration and Community*. Bristol: Policy Press.
Zolberg, A.R., Suhrke, A. and Aguayo, S. (1989) *Escape from Violence: Conflict and the Refugee Crisis in the Developing World*. New York: Oxford University Press.

30 Regional Integration and Migration

Definition: Regional integration (in connection with migration) refers to a limited set of instances in which groups of states have decided to lower the barriers to immigration of citizens of those countries.

The best-known example of regional integration as it relates to migration is the European Union, where citizens of member states can travel freely and take up residence under conditions much less onerous than those applied to non-Europeans (i.e., those from outside the EU). This 'internal' migration regime is part of a larger framework that began with efforts to reduce restrictions on trade and capital flows. There are several other instances, including the Nordic Common Labour Market, the North American Free Trade Agreement (NAFTA), and an agreement between Australia and New Zealand.

The term 'regional integration' implies a general process in which barriers between countries are reduced. That description is accurate only to the extent that one understands it as referring to an *ongoing* process rather than a completed one; indeed there is no reason to think that the various 'projects' listed above will ever be complete in the sense that the countries in question will no longer be separate countries. Ardent nationalists (e.g. the UK Independence Party) vociferously bemoan the 'loss of sovereignty' represented by European integration, asserting that Britain no longer controls its borders or its 'destiny' more generally. In reality, while Britain and other EU members have agreed to a supranational framework regulating some aspects of the migration of EU citizens, national governments implement the regulations themselves (there is no European border control agency, only the various national ones) and retain great independence to set policy for immigrants from outside the EU. The term integration is possibly too grand to describe the supranational agreements currently in force; the point is especially relevant to migration, where many barriers remain in place, in keeping with a desire among many policy-makers to retain 'national' control over migration policy (Lahav 2004; Brochmann 1996).

Even so, migration among members of the EU is now a much simpler process than it used to be, and member states normally cannot prevent immigration of citizens of other member states (or, rather, these states have chosen not to prevent such migration, via the various treaties they have signed). For most types of work, national citizens and citizens of other EU states compete on a level playing field (at least in legal terms), in contrast to the legal requirement to impose preferences for nationals (as with the job adverts one sees in Canada and many other countries). If a UK citizen receives a job offer in France, they can then take up residence in France under the same conditions that apply to French nationals, and with the various rights and benefits that French nationals enjoy. Some countries, anxious about 'benefit tourism', impose conditions designed to prevent residence where the individuals in question would likely become dependent on welfare payments. The British government, for example, is keen to demonstrate to British tabloid-readers and voters that it is vigilant against the prospect of people from Eastern Europe taking up residence in Britain with the intention of collecting unemployment benefits. But migration of workers, pensioners (retirees) and students is often a straightforward affair; one can reasonably start with the assumption that it will be possible (though there are exceptions, restrictions and conditions, on which see Hall 1995).

The Nordic Common Labour Market extends this logic to such an extent that Fischer and Straubhaar refer to 'complete freedom of movement' (1996: 103): people may move without restriction between Denmark, Finland, Sweden, Norway and Iceland. (The first three are now members of the EU; the agreement in question was adopted in 1954, formalizing practices that were already established, though Iceland joined only in 1982.) Historical associations (Sweden and Norway were ruled by Denmark in earlier centuries) and linguistic and cultural affinities mean that it is reasonable to think of regional integration as having progressed further in the Nordic region than in Europe as a whole. Even so, migration flows within the region have never been large (not even in percentage terms); the most significant migration flows were from Finland to Sweden, in the 1960s and 1970s, such that Finns are roughly 5 per cent of the Swedish population (some are from Finland's Swedish-speaking minority). Intra-Nordic migration is often a matter of short-term moves by younger people seeking adventure/experience (Fischer and Straubhaar 1996).

In some circumstances one observes regional integration frameworks that do not include significant provisions enabling migration. The most conspicuous instance of this pattern is NAFTA, encompassing Mexico, the USA and Canada, where beginning in 1994 some restrictions on trade and investment were lifted – but without concomitant measures for increased mobility of labour (there are provisions only for very small numbers of temporary work visas in specified professional occupations). The outcome in North America, however, has been quite different from what was intended. The particular mode of liberalization adopted for (some) goods and capital has resulted not in broad development and job creation but instead in displacement for Mexican workers, many of whom have then headed across the northern border to find alternative sources of income (Fernández-Kelly and Massey 2007; Martin 1998). Imports to the US of Mexican agricultural goods are still heavily restricted; the US continues, by all appearances, to prefer to import Mexican tomato pickers rather than Mexican tomatoes (Cornelius and Martin 1993). Stated goals for NAFTA included the reduction of migration pressures (in common with other regional integration efforts), but there is little evidence of success in this regard.

Regional integration frameworks can extend to a limited degree of harmonization of policy on immigration from other areas (as distinction from 'internal' migration/mobility), as attempted in the Maastricht Treaty (though with very limited success, see Brochmann 1996). Discussion of the EU in these terms is commonly framed in reference to the term 'Fortress Europe', which refers to the tightening of restrictions on immigration from outside Europe that has accompanied the lifting of internal restrictions. Some countries in northern Europe worry about the porous southern border, e.g. the Italian coast, sometimes a destination for migrants crossing the Mediterranean from northern Africa. Accession countries in central/Eastern Europe have had to agree to wholesale adoption of existing regulations touching on immigration, including a common entry visa regime (Jileva 2002). The rationale is that admission of external immigrants can have consequences for other EU member states. Occasionally decisions of this sort become a matter of open conflict, as when the Italian government in the spring of 2011 granted residence rights to 22,000 Tunisian asylum seekers, expecting that these French-speaking individuals would then move on to France (the former colonial power in Tunisia); France subsequently denied entry to several trains at the Italian border. Generally, however, immigrants in Europe (particularly those who gain citizenship of an EU member country) can migrate to other countries, though only a few secondary migration flows have reached non-negligible dimensions (e.g. Somalis who settled first in the Netherlands and subsequently moved to the UK, see van Liempt 2011).

Perhaps the most important observation to make about regional integration and migration is that regional integration does not generally lead to a great deal of migration, even when the agreements constituting integration include generous provisions for migration. Common labour market regimes have been adopted mainly by countries operating at broadly similar levels of economic development. The history of EU accession suggests that new countries are accepted when there is confidence that there will not be a mass exodus to wealthier member states. Sometimes predictions of this sort turn out to be wrong: Britain refrained from imposing a waiting period on nationals of 'A8' countries, i.e., the Eastern European countries that gained membership in 2004, only to find that inflows (especially from Poland) were much larger than anticipated. On this basis, Britain did impose a period of restrictions on Bulgarians and Romanians following A2 accession in 2007 (Sriskandarajah and Cooley 2009). The typical pattern is that other provisions of economic integration (freedom of trade and capital flows) are implemented first, often leading to a burst of economic development that reduces disparities and dampens enthusiasm for migration subsequent to the easing of migration restrictions (e.g. Tapinos 2000).

As with any proposition about migration, however, one must be cautious of over-generalizing, particularly on the basis of European and/or North American experience. Regional integration takes a variety of forms, sometimes quite different from the EU paradigm. Economic development in East Asia (with some countries organized under ASEAN, the Association of South East Asian Nations), for example, has contributed to distinctive migration flows that can be difficult to 'place' in perspectives constructed for Europe. 'Integration' in this instance has not generally meant the reduction of disparities but rather their deepening, with predictable consequences for migration (Jones and Findlay 1998). A number of frameworks exist in Africa, and although none of these involves explicit facilitation of unimpeded migration, cross-border migration is typically unimpeded, reflecting lack of state capacity as well as the shallower historical roots of African nation-states, with sometimes artificial borders imposed by colonial powers (Ouchu and Crush 2001). Regional integration is a frame for analysing complex processes, and expectations of uniform patterns at a global level are likely to be disappointed.

See also: *Borders*

KEY READINGS

Brochmann, G. (1996) *European Integration and Immigration from Third Countries*. Oslo: Scandinavian University Press.

Jones, H. and Findlay, A. (1998) 'Regional economic integration and the emergence of the East Asian international migration system', *Geoforum*, 29: 87–104.

Lahav, G. (2004) *Immigration and Politics in the New Europe: Reinventing Borders*. Cambridge: Cambridge University Press.

Martin, P.L. (1998) 'Economic integration and migration: the case of NAFTA', *UCLA Journal of International Law and Foreign Affairs*, 3: 419–32.

31 Remittances

Definition: Flows of money (and, as 'social remittances', other types of resources as well) from migrants to relatives and others in the country of origin.

The term remittances refers primarily to the money migrants send back to family (and perhaps other community members) in the country of origin (or, sometimes, third countries). When we recall that migrants are not abstract individuals but members of families and communities, it is unsurprising that significant numbers send significant amounts of money. The size of the flows suggests that the topic of remittances extends beyond the money itself, affecting migrant-sending countries in quite broad ways, i.e., not just the individuals who are the direct recipients.

The volume of recorded remittances to developing countries has soared over the last decade, reaching (according to the World Bank) US$440 billion in 2010; in the early 1990s remittances totalled less than US$50 billion annually (Ratha et al. 2010). Some migrants use informal channels for sending money home to avoid the high fees that result from monopolistic markets for transfers (Solimano 2010), so the total volume is undoubtedly higher and some portion of the increase just noted might consist of movement from informal to formal (measurable) channels. Remittance flows to developing countries are significantly larger than official development assistance and have grown much more quickly than the latter in recent years. With the global recession of the late 2000s, growth in remittances slowed, particularly in Latin America (Ruiz and Vargas-Silva 2011), but growth had already resumed in late 2010 (Migration Policy Institute 2011).

Remittances are a very significant portion of gross national product for some countries – 50 per cent for Tajikistan, more than 20 per cent in Nepal and Honduras, and more than 10 per cent in Nicaragua and the Philippines, for example. Some countries, notably the Philippines, encourage labour migration by their citizens as part of an official strategy to increase earnings of foreign exchange (Semyonov and Gorodzeisky 2008).

Remittances enable migrants' families to achieve a higher standard of living. But the effects are not limited to increased consumption. The 'new economics of labour migration' (NELM) demonstrates that pursuit of remittances is a household strategy to spread or diversify risk, particularly in settings where local insurance markets are underdeveloped and economic factors are subject to wide fluctuations (Lucas and Stark 1985). Some migration research emphasizes the notion that migrants are highly entrepreneurial, willing to take greater risks – but NELM approaches suggest that migration is also a strategy to manage risk, by providing an additional income source that is less likely to deteriorate if problems (e.g. unemployment, exchange rate deterioration, political unrest) arise in the migrant-sending country.

One key point of contention in research on remittances addresses the question of whether remittances are used 'productively' by those who receive them. The concern (one might call it an accusation) is that recipients use remittances primarily for consumption instead of investment (e.g. Dinerman 1982). This conclusion arguably depends on problematic categorizations of 'productive' (e.g. excluding expenditures on education) and is empirically dubious on other grounds as well (de Haas 2005). In addition, increases in local consumption (e.g. housing construction) can have local 'multiplier effects': that is, remittances to migrants' families can lead non-migrant families to make productive investments to satisfy increased local demand (Taylor 1999). The concern over whether remittances are invested productively vs. consumed is in any event slightly odd if one accepts that production is valuable not for its own sake but as a means of enabling consumption (though from a different angle one can find intrinsic value in work). Recent research suggests a robust and attractive conclusion: remittances enable greater consumption and reduce poverty (e.g. Adams and Page 2005; de Haas 2005), with fundamental benefits such as the improvement of children's nutritional status (e.g. in Ecuador; Antón 2010).

A related debate, in both scholarly and policy circles, addresses whether migrant remittances are a catalyst for or a hindrance to development – reflecting a long-standing concern with the relationship between migration and development more generally (e.g. Skeldon 1997; Papademetriou and Martin 1991; Appleyard 1989). In the early years of 'guestworker' migration to Europe (in the 1960s), some governments were keen to portray guestworker programmes as a contributor to the development process for sending countries, as migrants sent remittances and returned home with additional skills. These arguments were rooted in the prevailing modernization theory of that period, which taught that flows of all types from wealthy to poor countries could have only positive effects. Views about remittances took a pessimistic turn with the emergence of dependency theory and other versions of structuralism (de Haas 2007): in the 1970s and 1980s, a number of scholars argued that remittances deepened the dependence of poor countries on wealthy countries and reinforced dysfunctional social and economic structures of the former (e.g. Reichert 1981).

In recent years contributions to this debate have become more nuanced. Scholars studying remittances are now sceptical of the notion that one can provide a 'global' or general answer to the question of whether remittances help or hinder development; the answer depends on the specific characteristics of the country to which the remittances are sent (de Haas 2007). Remittances might help provide finance for investment where it would not otherwise be available (e.g. Giuliano and Ruiz-Arranz 2009), but if local conditions are such that investment of capital in general does not lead to productive outcomes, then those conditions (not lack of capital) are the real constraint on development, and remittances might not provide much benefit beyond the direct recipients. As noted above, people sometimes choose migration to overcome local difficulties such as poorly developed markets and infrastructure; those same difficulties can limit the development potential of remittances (Taylor 1999). This note of caution is different from the notion that remittances are actually harmful in development terms. Caution, however, is useful in the face of neo-liberal euphoria about remittances as a non-state (and therefore allegedly trouble-free) alternative to development aid (de Haas 2005, 2007).

A third issue is the effect of remittances on inequality in migrant-sending regions. Concerns about inequality arise from consideration of migrant selectivity: when there is a greater tendency towards migration among people who are relatively well-off in their own context, one would expect to find that remittances increase inequality, as non-migrant poor households fail to keep up with the advances of migrant households (e.g. Lipton 1980). This straightforward outcome is not the only possibility, however; here as well there is no universal pattern and the outcome depends on details of the local context. Non-migrant families can benefit from remittances via the same 'multiplier effects' discussed above (Stark et al. 1988), and changing patterns of selectivity over the evolution of a migration stream mean that remittances have time-varying effects on inequality, as poorer households follow migrant pioneers using networks created by the latter (Jones 1998). Since remittances generally reduce poverty at least in an absolute sense, one must consider how to balance that benefit against concerns regarding inequality, and evaluations of this sort depend inevitably on normative judgements for which there is no objective standard (de Haas 2007).

The concept of remittances has been extended beyond the conventional meaning of financial flows, to encompass the flow of other types of resources. Eckstein (2010) describes remittances in connection with social and symbolic capital: remittances (and the simple fact of being a migrant) can foster and reinforce reciprocity and prestige. Levitt (1998) introduced the term 'social remittances' to describe the diffusion of cultural forms, including normative structures, systems of practice, and social capital. For example, migrants might transmit ideas about gender roles and identities, or about political participation. Remittances in this broader sense might also extend to the way migrants sometimes return with skills acquired in the destination country, as noted above (Bloch 2005). The effect of social remittances does not always consist of wholesale adoption of destination-country cultural elements; in certain instances, migration to a wealthy Western country might catalyse movement towards more egalitarian gender relations, but in others migration might reinforce a more patriarchal or traditional framework (see Kunz 2008 on remittances and gender more generally).

As with remittances in the conventional sense, one finds that the impact of social remittances can be negative as well as positive: the transmission of ideas one considers positive might have unintended consequences that fail to express or actualize the ideas themselves. Judgements of this sort depend on a specific normative framework, and one might want to be wary of adopting a modernization-theory perspective that assumes that developing countries always benefit from the adoption of the cultural forms of wealthy destination countries (see Castles and Miller 2009).

Remittances are a core instance of the transnational social ties created by international migration. Several features of remittance flows and their effects (particularly in connection with development and inequality) demonstrate a key sociological argument about migration: migration is not merely the geographical relocation of individuals, it is a complex social process with wide-ranging consequences for both origin and destination societies. That more general point is true *a fortiori* for remittances: remittances are not merely money – it is highly consequential that remittances involve money transmitted by migrants in particular ways, to particular people, for particular purposes, etc.

See also: *Transnationalism; Migrant networks*

KEY READINGS

de Haas, H. (2005) 'International migration, remittances and development: myths and facts', *Third World Quarterly*, 26 (8): 1269–84.

Levitt, P. (1998) 'Social remittances: migration driven local-level forms of cultural diffusion', *International Migration Review*, 32 (4): 926–48.

Skeldon, R. (1997) *Migration and Development: A Global Perspective*. Harlow: Longman.

Taylor, J.E. (1999) 'The new economics of labour migration and the role of remittances in the migration process', *International Migration*, 37 (1): 63–88.

32 Restrictionism vs. Open Borders

Definition: A debate about immigration policies that includes a wide range of views, from those who think that any country may legitimately decide to admit or exclude immigrants as it pleases, to those who believe that national borders are artificial and that migration should be entirely free.

Some people become interested in the study of migration via engagement with a compelling political and ethical question: to what extent is it legitimate for a country to close its borders to immigrants? Most people believe that a country has the right to prevent non-citizens from entering, and/or to determine whom to admit. A minority view holds that restrictive borders are illegitimate and unjust: migration is seen as a human right – particularly migration of the poor to the world's wealthiest countries, given the vast inequalities that characterize our world.

In a context shaped by modern nationalism, the idea that countries have a right to exclude immigrants is taken for granted by many, as a matter of common sense ('England for the English'). This idea is, apparently, taken for granted in certain instances of political theory as well: John Rawls constructed 'a theory of justice' (1971) without any reference to migration, and *The Law of Peoples* (1999) considers 'peoples' as having fixed membership, and conveys his view that even justice considered at a global level does not require accommodation for migration.

Arguments in support of migration restrictions often point to a wide range of negative consequences for natives. These consequences fall into two categories. The first is economic: immigrants from poor countries are said to undercut wages for native workers, to the point that employers prefer to hire immigrants and natives end up unemployed. In the US, an important variant of this argument focuses on racial dimensions of economic consequences: Beck (1996) argues that mass immigration, with roots in legislation passed during the civil rights period of the 1960s, has undercut attempts to redress the disadvantages faced by African-Americans, whose presence in the US can be traced to a particularly cruel form of forced migration. Another variant considers the possibility that mass immigration undermines the social solidarity underpinning the advanced welfare states of Western Europe (e.g. Entzinger 2007; Goodhart 2013).

The second major consequence relates to culture and identity. Some natives believe that immigrants, particularly in large numbers, 'dilute' or threaten the destination country's culture and sense of identity (Glazer 1994). This concern is perhaps more keenly felt in an era where expectations of assimilation are arguably weaker. Walzer's classic statement of the argument asserts that immigration restrictions are justifiable as a means of preserving 'communal independence' and 'communities of character' (1983: 62 – though he also says there are inescapable obligations to admit refugees). The self-determination rights of democratic nation-states arguably would be undermined if they were unable to exercise control over membership (Miller 2007). People are not mere individuals, they are embedded in cultures, which in the modern period are typically constructed in part as nations; the nation-state might be essential not only for democracy as a process but for the (eventual?) realization of liberal egalitarian goals at least internally (Kymlicka 2001b). Even when culture is discounted, some writers assert that countries may control immigration on the basis that current citizens exercise a form of collective ownership over membership there (Pevnick 2011).

A notable feature of some restrictionist arguments is that they rest on the presumption that negative consequences for natives amount to a sufficient justification for immigration restrictions. In this perspective, the interests of natives count more than the interests of outsiders (if the latter count at all). This assumption – or at least the manner in which it is sometimes left implicit – is becoming increasingly untenable. A more cosmopolitan perspective on justice requires that the interests of potential migrants – indeed, of all 'foreigners' – be given weight, or at least consideration. A right of exclusion can no longer be assumed, it has to be argued (Booth 1997; Carens 1999). Some restrictionists do argue it: Blake (2002), for example, develops the view that we have lesser obligations to outsiders than to compatriots, because the former are not subject to the coercive power of our own state (see Nagel 2005). But for much public/political discourse on migration, the identification of negative consequences is the end of the argument.

For some, a cosmopolitan perspective leads directly and easily to the view that borders and immigration restrictions are artificial, arbitrary and unjust. The fact of being born in a particular country has enormous consequences for one's life chances. One cannot 'earn' the consequences of having been born in a particular place, and the attempts of people living in wealthy countries to preserve their standard of living by excluding immigrants originating in poor countries cannot be justified, in this view (Isbister 1996). In a watershed article, Carens (1987) argues that a Rawlsian perspective, in search of the choices people would make under the 'veil of ignorance' (i.e., without knowing in advance what the consequences would be for oneself), leads to the conclusion that individuals would choose to live in a world of open borders: not being able to count on birth in a wealthy country, people would prefer opportunities for mobility for themselves over the right to exclude others. Liberal societies, in particular, cannot endorse liberal ideals for their own citizens and then hold that those ideals are irrelevant when considering the interests of 'outsiders' (though Meilaender [1999] suggests that this argument might have nothing useful to say about immigration restrictions of societies that do not start from liberal premises).

Other open-borders arguments focus less on the interests of migrants than on the idea that there is a fundamental human right to free mobility (e.g. Sutcliffe 1998; Hayter 2000). Some draw an analogy between internal freedom of movement and (external) immigration, though Bader (2005) argues that this analogy is not very convincing. Others dispute the notion that consequences for natives are mostly negative, holding that receiving societies benefit from the fact that those who choose to migrate typically have high levels of initiative and ambition (Riley 2008; Legrain 2007). In addition, efforts to control migration are very costly (Martin 2003), not only economically but in the way they generate tensions and feelings of insecurity as well as the inevitable 'illegality' of unauthorized immigration (Pécoud and de Guchteneire 2006; Wihtol de Wenden 2007).

The normative terms of debates regarding immigration restrictions are not always well specified. The implicit philosophical orientation of most ethical discussions about migration is 'consequentialist' (though some arguments about culture are rooted more in 'perfectionism') – but what kinds of consequences matter? Many contributors emphasize economic and cultural consequences, as noted above, but here as well a great deal is assumed instead of argued. Why do economics and culture figure so prominently? An easy answer is: because most people consider them important. But the question bears pressing: why?

An intriguing argument emerges from the possibility that economic (and perhaps other 'objective') factors are not intrinsically valuable but are only means towards the more fundamental end of happiness (subjective well-being). The empirical study of happiness suggests that increases in income do not reliably lead to increases in happiness (e.g. Easterlin 2001). Perhaps, then, economic migration does not generally result in greater happiness for the migrants (Bartram 2010, 2013). The widespread belief that migration is beneficial might be mistaken, if the benefit is specified as happiness; there is no shortage of mistaken beliefs about paths to happiness (Gilbert 2006).

Does that possibility undercut the open borders view? Perhaps, to a degree – though care is required here. One can hardly argue that immigration restrictions contribute to the well-being of those who are excluded; the paternalism of such a conclusion would be absurd. Even if some migrants have mistaken beliefs about life in the destination country, perhaps a proper conception of freedom includes the freedom to make mistakes (in the course of trying to make things better). Additionally, a great many migrants have non-economic reasons for choosing migration, and there would be no practical bureaucratic way of distinguishing between different types in admissions decisions. Even so, a consideration of migration and happiness suggests that the open borders view might entail excessive optimism about the notion that migration can lead to greater happiness in the lives of significant numbers of people. Improvement in objective well-being might be a more reliable consequence of migration to a wealthy country, but it is not obvious how to value objective vs. subjective outcomes.

Even on objective measures, the impact of open borders might be limited and poorly distributed, with the benefits going mainly to people whose relative position is quite good in comparison to those who would still lack the resources to move (Bader 2005). Migration might also be an inferior strategy for addressing the problems that lead some people to choose migration (Seglow 2005; Carens 1992). Significantly, the position of open borders is embraced with particular fervour by neoclassical economists and employers; the fact that some left-wing groups sometimes join them shows an uncharacteristic faith in the power of markets to improve the lives of disadvantaged people (Castles 2003b).

In practice, states adopt immigration policies that occupy a diverse middle ground between open borders and complete closure. Borders and restrictions are regularly breached and regularly reinforced, and no wealthy country tries or even wants to exclude immigrants altogether. A sharp review of the literature (Bader 2005) notes that arguments for closure become convincing only when receiving countries are otherwise meeting their 'global moral obligations' – a condition that is by no means satisfied to a measure that justifies existing restrictions (see Tan 2004). It is, however, far from obvious that debates about the ethics of migration restrictions have a significant impact on the evolution of policies. Politicians negotiate a balance (different for different countries) between the desire of many voters for greater closure (though some significant subgroups oppose this) and the demands of employers for greater openness. Mostly the relevant decision-makers pay attention only to the interests of domestic actors, though the cosmopolitan idea has found increasing expression in court rulings and international institutions.

KEY READINGS

Bader, V. (2005) 'The ethics of immigration', *Constellations*, 12: 331–61.

Carens, J.H. (1987) 'Aliens and citizens: the case for open borders', *Review of Politics*, 49: 251–73.

Hayter, T. (2000) *Open Borders: The Case Against Immigration Controls*. London: Pluto Press.

Tan, K.-C. (2004) *Justice Without Borders: Cosmopolitanism, Nationalism, and Patriotism*. Cambridge: Cambridge University Press.

33 Return Migration

Definition: The return of migrants to their country of origin – sometimes as fulfilment of original intentions, sometimes as a consequence of revised intentions. Far from being the opposite or reversal of 'outward' migration, it has much in common with outward migration.

On reflection, it is no great surprise that significant numbers of migrants choose not to remain in the destination country. Return migration has received less attention from researchers than 'outward' migration, in part because of data limitations (Khoser 2000): many destination countries do not record departures, and origin countries often do not treat the entry of their own citizens as 'immigration'. To the extent that research is meant to help us overcome misconceptions arising from 'common sense', the research we do have about return migration shows that there is a great deal we can learn. Many of the interesting issues have to do with the notion that return migration is a simple matter of returning 'home': many returning migrants find that matters are a great deal more complicated than the idea of 'home' would imply. Other key topics include the relation between return and development, and the specific challenges faced by returning refugees.

An important argument about migration generally is that flows take place in 'migration systems' that connect countries and regions (Fawcett 1989); Morawska (1991) observes that migration systems can facilitate not just outward migration but return as well. In an era of transnationalism, with cheaper and faster transportation, return migration is common. Even in earlier periods, return migration was more common than is often realized: roughly one-fourth of the 16 million European immigrants who arrived in the USA in the early twentieth century returned (Gmelch 1980). For the contemporary period, Dustmann and Weiss (2007) estimate that more than half of immigrants to the UK leave within five years of arrival, with higher rates for those originating from other wealthy countries. Trends of return at present have likely been affected by the global economic crisis that has reduced employment levels in most wealthy countries, with disproportionate impact on jobs held by immigrants. On the other hand, increasing scholarly attention to return in recent years probably arises as much from the popularity of the transnationalism perspective as from any actual increase in return.

A variety of typologies are available to summarize the different modes of return migration. An oft-cited one is that of Cerase (1974): return migration is characterized here as retirement, failure, conservatism or innovation. The first two are self-explanatory, while 'conservatism' indicates return by someone who never really tried to integrate thoroughly in the destination country and returns without having been much affected by the migration experience. 'Innovation' denotes a migrant who did absorb some of the values and practices of the destination country and returns intending to catalyse changes at 'home' using what they have learned while away (an intention Cerase says is typically frustrated). Another approach is found in Piore (1979), who distinguishes between different types of success and failure. Migrants often arrive with the intention to return after having met a goal (usually financial, e.g. accumulation of savings), and return can then be an indication of success. In other instances migrants intend their move to be permanent, but economic hardships in the destination lead to return as a matter of failure. The complication in this scheme is that intentions can change after arrival: people who intended to remain permanently might decide to return even in the absence of hardship, while someone who intended only a temporary sojourn can find that accumulation of savings is much more difficult than they had expected and then postpone return, perhaps indefinitely.

In some destination countries governments have not been content to treat return as a wholly voluntary matter for the migrants themselves. In democratic countries where deportation was typically not an available policy option, some governments (e.g. in France and Germany in the 1970s and 1980s) offered financial incentives and other forms of assistance, hoping to persuade immigrants (especially those who were unemployed) to depart. These programmes were generally not very successful: there were fewer takers than anticipated, and some of those who took the incentives likely would have returned even without them (Rogers 1997). King (2000) writes that decisions about return often have more to do with family or other non-economic considerations, in contrast to the economic basis of outward migration decisions. Other forms of government policy are rife with unintended consequences related to return: American efforts to reinforce borders against unauthorized crossing in recent years are widely acknowledged to have reduced the likelihood of return among undocumented Mexican immigrants, who fear that if they leave they will find it more difficult to gain re-entry to the US (e.g. Massey et al. 2003).

A central area of concern is what migrants experience after return to their country of origin. Many returning migrants invest a great deal of hope and optimism in return, in no small measure because of the notion that they are going home. The word 'home', however, can be misleading, particularly when one has lived abroad for an extended period. Sometimes returnees fail to anticipate how much 'home' has changed (or alternatively are frustrated at how little it has changed, see Boccagni 2011). They might also fail to perceive how much they themselves have changed and find it difficult to connect with old friends and family. For outward migration, one perhaps expects loneliness and other challenges of adaptation – but 'returning home' can be all the more difficult for the way one expects it to be easier than it is (Tannenbaum 2007). Boccagni (2011) found a significant level of misunderstanding and mistrust between returnees and stayers in Ecuador, and some disappointed returnees (unhappy with their economic situation as well) ended up migrating outwards again. Return need not be the end of a migration cycle; in some cases it is a stage in 'circular migration' (Cassarino 2004).

Such experiences raise questions about the meaning of migration and return in a world of nation-states. In a conventional understanding, migration creates an anomaly: someone attempts to gain membership in a different society, and that process entails a difficult transformation from 'foreigner' to 'national'. At least in highly ethnonationalist contexts, that transformation can be difficult to the point that it is never complete: even with naturalization, an immigrant might always be perceived (even perceive themself) as a foreigner. Immigrants who experience discomfort in this situation might decide to try to resolve the anomaly by returning to the place where their nationality indicates that 'this is home'; Boccagni suggests that some migrants think of return as 'a restoration of the natural order of things' (2011: 11). The research noted in the previous paragraph suggests that there might be limits on the effectiveness of this resolution: by virtue of living abroad for an extended period, a migrant arguably becomes, to a certain extent, a foreigner with respect to their country of origin. For some migrants, return is not difficult in these terms: they meet their goals and generally find satisfaction in return. But for others, return brings to mind the phrase 'you can't go home again'. In this perspective, return is not the reverse of outward migration; instead, it shares some essential features with outward migration (see Lee 2009).

Some researchers apply the notion of 'return' to the migration of immigrants' children (and subsequent generations) when they move to their parents' country of origin. Often the word return is enclosed in quotation marks (as with King and Christou [2010], writing about 'second-generation "returnees"'), indicating the challenges of applying it to the migration of those who did not themselves originate in the country in question. In such instances the word 'home' is even more ambiguous: such migrants can experience significant uncertainty as to where they really belong (King et al. 2011). Different contexts contribute to different outcomes for 'counter-diasporic migration': Jewish immigrants in Israel (whose families have lived elsewhere for many generations) can become Israelis with relative ease in a context of shared religious/ethnic identity and sustained large-scale immigration. Brazilian descendants of Japanese emigrants, on the other hand, typically remain 'Brazilians' as *Nikkeijin* (immigrants of Japanese ancestry) in Japan, given persistent disparities of language and culture (Tsuda 2003).

Research on return migration also considers its implications for development in the country of origin. In an older perspective rooted in neoclassical economics, return migration was expected to catalyse development insofar as migrants returned with useful skills and experience acquired in a developed ('modern') country (and perhaps some capital as well). Many scholars have long been sceptical of this claim, noting that migrant workers were often employed in unskilled jobs in the destination and sometimes experienced downward occupational mobility via migration; they might even have been skilled workers prior to emigration, such that their departure was a loss for the local economy. Other research has produced more optimistic results: Conway and Potter (2007) find that migrants (even those at or near retirement age) often return with relevant human capital that contributes to the local economy. Ammassari (2004) reached a similar conclusion about elite migrants who returned to West African countries and used connections developed while abroad to support their entrepreneurial efforts. In some instances, governments in sending countries encourage emigration with the expectation of eventual return; migration can even be part of a diaspora-building strategy, with governments and other actors encouraging development of transnational ties among emigrants and their descendants, with these links perhaps leading to various types of remittances.

The return of refugees and asylum seekers likely requires a different analytical focus. Return in such cases could be considered more unambiguously attractive (assuming the threat leading to their flight has passed), given that refugees didn't want to leave in the first place. As with other types of migrants, however, it would be unwise to expect return to be a restoration of the *status quo ante*. Situations for returned refugees might no longer be dangerous, but they can still be very difficult – as discovered by Blitz (2005) in research on the return of Serbian minorities to eastern Croatia in the 1990s and 2000s, who encountered state discrimination as well as displacement by Bosnian Croats, themselves refugees from Bosnia. For failed asylum seekers, 'return' (e.g. deportation) might take place while the origin country is still dangerous – though some destination countries attempt to coordinate return with origin countries in hopes of reducing the likelihood that the migrants will try to gain entry again (Khoser 2001).

See also: *Transnationalism; Circular migration*

KEY READINGS

Conway, D. and Potter, R.B. (eds) (2009) *Return Migration of the Next Generations: 21st Century Transnational Mobility*. Farnham: Ashgate Publishing.

Ghosh, B. (ed.) (2000) *Return Migration: Journey of Hope or Despair?* Geneva: International Organization for Migration.

Tannenbaum, M. (2007) 'Back and forth: immigrants' stories of migration and return', *International Migration*, 45: 147–75.

34 Second Generation

Definition: The children of immigrants, born in the country to which their parents have migrated.

Immigration has transformed many societies around the world, in some cases over many decades. The children of immigrants hold a special place in those transformations. They generally have greater rights of residence and membership (sometimes including automatic/birthright citizenship) and encounter local schools and other institutions of socialization. They therefore ought to have better prospects for integration and/or assimilation, and they are perhaps even the main 'agents' of the integration process. How and to what extent the second generation becomes integrated is thus a core question of immigration research. This question is multifaceted and includes: the processes by which the second generation learns the language and culture of the new society and/or maintains the parent language; schooling and educational achievement; employment and experiences in the labour market; and the cultural, national and ethnic identification of these children as they make their way into adulthood and across the life course.

The label second generation, as used to refer to the children of immigrants, has sometimes been criticized because it implies that the second (and perhaps subsequent) generation(s) will always be immigrants, never truly integrated or accepted into the country in which they were born (Durmelat and Swamy 2013). This implication reflects the concern in popular and academic discourse about how immigrants and the subsequent generations will fare in the societies in which they now live. Accompanying these discourses are two general, if not crudely imagined, views. The first is that the second (and subsequent) generations in many countries of immigration, such as the United States, Canada, Australia, the UK, and even France and Germany, generally adapt well to the destination society by learning its language and adopting its mores, norms, values and civic responsibilities through positive engagement with the main institutions of education and employment. The other view is that the second generation's attachment to the parental culture, norms and values prevents these children (and the adults they become) from fully integrating despite positive or, at worst, neutral engagement with host institutions (as judged by the host society). Empirical realities are of course usually much more complex, at least for the so-called 'new' second generation, which is the focus here.

One of the most pressing questions about the second generation in many countries centres on language and education. Understanding and becoming a full participant in a society is difficult if not impossible unless one can communicate in a common language. Learning a new language can be much more difficult for immigrant adults than for their children, who tend to have far more contact with the native institutions that require them to use the dominant language. Thus, even if second-generation children speak only their parents' language at home and in their neighbourhoods (e.g. if those are dense ethnic enclaves), the children will nonetheless usually adopt the host society language(s) via schooling and other institutions where socialization takes place. In the United States, this process has been severely questioned by anti-immigration supporters who disdain the bi- or multilingualism of the second generation and their 'corruption' of English via code-switching (between their home language and English) and the creation of hybrid words or expressions. Some even view public spending on ESL or ELL (English as a Second Language or English Language Learners) classes as wasteful, pointing to low expectations and low achievement among some children of immigrants (many of whom are enrolled in poorly resourced public schools). Yet research indicates that the second generation adopts English as the primary language almost universally, and many in the second generation are unable to speak or read and write well in their parents' language (Portes and Rumbaut 2001). True, bilingual children do engage in code-switching and hybridization. However, Portes and his colleagues also found that fully bilingual children show better achievement in school than do children who are only partially fluent in more than one language. Even the American Pediatric Association recommends that, when possible, children should be exposed to multiple languages to benefit brain development, cognitive functioning and school achievement.

In the US, second-generation educational attainment is equivalent to or surpasses comparable native whites, with the notable exception of Mexicans (Waldinger and Reichl 2007). On one end of the continuum, second-generation children from Asian backgrounds (whose immigrant parents have often arrived in the US with higher education qualifications) tend to surpass native whites in education. On the other end, Mexicans are still 'catching up'. Although they have made great strides compared to their parents (many of whom have, at best, only a few years of secondary schooling) in having greater high school completion rates, they still lag significantly behind native whites. In their study of New York's second generation, Kasinitz et al. (2008) describe similar outcomes, punctuated by differences in race, class and culture. Second-generation Russian Jews and Chinese have moved ahead of comparable native whites, while second-generation Dominicans lagged behind along with the Puerto Ricans and African-Americans who were included as control group comparisons. These findings have recently been supported by national-level studies that find second-generation advancement for children of many immigrants backgrounds (Pew Research Center 2013).

In Europe, we now have excellent comparative data from the TIES – The Integration of the European Second Generation – study about how the second generation is faring in education and employment (see Crul et al. 2012). TIES surveyed almost 10,000 children of immigrants from the former Yugoslavia, Morocco and Turkey, living in eight European countries. Its findings diverge in some important ways from the American debate, which tends to emphasize differences between immigrant groups (e.g. Asians vs. Mexicans), rather than exploring variation within them. Perhaps unsurprisingly, the TIES study finds significant differences in the way national contexts affect these children of immigrants. In Germany and Austria, for instance, where the educational systems are more stratified than in the more open systems (France and Sweden), second-generation students were often tracked into vocational secondary education quite early. The vocational track of this highly stratified system promises more job opportunity (as it coincides with specific types of jobs) even if these jobs are clearly low status and low paid. In France and Sweden, by contrast, and although second-generation respondents as a whole had lower educational attainment than their native peers there, a higher proportion of second-generation students could be found pursuing and completing tertiary education than in the other European countries. Thus, Turkish students from similar backgrounds might have much greater mobility in France and Sweden than in Germany and Austria.

In the US, research has shown that many young second-generation adults have labour market attachment and outcomes equivalent (or nearly so) to that of comparable native-born whites (Portes and Rumbaut 2001; Kasinitz et al. 2008; Waldinger and Riechl 2007). However, for some groups, such as second-generation Mexicans, the openness of the American labour market is a double-edged sword. On the one hand, there seems to be ample job opportunity at a lower skill level. On the other hand, many of those opportunities are poorly compensated, flexible and temporary, offering little stability to young adults trying to get a foothold in the formal labour market, much less allowing them to match their native peers. Culture can also be a constraint, as in the case of many Turkish women in Amsterdam and Frankfurt whose parents have little education and who are sometimes encouraged or allowed to leave school early to marry and form families (Crul et al. 2012). Thus, although racial discrimination still marks the educational and employment experiences of the second generation (especially of children from certain backgrounds), it does not define their experiences altogether. Ethnicity can be an advantage, as can certain cultural practices, such as delaying marriage and childbearing and living in the parental home until one's educational goals have been met or until marriage (see Kasinitz et al. 2008). However, one's specific immigrant background can also be a deterrent to upward mobility, for women especially.

Second-generation identity is not an 'either/or' proposition as implied by the conventional assimilation perspective. Second-generation immigrants in many countries hold multiple identities simultaneously without apparent inner conflict. In the US, the 'hyphenated American' identity is still prominent for many in the second generation, as in Mexican-American or Asian-American. Pan-ethnic labels created as part and parcel of the American context are also common. Thus, the terms 'Latinos' or 'Asians' signal a kind of unity among immigrants, their children and subsequent generations – an identity that is both separate from and part of the broader American society. In France, by contrast, a hyphenated identity is almost inconceivable given the prevailing assimilationist model of belonging. Nonetheless, a high proportion of second-generation children maintain multiple identities that include feeling French as well as an attachment to their parent's country or place of origin (Simon 2012). Some 30 per cent of France's second-generation children also have dual nationality. Some of these children even lead transnational lives, for instance by marrying someone from 'back home' or choosing an occupation that can benefit their families and extend the transnational space in which they have grown up (Levitt 2009). The transnational lives of some in the second generation and their attachment to multiple identities complicates the picture of assimilation put forth by some of its main proponents (see Kasinitz et al. 2008 and Alba and Nee 2003).

The often stark divisions of race in white-dominated societies in Europe, the US, Canada and Australia have led to new forms of identification and changing boundaries as the children of immigrants negotiate their place in these societies. Interestingly, in many of the largest cities in these countries (e.g. London, New York, Toronto) immigrants and their children now outnumber the native born (or will do so soon) – creating 'minority-majority' cities that present an entirely new way of thinking about what sort of society the second generation has been (or will be) integrating into. Are they becoming 'American' if nearly all of the reference groups around them are from immigrant origins? What does it mean to be Canadian, American or British in a context in which one's environment is dominated by immigrants and other non-native ethnic groups? As Kasinitz and his colleagues found in their study, urban identities such as 'New Yorker' may in fact become the most salient ones for the second generation in the near future, overshadowing national identities altogether.

See also: *Acculturation; Assimilation; Integration; Ethnicity and ethnic minorities; Multiculturalism; Transnationalism*

KEY READINGS

Alba, R.D. and Nee, V. (2003) *Remaking the American Mainstream: Assimilation and Contemporary Immigration*. Cambridge, MA: Harvard University Press.

Crul, M., Schneider, J. and Lelie, F. (eds) (2012) *The European Second Generation Compared: Does the Integration Context Matter?* Amsterdam: Amsterdam University Press.

Kasinitz, P., Waters, M.C., Mollenkopf, J.H. and Holdaway, J. (2008) *Inheriting the City: The Children of Immigrants Come of Age*. New York and Cambridge: Russell Sage Foundation and Harvard University Press.

Pew Research Center (2013) *Second-generation Americans: A Portrait of the Adult Children of Immigrants*. Washington, DC: Pew Research Center.

Simon, P. (2012) *French National Identity and Integration: Who Belongs to the National Community?* Washington, DC: Migration Policy Institute.

35 Selectivity

Definition: A process that determines whether certain types of individuals are more likely to migrate than others from the same sending region, whether as part of regulated recruitment or via self-selection.

It is well established that migration is selective. Not just anybody moves from their home to a new destination. About 3 per cent of the world's population (or 214 million persons) in 2010 consisted of individuals who had moved internationally, according to the International Organization for Migration (IOM). That proportion might seem quite small. Even so, international migration has had a tremendous impact on states and societies. Immigrants sent remittances totalling

US$440 billion in 2010, for instance. In some countries, especially in the Middle East, immigrants constitute as much as half or more of the population (e.g. 87 per cent in Qatar and 70 per cent in the United Arab Emirates). Immigrants everywhere have had an enormous social impact on the societies to which they have migrated. The national mythology of some countries, such as the United States, is built on the idea that immigrants constitute the nation. Who moves, therefore, is one of the key questions in research on international migration – and that question is addressed by the concept of selectivity. Why do some individuals migrate while others in their communities and places of origin stay put? What are the self-selecting characteristics of individuals who move internationally? Which state policies or recruitment strategies promote selective migration flows, and what are their consequences?

The idea of selectivity starts with the observation that those who migrate are different from those who don't, on three related dimensions: who is inclined to migrate; who is able to accomplish it; and who is deemed appropriate for admission by the destination country. The concept has been developed primarily by economists and demographers to examine the costs and benefits of immigration for destination countries. It has gone hand in hand with human capital theories of migration, which focus on economic migrants and their human capital characteristics, primarily their level of education and work experience. Economists have debated whether migrant self-selection, in particular voluntary migration for the purpose of economic advancement, is positive or negative with respect to economic outcomes in the destination (see Borjas 1987; Chiswick 1999). Do these migrants have human capital characteristics that will bring success at the destination – or will they falter or fail (and thus impose costs on the destination society in general)? The question is politically charged. Politicians and policymakers in favour of reduced immigration have often argued that migrants are by and large negatively self-selected – a view that was reinforced by Borjas's arguments (e.g. 1985) about a decline in the 'quality' of immigrants in the USA. This position supports their policy of raising the minimum skill levels of future immigrants and reducing family-based immigration and asylum. Similarly, they favour economic migrants because they are perceived as less likely to settle permanently and to rely on public resources while they are resident in the destination country. Family-based migrants, chain migrants, and refugees and asylees are considered to be more 'negatively selected' and more likely to rely on public resources because they might not be able to work or might have difficulty finding work to support themselves and their families.

Historically, formal immigrant selection has occurred at the level of national policies directed at sending countries or has been based on the demand for certain skills and labour needs. Immigration policies, such as the United States Immigration Act of 1924, selected future immigrants by instituting 'cultural preferences' in the form of country quotas. The 1924 Act virtually halted total immigration compared to previous years by implementing country quotas that allowed only very limited immigration from racially 'undesirable' populations – principally southern and Eastern Europeans and Asians – while continuing to welcome immigration from northern Europe. Guestworker programmes have also been used as a mechanism for selecting migrants. These programmes have targeted individuals with specific skills or characteristics to move temporarily to the countries that required their labour, expecting the migrants to return home once they were no longer needed. A key example is Turkish guestworker immigration to northern Europe – primarily Germany, Austria, France, Belgium and the Netherlands – beginning in the 1960s. However, most of those Turkish immigrants stayed in northern Europe rather than returning home after the programmes were discontinued. Today, these countries have a large second and third generation population of Turkish background, who have often been deemed by native Europeans as problematic, 'a great mistake never to be repeated', as one report put it (Doomernik et al. 2009: ix). Similarly, the United States Bracero programme, which brought several million Mexicans to the south-western part of the country beginning in the 1940s, also resulted in more permanent flows that have viewed as problematic by some policy-makers. These historical selective migration models set the stage for current policy debates about migration and how to select migrants successfully using policy. Those debates have begun to focus attention on integration, asking whether and how states can select migrants so that they will be 'better integrated' into the destination societies.

States' policy emphasis on integration has, unsurprisingly, led to a focus on highly skilled, educated workers rather than the low-skilled labour of the past. Points-based immigration policies and skill-based visas or other labour market criteria have been designed by many countries to positively select immigrants. These countries have assumed that higher-skilled or educated migrants are easier to integrate into their societies. Undoubtedly, low-skill labour is still needed in certain sectors in wealthy, developed countries, but the political atmosphere has not been conducive to creating productive policies that address the needs of employers and low-skill migrant workers, as well as social cohesion in the larger society. This disjuncture has led to skewed ideas about whom to recruit and what makes a migrant desirable in the long term.

Canada is often cited as a success story for its positive selection of immigrants. It has one of the oldest points-based systems, which has been in effect since the 1970s. The system is designed to recruit about 60 per cent of Canada's immigrants based on skill level, educational and linguistic criteria, with the remaining 40 per cent based on family relationships and asylum protection. Canada's points system became so successful that it caused an enormous backlog in immigration admissions. Thus, Citizenship and Immigration Canada (the government agency responsible for regulating immigration) has given priority to Canadian-educated applicants and those with experience in the Canadian labour market. Other countries have followed the Canadian example. The United Kingdom instituted a points-based system in 2008. It is divided into five tiers and is based on skill and educational levels, English-language ability, age and previous earnings. In contrast, the USA, Germany and Ireland have primarily used indirect means, such as employment and skill-based visas, as tools for recruiting selective streams of migrants, both temporary and permanent (especially in the case of the US and

Ireland). The US H-1B visa for highly skilled migrants and the German 'green card' initiated in 2000 have primarily served to recruit temporary high-skill labour in those countries.

The result of these formal policies designed to correct the migration 'mistakes' of earlier eras is that selective migration is purported to be almost exclusively based on economic criteria (imagined as 'neutral'). The country origins of selected immigrants do, however, play a large role in policy and recruitment strategies. Germany's 'green card' scheme specifically targeted Indian IT workers as well as smaller numbers of workers from other countries. After failing to attract significant numbers of Indian workers, however, the scheme turned its sights back onto Europeans. Ironically, high-skill mobility among Europeans has been even more difficult to attract despite the fact that labour mobility is one of the cornerstones of the European Union. Nevertheless, European countries have resisted recruiting immigrants from outside the EU even though this has disadvantaged their high-tech industries relative to the USA (Poros 2011). European countries may lament their position; however, without paths to permanent immigration and an openness towards non-European labour, Europe is unlikely to compete with the USA's enviable position of attracting large amounts of high-tech talent from India and China.

The problem of integration and the lower skill levels of past flows seems to haunt Europe in its pursuit of positively selected migration streams. In France, the slogan 'immigration choisie, intégration réussie' ('selective immigration, successful integration') was used by Nicolas Sarkozy's recent government to signal his intention to rectify the perceived deficiencies of past immigration flows (Doomernik et al. 2009). European governments in general have also neglected to develop integration policies and programmes for the highly skilled, assuming that highly educated and skilled migrants would adjust to a new society without them. Positively selected immigrants can, however, experience problems of integration. Highly skilled immigrants have experienced lower earnings than their occupational peers because of difficulty in transferring their education and skills. Their schooling and labour market experiences in other countries generally have lower pay-offs than if they had been educated and had previously worked in the destination country. Poros (2001) has suggested that organizational ties to firms, educational institutions and certifying agencies are crucial for many highly skilled migrants to attain equivalent work and occupational status; human capital characteristics are not usually enough to achieve parity with home country status. The highly skilled may also lack the support of family and friends (i.e., social capital) to provide a smooth transition to a new society (Jasso and Rosenzweig 1995). And they may experience discrimination based on race, national origins or other characteristics that stigmatize them as 'foreigners' in a new society.

Selectivity can also be viewed from the perspective of migrants and not only the recruitment strategies of states and organizations. Sociologists and anthropologists have tended to see selectivity in this way, adding to the conventional human capital models of economists and demographers. Migrants move for many different reasons, including economic, cultural, familial and political ones. They may self-select based on the 'culture of migration' (Kandel and Massey 2002) prevalent in their communities. Cultures of migration can influence whether movement is undertaken mainly by men, women or whole families. Birth order is sometimes important in family decisions about who moves, as are the comparative economic prospects of siblings.

Selectivity has also been viewed from the perspective of how the second generation is faring in North American and European societies. Here, the question of second-generation integration rests squarely on the origins of the parents. In part, the perceived failure of integration of guestworkers in northern Europe is based on perceptions of a 'problematic' second generation, and some believe it can be avoided by limiting future recruitment of lower-skilled and -educated workers (who are potential first-generation parents). The assumption is that positively selected (highly skilled) first-generation immigrants will create a positively selected second generation. Although the second generation from educated backgrounds has demonstrated many achievements in schooling and occupational status, their integration cannot simply be taken for granted. Political participation by some of these groups still remains low, effectively keeping them out of important political decisions for their communities and the nation as a whole. Researchers often cite the low political participation among second-generation Asian-Americans, for example (e.g. Kasinitz et al. 2008). Middle-Eastern Americans, most of whom are highly educated (many with US qualifications as well), have also had low levels of political participation in the American political system, notwithstanding their mobilization after the attacks of 9/11 (see Bakalian and Bozorgmehr 2009). In contrast, there is evidence that many working-class second-generation children in Europe do participate in local-level politics and have provided effective grass-roots organization for their communities (Doomernik et al. 2009). Thus, it seems time to throw out the ideological predisposition against lower-skilled migrants for a more balanced view on selectivity and integration that does not draw simplistic connections between the two.

See also: *Family migration and reunification; Guestworkers; Labour migration; Integration; Second generation*

KEY READINGS

Borjas, G.J. (1987) 'Self-selection and earnings of immigrants', *American Economic Review*, 77: 531–53.

Chiswick, B.R. (1999) 'Are immigrants favorably self-selected?', *American Economic Review*, 89 (2):181–5.

Doomernik, J., Koslowski, R., Laurence, J., Maxwell, R., Michalowski, I. and Thranhardt, D. (2009) *No Shortcuts: Selective Migration and Integration*. Washington, DC: Transatlantic Academy.

Jasso, G. and Rosenzweig, M.R. (1995) 'Do immigrants screened for skills do better than family reunification migrants?', *International Migration Review*, 29 (1): 85–111.

Poros, M.V. (2001) 'Linking local labour markets: the social networks of Gujarati Indians in New York and London', *Global Networks*, 1 (3): 243–60.

36 Social Capital

> *Definition: Access to actual or potential resources via membership in a social network or other social structures.*

The concept of social capital represents perhaps one of the oldest and most important ideas in the social sciences that articulates the relationship between economy and society. It has been revived in recent decades to address a wide range of concerns, including crime, education, poverty and development, and community, to name just a few. Despite disagreement and criticism concerning its definition across disciplines such as sociology, political science and psychology, the main idea behind social capital is that an investment in social relations produces expected returns (Lin 1999: 30). In other words, social capital captures the idea that various kinds of resources – economic ones, in particular – are embedded in social relations. Thus, investing in social relations can produce 'returns' (or benefits) of various types.

The first use of the concept can be found in Marx's writings, and contemporary uses of the term take their inspiration from it to varying degrees. For Marx, capital itself is a social relation, between the working class and the capitalist class. However, Marx's notion of 'social capital' is quite different from contemporary uses of the term. Marx saw social capital as the aggregate of all individual capitals that emerged from the processes of reproduction and circulation of (money) capital (Marx 1978 [1885]). Social capital, for Marx, then, is a structural element of society, not something that exists within classes, groups, networks or institutions as proposed by contemporary theorists. Nevertheless, Marx's idea that there could be different sorts of capital seems to have provided the inspiration for the current term.

Differences in the meanings of social capital in current usage have emerged in different theoretical perspectives. The liberal perspective (represented by social exchange theory, network analysis and rational choice) focuses on the individual and individual-level transactions in which social capital arises; consequences of having social capital are then mainly consequences for individuals. This perspective is represented in whole or in part by authors such as Pierre Bourdieu, Glen Loury, James Coleman and Nan Lin (although each also has differences with the others). The communitarian perspective, which focuses on social capital as a collective good rather than an individual one, is represented most famously in Robert Putnam's (2000) work, which draws on predecessors such as Alexis de Tocqueville and his concern with civic participation and excessive individualism, as well as Emile Durkheim's concern with societal integration and social solidarity. We can also say, however, that this broad contrast coexists with broad commonalities as well.

Pierre Bourdieu, for instance, defined social capital as 'the aggregate of the actual or potential resources which are linked to possession of a durable network of more or less institutionalized relationships of mutual acquaintance or recognition' (1986: 248). This instrumentalist view, although focused on individual mobilization of social capital through investment strategies that increase one's cultural capital (e.g. through association with experts or upper-class affiliates), treats social capital as institutionalized social relations, not simply as relations embodied in an individual's social ties. Thus, Bourdieu saw social relations as class-based relations that can be mobilized in class struggles. The economist Glen Loury also used the term, though only in passing, to launch an anti-individualist argument against the notion of meritocracy which is so strongly embedded in rational-choice models of socio-economic mobility. Loury thus attributes many racial inequalities to differential social capital. James Coleman built his analysis of social capital drawing on Loury and others such as Nan Lin and Mark Granovetter. Coleman viewed social capital as part of larger social structures that could facilitate certain kinds of action to acquire valuable resources and paved the way for the idea that social capital could be used to enhance other kinds of capital such as economic and human capital. Although these three theorists see social capital as part of larger social structures, they all embody instrumentalist views of the concept and tend to discuss many of the consequences of social capital at the individual level. Putnam's communitarian view is much the same in this respect, although offering a structural place for social capital as institutionalized and belonging not only to individuals but also to communities, nations and even states.

The concept of social capital most certainly has its critics. Beyond general criticisms about the ambiguity of the term, which seem to appear in almost every paper or book on it, the concept has been criticized for being too instrumentalist, individualistic, apolitical, positive and tautological (confusing its causes with its effects) (Daly and Silver 2008). These criticisms are well founded. For instance, the concept relies on the idea that social relations are 'investments', even with close friends and family, who are seen almost exclusively as the holders of potential resources rather than, say, sources of emotional support or shared companionship. Individual social ties are often considered the most important way to perceive social capital. And the growth or development of social capital (almost always conceived as positive) is understood to emerge from the actions of individuals rather than the state. (Examples of dense social ties that might indicate 'negative' social capital include the mafia, gangs or oligarchic groups – closed circles of people that exclude others from power, wealth or even safety.) This individualistic, rational-choice approach promotes social capital as a technical tool in development, leaving the poor and disadvantaged with the responsibility of creating social capital themselves to improve their lives. Witness, for instance, the recent popularity of micro-development and micro-finance in development policy circles as means of raising capital (Woolcock 1998). In general, the role of the state is minimized. Not only that; politics, too, is grossly underplayed, especially in the communitarian perspective. Organizations that indicate 'high' social capital in Robert Putnam's influential work, for instance, do not include unions, political parties or social movements, but rather only civic and voluntary associations. Moreover, in Putnam's rendition of social capital, cause and effect are often confused such that social capital stands in for both. Civic communities, such as in the northern regions of Italy, do civic things, value solidarity, and express democracy well – while 'uncivic' communities in the south do uncivic things and do not demonstrate civic or democratic principles (Daly and Silver 2008; Portes 1998; Putnam et al. 1993; Putnam 2000). In Putnam's view, then, cities with low social capital result in less democracy and cities with high social capital result in more or better democracy, making social capital both the cause of democracy and part of its effect.

Nonetheless, a number of authors argue that the concept still has value as an analytical tool and should be redeemed (Portes 1998; Daly and Silver 2008). One area in which the social capital concept has been used to good effect is the field of migration studies, especially regarding the consequences of migration.

Portes (1998) argues that one can distinguish three effects of social capital relevant to the analysis of immigrants. Social capital can be a source of social control, family support, and benefits gained through extrafamilial networks. Many immigrant populations and communities exhibit social control within their densely woven networks of family, friends, co-ethnics and co-religionists. For Portes and others, the sources of this social capital are located in these tightly bounded communities in which mutual obligations and trust run high, exerting significant controls on individual behaviour. Social capital is also most obviously a source of family support and, as documented by many studies, confers benefits also through networks outside of one's family. Although dense networks of close friends and community members are thought to provide multiple benefits to network members, 'weak ties' to acquaintances or friends of friends, first identified and explicated by Mark Granovetter (1995), have been found to provide significant resources as well, such as information and access to good jobs (see also Burt 1995).

Many studies of immigrants (e.g. Griffiths et al. 2005; Min 2008; Poros 2011; Waldinger 1999; Waldinger and Lichter 2003) have demonstrated these effects of social capital by documenting how the social networks of immigrants are used to facilitate migration, border crossing and settlement in destination countries. Without the networks that constitute social capital for immigrants, migration would be too costly and risky for many. Thus, many network theories of migration have generally viewed networks as a form of social capital based on co-ethnicity. Network membership by virtue of co-ethnicity is thought to grant access to the tangible and intangible benefits of network-mediated social capital, which can aid settlement and integration in the destination country. Social capital can be converted into other positive forms of capital, such as economic capital in the form of migrant remittances (see Massey et al. 1998). The study of ethnic economies has equally shown that social capital can have significant positive effects on the co-ethnic populations that form those communities (Light and Gold 2000). Thus, ethnic businesses in enclaves such as the Chinatowns, Koreatowns and Little Italies of many cities around the world arise via the social networks of these immigrants. Immigrants mobilize their networks to create opportunities and access to resources, such as loans, jobs and housing or the crucial information needed to secure them.

There are constraints in belonging to such networks, however. One of the criticisms of the social capital concept is that it focuses excessively on the positive effects of social capital. Migration researchers have shown that social capital can also be 'negative' (Faist 2000; Griffiths et al. 2005; Kyle 2000; Levitt 2001; Mahler 1995; Menjívar 2000; Poros 2011; Portes and Sensenbrenner 1993). The resources that accrue or are attributed to the social network are often not distributed equally or made equally accessible to a network's members. Networks may impose excessive social obligations on and control over their members, which can cause conflict and resistance, or capitulation and resentment. The resources that networks do produce for some, such as employment by co-ethnics in an ethnic economy, can also involve exploitation and unequal treatment. The negative or unequal effects of social capital deserve to be understood and explored in social capital research lest we fall into the trap of prescribing social capital as the antidote to all of our social ills (something that has become common in policy circles).

Many questions about social capital remain underexplored. Much attention has been paid to the characteristics of networks, their structure and configuration, but less is known about the quality of social ties within a network and the different environmental contexts within which networks exist and produce resources. How does exchange take place within networks, and how do networks operate? How does 'bonding social capital' (the kind associated with strongly bounded, dense networks of ties) differ from 'bridging social capital', which includes the kinds of weak ties that Granovetter identified? Even if we discover just how different kinds of social capital produce access to different sorts of resources, what about context? What is the historical and cultural context of particular social networks and their ties? Surely differences across space and time also matter. Nevertheless, the concept of social capital, with needed attention to its drawbacks and difficulties, provides a fruitful area of continued research across the social sciences – especially in migration studies.

See also: *Ethnic enclaves and ethnic economies; Migrant networks*

KEY READINGS

Bourdieu, P. (1986) 'The forms of capital', in J.G. Richardson (ed.), *Handbook of Theory and Research for the Sociology of Education*. New York: Greenwood Press, pp. 241–58.

Daly, M. and Silver, H. (2008) 'Social exclusion and social capital: a comparison and critique', *Theory and Society*, 37 (6): 537–66.

Lin, N. (1999) 'Building a network theory of social capital', *Connections*, 22 (1): 28–51.

Portes, A. (1998) 'Social capital: its origins and applications in modern sociology', *Annual Review of Sociology*, 24: 1–24.

Putnam, R. (2000) *Bowling Alone: The Collapse and Revival of American Community*. New York: Simon & Schuster.

37 Social Cohesion

Definition: A set of ideas that problematizes differences between immigrants and natives and seeks (typically via government policies) to resolve such problems by fostering 'shared values' and 'common identities'.

In the experience of people in destination countries, immigration involves the arrival and settlement of individuals who are inevitably different from natives, in ways commonly identified as significant. In 'social cohesion' discourses and initiatives, these differences constitute a challenge, and perhaps even a threat. Societies must be 'cohesive' to some minimal degree (a lack of social cohesion might amount to disintegration and breakdown), and common values and/or culture are sometimes considered an essential condition for cohesion. In some countries, then, one finds efforts to redress perceived deficits of cohesion by attempting to diminish the salient differences that (apparently) follow from large-scale immigration. These efforts have, in turn, become targets of critique by scholars and activists who believe that social cohesion discourses herald a return to a discredited assimilationist orientation towards immigrants; in some instances these critiques include accusations of ethnocentrism and racism, particularly towards non-white Muslims.

The social cohesion concept, a topic of concern more in Europe (and particularly Britain) than in North America, emerged in reaction to what some perceived as the excesses or even failures of multiculturalism. Older assimilationist approaches had been discredited in part because of the ethnocentrism of their insistence that immigrants adopt the 'superior' culture of their adopted homelands; in a multiculturalist orientation, differences were to be sustained and celebrated – and doing so was considered to advance immigrant integration rather than to hinder it (e.g. Kymlicka 2001a). In the 2000s, however, some observers took the view that multiculturalism had 'gone too far'. This perception gained credence in the UK following riots in several northern cities in the summer of 2001: clashes between young white and Asian men were attributed to the notion that the different groups lived 'parallel lives', in part because of residential segregation but (more significantly) because multiculturalist public policy seemingly encouraged ethnic/religious groups to isolate themselves in other ways as well. Another factor was white-British resentment rooted in perceptions of government favouritism towards minorities (Modood and Salt 2011). Concerns of this sort gained strength with the London Tube bombings of July 2005, such that social cohesion was defined also as a security matter and linked with the government's anti-terrorism agenda (Cheong et al. 2007). Dissension and violence between immigrants and natives has occurred in recent decades also in a number of European countries, beyond the UK (Taran et al. 2009).

In practice, efforts to reinforce social cohesion have consisted of programmes and regulations primarily affecting immigrants as well as established minority communities (e.g. in Britain and the Netherlands). Immigrants wanting to become naturalized UK citizens were required to pass a test demonstrating linguistic competence in English as well as familiarity with 'Life in the UK' (this is now required at an earlier stage, with applications for permanent residence). The final stage of the naturalization process is a citizenship ceremony, signalling an attempt to transform naturalization from a merely bureaucratic act into one that also expresses and deepens a new loyalty and identification (Shukra et al. 2004). (One of the present authors [Bartram] completed this process in 2010: the attempt at stagecraft was half-hearted at best, featuring officials who fiddled openly with their mobile phones and a puzzling musical backdrop consisting of Dvořák rather than Elgar, Vaughan Williams or the Beatles.) In addition, the New Labour government developed a number of community programmes designed to increase contact across community lines, such as meetings of umbrella organizations with representatives from different 'faith groups'. Local authorities were required to develop a 'local community cohesion plan', seeking to increase cross-cultural contact more comprehensively (Worley 2005).

As noted above, this policy orientation has provoked a great deal of critique. A number of writers have asserted that social cohesion on the basis of 'shared values' in reality amounts to an exercise of power over immigrants and minorities: beyond the lip-service paid to the merits of diversity (perhaps amounting to little more than tastier food), immigrants are meant to 'share' the values of the dominant/majority (e.g. white-British) group rather than vice versa. While explicit declarations of cultural superiority are no longer acceptable in polite company, an implicit hierarchy operates all the same, with Islam in particular identified as problematic and inferior (e.g. Kalra and Kapoor 2009; Robinson 2008). Some observers frame these claims in terms of racism, on the basis that a highly diverse group (Muslims) is reduced to a putative sameness, in a context where Islamist-inspired terrorism has become a major political issue. That is, despite the differences among Muslims of different national origins – not to mention the diversity *within* a 'community' such as British Muslims of Pakistani origin – to be a Muslim in contemporary Britain is to be an object of presumptive suspicion, i.e., a potential terrorist or other form of criminal (Kundnani 2007; Burnett 2004; Yuval-Davis et al. 2005).

These critiques work with a different set of assumptions about the roots of disorder and dissension (lack of social cohesion). Instead of 'excessive' cultural difference, the problem in this perspective has more to do with economic deprivation and exclusion from the mainstream of British society, rooted partly in prejudice and discrimination (e.g. Pilkington 2007). When immigrants and their descendants absorb the consumerist expectations that are said to characterize British culture, they share a great deal with native Britons – but those of immigrant background often find themselves unable to satisfy those aspirations. The point extends beyond consumerism: Back et al. assert that

> the young men of Burnley, Bradford and Oldham who took to the streets in the summer of 2001 … are all too well assimilated into a society divided by racism and discrimination … [I]t is not a matter of 'difference,' but rather, of marking divisions within shared patterns of masculine culture. (2002, §5.4)

Conflict in this context arguably has more to do with commonalities across racial lines (including economic deprivation among whites as well) than with cultural differences and lack of contact. If this mode of analysis is right, then one would expect little good to come from 'social cohesion' initiatives, particularly if non-white Muslims experience them as denigrating and even racist.

Debates in the US on these issues have been framed more in terms of 'social capital' than of social cohesion. The use of the word capital in this context refers to the value one can derive from social connections and networks: with higher amounts of social capital, one can draw more productively on norms of reciprocity and trustworthiness. Robert Putnam argues (e.g. 2007) that increases in ethnic diversity resulting from mass immigration have led to a broad decline in social capital, both within groups ('bonding social capital') and across groups ('bridging social capital'). Among the consequences of this decline, Putnam finds increasing social isolation and decreasing levels of trust – deficits that might be remedied only over the long term (as they were for earlier immigration waves), in part via public policies that encourage development of shared identities transcending ethnic boundaries. Unsurprisingly, claims about negative effects of diversity have been contentious, not least for being overly broad: Kesler and Bloemraad (2010), for example, find that effects of increasing diversity vary according to context and are positive when supported by an active multiculturalist policy orientation.

Research on 'social cohesion' in the UK has consisted, to a greater extent than in North America, of analysis of policy documents, speeches, reports, etc.; one finds a focus on 'discourse', with the premise that 'Discourses are of course powerful' (McGhee 2005, §6.1). While discourses can indeed be powerful, it is more constructive and revealing to concentrate empirical analysis on consequences, determining which discourses have been powerful and in what ways. A model for empirical research in this mode is available in Reitz et al. (2009), who arrive at a conclusion characterized by a great deal of nuance. They find that among immigrants in Canada strong attachment to an 'original' ethnic identity is often consistent with a strong sense of 'belonging' in Canada; however, for some groups (particularly 'visible minorities') that attachment can delay the development of a Canadian identity. An important contextual factor is discrimination: ethnic identity can function as a resource for those who encounter prejudice – but at the price of weakening attachment to Canadian identity when it is perhaps most needed. A key policy implication is that while multiculturalism in general does not weaken social cohesion, support for integration in a more general sense (above the level of distinct ethnic identities) is an essential complement to multiculturalism.

Several points made in earlier paragraphs merit greater emphasis. Debates about social cohesion and social capital are often framed in terms of stark oppositions and broad 'global' relationships, e.g. 'increasing diversity undermines social cohesion'. In some instances, particularly when debates have become highly politicized (as in the UK), these assertions extend to the notion that reinforcing social cohesion requires more drastic limits on immigration; it isn't sufficient to facilitate or induce assimilation of those who arrive, instead (the argument goes) governments must reinforce cohesion in a more direct way, preventing an increase in diversity by minimizing immigration itself. While some individual studies might support such views, it is far from clear that empirical research on immigration viewed more broadly warrants conclusions of that sort. Politicization operates in different directions in this context; it is perhaps apparent also in accusations that the social cohesion agenda is racist. While there is obviously value in constructing social science research to address inevitably politicized issues such as these, the prospects for doing this well will surely be greater when one's research shows attention to complexity and is not limited to the more simplistic notions of politicians and activists.

See also: *Social capital; Integration; Assimilation; Multiculturalism*

KEY READINGS

Back, L., Keith, M., Khan, A., Shukra, K. and Solomos, J. (2002) 'The return of assimilationism: race, multiculturalism and New Labour', *Sociological Research Online*, 7 (2).

Burnett, J. (2004) 'Community, cohesion and the state', *Race & Class*, 45 (3): 1–18.

McGhee, D. (2005) 'Patriots of the future? A critical examination of community cohesion strategies in contemporary Britain', *Sociological Research Online*, 10 (3).

Modood, T. and Salt, J. (eds) (2011) *Global Migration, Ethnicity and Britishness*. Basingstoke: Palgrave Macmillan.

38 Transnationalism

Definition: The tendency among immigrants particularly in recent decades to maintain ties with their country of origin while also integrating in the destination country.

Transnationalism refers to the increasing tendency among migrants to maintain ties with their country of origin – and thus to develop identities and social relations in multiple national contexts rather than being rooted in only one country at any given time. Some migrants now travel back and forth as a matter of routine, send remittances on a regular basis, communicate routinely with family and friends (via telephone, email, Skype, etc.), and even engage in political actions such as voting in two (or more) different countries. It is then less plausible to use national-level concepts in a straightforward way when describing migrants' activities and identities: the geographical boundaries implied by such concepts arguably no longer actually 'bound' what migrants do (Basch et al. 1994). One can perceive here affinities with the concept of diasporas (see Vertovec 2009) – but while that term in the past was applied to a limited number of specific groups (e.g. Jews and Armenians), transnationalism describes a more general tendency in which migrants increasingly have loyalties and engagements that span national boundaries in pervasive and durable ways.

Certain ethnographic descriptions can be read as emblematic of the transnationalism perspective. Smith (2006) describes a trip undertaken by immigrants living in Brooklyn to their community of origin in Mexico to help with a project for installing new water pipes in that community's municipal water system: after having raised the majority of the funds for the project from other Mexican immigrants in Brooklyn, they travelled over a weekend to inspect the pipes and meet with contractors, returning in time to arrive at their New York jobs on the Monday. This story demonstrates a key element of transnationalism: emigrants often continue to be members of the communities they have left behind – and perhaps it is then inaccurate to say that emigration means they have left these communities behind.

As with most new concepts, arguments about transnationalism were developed in explicit opposition to earlier understandings of how immigrants adapted to their new circumstances. In earlier perspectives (developed in research on earlier migration streams), immigrants typically embarked on a one-way trip, often travelling for weeks by boat to a destination which they then never left; ties with the origin country were (so it seemed) severed as immigrants focused on making new lives for themselves in the destination. Immigrants in the US, for example, thus became 'hyphenated Americans': an 'Italian-American' was first and foremost an American, someone in the process of shedding a part of their identity that was becoming irrelevant. A return trip to the country of origin, either to visit or to stay, would have been expensive and time-consuming – but more importantly it would have been a step backwards, a sign of failure to assimilate and to adopt a new loyalty appropriate to one's new situation.

In part as a result of new technologies reducing the cost of travel and communications, migrants now are increasingly inclined to engage with their country of origin in a variety of ways – and in the transnationalism perspective doing so is by no means a step backwards. Transnationalism has at least three distinct dimensions: economic, political and cultural (Portes et al. 1999). The economic dimension is embodied in the vastly increased flows of migrant remittances. Some 'transmigrants' (as they are sometimes described) have also developed a distinctive form of entrepreneurship, selling goods from the origin to fellow migrants (and, subsequently, to natives) in the destination – as well as selling goods produced in the destination to non-migrants in the origin country (e.g. Landolt et al. 1999). Transnationalism also has a political dimension, as when migrants continue to vote in the country of origin – perhaps while also voting in the destination country, if they have dual citizenship (e.g. Østergaard-Nielsen 2003). The cultural dimension of transnationalism follows from and reinforces the other two components: in maintaining economic and political ties with their country of origin, migrants are less likely to discard cultural endowments such as language, music and arts, and a more pervasive sense of identity. Instead of becoming a 'Dominican-American', then, a migrant might consider herself both a Dominican and an American, with neither element dominating the other.

That latter point carries significant implications regarding tendencies towards assimilation – implications that some in destination countries are inclined to find troubling. In a more conventional perspective that seeks to take the nation-state for granted, immigration (of foreigners, inevitably) creates an anomaly that can only be resolved to the extent that the immigrants themselves (if they are to remain) become fully a part of the *nation* in their new home. Concepts like 'dual loyalty' signal a problem for some: a 'disloyal' (i.e., less than fully loyal) citizen is perhaps a contradiction in terms, though of course that view is fervently contested. The rise of transnationalism no doubt exacerbates the concerns some observers have expressed concerning related trends towards multiculturalism (e.g. Schlesinger 1992). On the other hand, those who are inclined toward greater involvement in transnational activities often participate more fully in the collective life of their destination country as well (Smith 2006; Portes 2003). Assimilation is no longer the sole path to successful integration; indeed, success sometimes emerges instead from preservation and active maintenance of one's 'cultural endowment' (Portes et al. 1999).

Discussions of transnationalism commonly describe the activities of migrants at a 'grass roots' level. But these practices also have consequences at the macro-social level (Portes 2003). The previous paragraph indicates consequences in relation to national identity – arguably, transnationalism among individuals contributes to a process of fragmentation for the nation writ large, and to new modes of identity that bind populations across borders (rather than allowing borders merely to *divide* populations). There are also macro-economic impacts: for example, rising volumes of remittances have enhanced origin countries' credit ratings, enabling access to credit at lower cost (Guarnizo 2003). The on-going involvement of migrants in their communities of origin also means that transnationalism affects the lives not just of migrants but of non-migrants as well, as Levitt (2001) shows in her analysis of 'social remittances' (a concept that suggests a fourth dimension, social transnationalism, in addition to the three identified above).

Another macro-level consequence can be discerned in the concept of 'transnational citizenship' – a significant departure from more conventional notions of exclusivity in national belonging (Bauböck 1994b, 2003). As noted above, immigrants can engage in political action in different jurisdictions; such action does not even require physical presence (Martiniello and Lafleur 2008). Mexican voters living in the US, for example, are actively courted by Mexican candidates, who sometimes engage in cross-border campaigning (Smith 2008). Basch et al. (1994) argue that migrant transnationalism thus results in 'deterritorialized' nation-states – though this point seems overstated insofar as most nation-states remain firmly rooted in particular territories even while cultivating ties with emigrant populations.

The trends described as transnationalism are obviously important. Even so, early research on transnationalism arguably exaggerated the newness of the tendencies discussed here. Assertions about assimilation and the severing of ties among earlier immigrant cohorts were themselves overdrawn: for example, some immigrants from Italy in the early twentieth century also maintained ties with origin communities and travelled home for visits or for good (Foner 1997b). On reflection, it would be puzzling if migrants generally engaged in a wholesale purge of previously held identities and attachments; a well-known folk song ('Kilkelly, Ireland') uses a series of verses based on letters sent between nineteenth-century immigrants in the US and family in Ireland to portray both the pain of separation and the sustained effort to preserve relationships – including a transatlantic visit.

But the lower costs of travel and communication have undeniably enabled migrants to engage more intensively in the patterns described by scholars as transnationalism. Moreover, some components of transnationalism seem genuinely new, or at least so much more prevalent as to constitute a qualitative change, as with the significant increase in provisions for dual citizenship, for example. If nothing else, the transnationalism perspective has enabled scholars and others to *perceive* something we were unable to see clearly before, not only in current trends but in historical patterns as well (Smith 2003). That is, transnationalism has helped us not only to understand recent changes in migration patterns but also to see that earlier arguments about assimilation had overlooked patterns of transnationalism in earlier migration streams.

Scholars have also come to recognize that current trends towards transnationalism themselves have limits. Many (perhaps even a majority of) migrants engage in transnational behaviours only sporadically if at all; ties may not be severed, but frequently they do fade over time. Transnationalism in a political sense is especially rare – and in most migrant groups it is limited particularly to educated middle-aged men (Guarnizo et al. 2003). In earlier contributions to the transnationalism literature, some migration scholars argued that transnationalism held potential for emancipatory social change, insofar as it embodied a new form of social action embraced particularly by previously marginalized groups such as migrant women. More recent research suggests that these hopes were probably overstated; instead, in many instances transnationalism might only reinforce existing inequalities and hierarchies. In other respects as well it would be a mistake to imagine that transnational involvements always have positive consequences, a point apparent in the activities of transnationalized gangs (Smith 2006) and in the dysfunctions and travails of many transnationalized (i.e., separated) families (see Dreby 2010).

Early work on this topic relied heavily on ethnographic studies of what we can call 'positive cases' of transnationalism. But ethnography is probably not the right technique to identify or explain variation in broader patterns of transnationalism. Portes (2003) therefore encourages further research using comparative and quantitative methods, particularly to investigate why some migrants are more inclined than others to live in a transnationalized mode. A closely related point emerges from the observation that there is no single mode of migrant transnationalism: there is significant scope for research exploring heterogeneity, differentiation, etc. (Vertovec 2009). In any event, the concept itself is now firmly established in migration studies (as in other fields – see transnational corporations), with ongoing research that demonstrates increasing nuance and a healthy appreciation of limits. The concept of transnationalism has also been adapted for research on topics other than migration: a wide range of social processes are now understood to operate outside the confines of the nation-state, such that researchers need to transcend the 'methodological nationalism' that has long framed a great deal of social science (Amelina and Faist 2012).

See also: *Integration; Assimilation; Circular migration*

KEY READINGS

Foner, N. (1997b) 'What's new about transnationalism? New York immigrants today and at the turn of the century', *Diaspora*, 6 (3): 355–75.

Levitt, P. (2001) *The Transnational Villagers*. Berkeley, CA: University of California Press.

Portes, A., Guarnizo, L.E. and Landolt, P. (1999) 'The study of transnationalism: pitfalls and promise of an emergent research field', *Ethnic and Racial Studies*, 22 (2): 217–37.

Smith, R.C. (2006) *Mexican New York: Transnational Lives of New Immigrants*. Berkeley, CA: University of California Press.

Vertovec, S. (2009) *Transnationalism*. Abingdon: Routledge.

39 Undocumented (Illegal) Migration

Definition: Migration that is not officially sanctioned by the state in the destination country; it results from clandestine entry or (more commonly) from overstaying one's visa and/or engaging in activities (e.g. employment) not authorized by one's visa.

The common-sense understanding of 'illegal immigration' available in most instances of public discourse (e.g. politicians' speeches) on the topic is lamentably inadequate. In a 'lay' perspective, those who enter a country without authorization are in essence criminals, and the government has a responsibility to 'do something' to address the threat they pose. That threat is taken to be dire in some quarters: among other evils, illegal immigration allegedly damages national security, undermines national identity, and embodies the state's loss of control over its borders.

The first difficulty with this perspective appears in a consideration of terminology. Governments and certain types of interest groups are content with the term 'illegal immigration', in part because it legitimizes the 'law and order' response these groups embrace ('illegal aliens', popular in the US, makes the point even more clearly). Others, however, believe it is unacceptable to describe *people* as 'illegal' (thus the slogan, 'no one is illegal', Cohen et al. 2003). An alternative term, 'undocumented immigration', suggests that some immigrants merely lack certain documents and signals a greater acceptance of immigration more generally, even when it is not legally authorized. Scholars might prefer to use neutral terms that avoid these political commitments, but it isn't clear that there *are* any genuinely neutral terms. Carens (2008) suggests that 'irregular' or 'unauthorized' are less loaded than 'illegal' or 'undocumented', but he allows that one can discern political or normative connotations for those alternatives as well. 'Clandestine' migration has some currency (e.g. Spener 2009), though it suggests furtive and thus perhaps shady behaviour. In addition, irregular migration (like all migration) is much more than a matter of individual behaviour: individual actions acquire meaning via social context, as when some irregular Romanian migrants in Western Europe stood to suddenly become 'regular' by virtue of Romanian accession to the European Union (Triandafyllidou 2010).

The demand for a 'law and order' response noted above has led in recent years to just that, particularly in the USA, with vast increases in expenditure on border-control efforts, a high-tech fence (actually a high metal wall in sections of the border with Mexico – the 'Iron Curtain'), etc. The phrase 'just that' in the previous sentence has a double meaning, however: there is much evidence that this response has been ineffective in deterring unauthorized crossings. Instead, it has driven migrants to cross in more remote desert regions, leading to thousands of deaths from heat exhaustion and dehydration (Johnson 2007). Reinvigorated border control (with its uniforms, gadgets, etc.) is perhaps better understood primarily as a form of political 'performance', a 'symbolic representation of state authority' (Andreas 2000: 8) that seeks to mollify voters (see Newton 2008).

The ineffectiveness of control efforts focused on the border is only one of the factors contributing to immigration described variously as illegal or undocumented. Many undocumented immigrants enter the destination country via perfectly legal means but then become 'undocumented' when they engage in activities not permitted by the visa allowing their entry: for example, students who abandon their studies and find full-time jobs, or 'temporary' workers who overstay their visas (e.g. Dauvergne 2008). Another route involves the failure of asylum seekers to leave when their applications for refugee status are rejected. The problem of illegal immigration is by no means solely a failure to control the border.

Another drawback of the 'illegal' terminology emerges in the fact that many countries do not in fact treat undocumented immigrants as criminals. Government agencies typically approach detention and deportation as administrative rather than criminal justice procedures – in no small measure because they then require a lower burden of proof to satisfy 'due process' requirements (Carens 2008). On the other hand, the US government (perhaps recognizing limitations of border controls) in recent years has begun redirecting enforcement efforts to 'internal' sites, sometimes prosecuting (and then imprisoning) undocumented workers for identity theft, i.e., for having provided someone else's Social Security number to their employer (Bacon 2008).

More attention is typically focused on 'supply' (the migrants) than on 'demand' (the employers), particularly in the USA (Andreas 2000; Kwong 1997). Some European countries, on the other hand, have long imposed significant penalties on employers of undocumented workers and generally experience lower levels of undocumented immigration, though sanctions are by no means a panacea (Freeman 1994; Martin and Miller 2000). Early American attempts to implement sanctions, in 1986, were conspicuously unsuccessful (e.g. Fix 1991); they were perhaps even counterproductive, in that employers, who were not required to verify the authenticity of documents presented by their workers, were protected from prosecution for merely having 'checked' them.

Political and moral debates about undocumented immigrants are unsurprisingly quite complex. Carens (2008) argues that lack of legal status does not justify denying migrants' basic human rights such as emergency medical treatment, education for children, and work-related rights (e.g. minimum wages and safe conditions). Failing to guarantee these rights can be counterproductive with respect to the goal of reducing incentives for migration, insofar as it renders immigrants more exploitable and thus more attractive to employers. Some observers are particularly troubled by provision of education for undocumented children because it enhances their identification with the 'host' country, making departure/deportation both less likely and more traumatic. But Carens notes that the children cannot be held responsible for illegal entry and argues that uneducated children would only become marginalized adults, as the feasibility and legitimacy of deportation declines the longer they stay. California voters expressed their displeasure with these matters by approving Proposition 187 in 1994 (excluding undocumented children from schools and undocumented immigrants generally from a variety of public services and facilities), but its subsequent invalidation by a federal court demonstrated that liberal states (and their electorates) face substantial limits in their ability to deny basic rights to illegal immigrants. Even so, undocumented immigrants are typically quite vulnerable, unable or unwilling to access rights they formally have, out of fear that contact with authorities will lead to deportation (Bosniak 2008; Clark 2013).

The rhetoric of 'illegality' suggests that the destination country genuinely rejects the immigrants who carry this label: this migration violates the law, ostensibly the expression of the public will (at least in democratic countries). But some elements of the destination country plainly want illegal immigrants – and it is often their very illegality that makes them attractive (e.g. Bacon 2008). Again, lacking proper documents, the immigrants are vulnerable and thus more easily exploited; if they complain, the employer might dispose of the problem by alerting the authorities (who can detain and deport), and so there are fewer complaints. In the USA, members of Congress, governors and others have sometimes interfered in federal enforcement efforts, forcing the Immigration and Naturalization Service (whose successor is now part of the Department of Homeland Security) to withdraw from workplace raids (Martin and Miller 2000). Large numbers of private individuals employ undocumented housekeepers, gardeners, nannies, etc., and some social movement groups embrace undocumented immigrants on humanitarian and civil rights grounds.

In addition, wealthy countries' policies on trade and other economic matters arguably displace workers in countries like Mexico, leading them to perceive no alternative to migration to the USA, where many employers prefer them to native workers (Johnson 2007). Some observers, highlighting the racial dimension of migration restrictions, argue that migration control regimes are a component of 'global apartheid', such that clandestine migration is a legitimate form of resistance (Spener 2009).

On occasion, some countries have in essence conceded defeat, offering opportunities for regularization (amnesties) to large numbers of undocumented immigrants. The USA in 1986 offered amnesty to more than 3 million people, and Spain has undertaken no fewer than five episodes of 'normalization' since 1984 (López 2008). As Newton (2008) shows, while 'illegal immigrants' are usually constructed as targets of demonization, more positive forms of political constructions do sometimes gain sway. Critics worry that these decisions only increase incentives for illegal immigration, and there is currently significant opposition (though some significant support as well) in the USA to proposals for another amnesty to address the situation of roughly 11 million undocumented immigrants. On the other hand, this opposition can be framed as an implicit decision to carry on living with this large number: deportation on this scale would be wildly unrealistic, many employers are happy to have them, and many migrants themselves would face difficult prospects upon return (though as noted in other chapters, many migrants do choose to return).

The experiences of undocumented immigrants show that there are limits to what some scholars describe as a human rights revolution in recent decades. While some forms of migration have led to an expansion and diversification of citizenship, this transformation has had only limited impact on the situation of migrants lacking legal status, with many experiencing increasing insecurity (Verduzco and de Lozano 2011). One sign of this limited scope is the fact that the International Convention on the Protection of All Migrant Workers and Members of Their Families, proposing to guarantee key rights for migrants regardless of legal status, has been ratified by very few countries. The major destination countries in particular have declined to adopt it – in essence confirming their position that legal immigration status is a precondition for holding many basic rights (Dauvergne 2008).

One commonly thinks of illegal immigration as a challenge faced by wealthy countries, potentially overrun or swamped by migrants originating in poor countries – but this picture is incomplete (if not simply wrong). Other chapters have noted that migration flows among poorer countries are substantial, and many of these flows contain large numbers of undocumented immigrants. Individuals from wealthy countries can also become illegal immigrants, though usually without the same risks or stigma: Europeans living in another EU country are required to register their new residence but are not commonly considered illegal when they do not (Triandafyllidou 2010). One of the biggest groups of undocumented immigrants in Australia consists of Americans who have overstayed their tourist visas (Dauvergne 2008).

See also: *Human trafficking and smuggling; Deportation*

KEY READINGS

Bacon, D. (2008) *Illegal People: How Globalization Creates Migration and Criminalizes Immigrants*. Boston, MA: Beacon Press.

Newton, L. (2008) *Illegal, Alien, or Immigrant: The Politics of Immigration Reform*. New York: New York University Press.

Spener, D. (2009) *Clandestine Crossings: Migrants and Coyotes on the Texas–Mexico Border*. Ithaca, NY: Cornell University Press.

Triandafyllidou, A. and Lundqvist, A. (eds) (2010) *Irregular Migration in Europe: Myths and Realities*. Farnham: Ashgate Publishing Group.

references

Achvarina, V. and Reich, S.F. (2006) 'No place to hide: refugees, displaced persons, and the recruitment of child soldiers', *International Security*, 31: 127–64.

Adams Jr., R.H. and Page, J. (2005) 'Do international migration and remittances reduce poverty in developing countries?', *World Development*, 33: 1645–69.

Adepoju, A. (1998) 'Linkages between internal and international migration: the African situation', *International Social Science Journal*, 50: 387–96.

Afsar, R. (2011) 'Contextualizing gender and migration in South Asia: critical insights', *Gender, Technology and Development*, 15: 389–410.

Agunias, D.R. (2009) *Committed to the Diaspora: More Developing Countries Setting up Diaspora Institutions*. Washington, DC: Migration Policy Institute.

Agustín, L. (2005) 'Migrants in the mistress's house: other voices in the "trafficking" debate', *Social Politics*, 12: 96–117.

Alba, R. (2005) 'Bright vs. blurred boundaries: second-generation assimilation and exclusion in France, Germany, and the United States', *Ethnic and Racial Studies*, 28: 20–49.

Alba, R.D. and Nee, V. (1997) 'Rethinking assimilation theory for a new era of immigrants', *International Migration Review*, 31: 826–74.

Alba, R.D. and Nee, V. (2003) *Remaking the American Mainstream: Assimilation and Contemporary Immigration*. Cambridge, MA: Harvard University Press.

Amelina, A. and Faist, T. (2012) 'De-naturalizing the national in research methodologies: key concepts of transnational studies in migration', *Ethnic and Racial Studies*, 35: 1707–24.

Amir, S. (2002) 'Overseas foreign workers in Israel: policy aims and labor market outcomes', *International Migration Review*, 36: 41–57.

Ammassari, S. (2004) 'From nation-building to entrepreneurship: the impact of élite return migrants in Côte d'Ivoire and Ghana', *Population, Space and Place*, 10: 133–54.

Andall, J. (1992) 'Women migrant workers in Italy', *Women's Studies International Forum*, 15: 41–8.

Andersen, U. (1990) 'Consultative institutions for migrant workers', in Z. Layton-Henry (ed.), *The Political Rights of Migrant Workers in Europe*. London: SAGE, pp. 113–26.

Anderson, B. (1983) *Imagined Communities: Reflections on the Origin and Spread of Nationalism*. London: Verso.

Anderson, B. and Blinder, S. (2011) *Who Counts as a Migrant? Definitions and Their Consequences*. Briefing, The Migration Observatory at the University of Oxford. Oxford: University of Oxford.

Anderson, B., Gibney, M.J. and Paoletti, E. (2011) 'Citizenship, deportation and the boundaries of belonging', *Citizenship Studies*, 15: 547–63.

Andreas, P. (2000) *Border Games: Policing the U.S.–Mexico Divide*. Ithaca, NY: Cornell University Press.

Andrijasevic, R. (2010) *Migration, Agency and Citizenship in Sex Trafficking*. Basingstoke: Palgrave.

Anthias, F. (1998) 'Evaluating "diaspora": beyond ethnicity', *Sociology*, 32: 557–80.

Antón, J.-I. (2010) 'The impact of remittances on nutritional status of children in Ecuador', *International Migration Review*, 44: 269–99.

Appleyard, R. (1989) 'Migration and development: myths and realities', *International Migration Review*, 23: 486–99.

Back, L., Keith, M., Khan, A., Shukra, K. and Solomos, J. (2002) 'The return of assimilationism: race, multiculturalism and New Labour', *Sociological Research Online*, 7 (2).

Bacon, D. (2008) *Illegal People: How Globalization Creates Migration and Criminalizes Immigrants*. Boston, MA: Beacon Press.

Bader, V. (2005) 'The ethics of immigration', *Constellations*, 12: 331–61.
Bakalian, A.P. and Bozorgmehr, M. (2009) *Backlash 9/11: Middle Eastern and Muslim Americans Respond*. Berkeley, CA: University of California Press.
Baker, P., Gabrielatos, C., KhosraviNik, M., Krzyzanowski, M., McEnery, T. and Wodak, R. (2008) 'A useful methodological synergy? Combining critical discourse analysis and corpus linguistics to examine discourses of refugees and asylum seekers in the UK press', *Discourse and Society*, 19: 273–306.
Bakewell, O. (2008) 'Research beyond the categories: the importance of policy irrelevant research into forced migration', *Journal of Refugee Studies*, 21: 432–53.
Baldassar, L. (2007) 'Transnational families and the provision of moral and emotional support: the relationship between truth and distance', *Identities*, 14: 385–409.
Banerjee, B. (1983) 'Social networks in the migration process: empirical evidence on chain migration in India', *Journal of Developing Areas*, 17: 185–96.
Banton, M. (2001) 'National integration in France and Britain', *Journal of Ethnic and Migration Studies*, 27: 151–68.
Barcus, H.R. (2004) 'Urban–rural migration in the USA: an analysis of residential satisfaction', *Regional Studies*, 38: 643–58.
Barry, B. (2001) *Culture and Equality: An Egalitarian Critique of Multiculturalism*, Cambridge, MA: Harvard University Press.
Barth, F. (1969) (ed.) *Ethnic Groups and Boundaries. The Social Organization of Culture Difference*. Bergen and London: Allen & Unwin.
Bartram, D. (2005) *International Labor Migration: Foreign Workers and Public Policy*. New York: Palgrave Macmillan.
Bartram, D. (2010) 'International migration, open borders debates, and happiness', *International Studies Review*, 12: 339–61.
Bartram, D. (2012) 'Migration, methods and innovation: a reconsideration of variation and conceptualization in research on foreign workers', in C. Vargas-Silva (ed.), *Handbook of Research Methods in Migration*. Cheltenham: Edward Elgar, pp. 50–68.
Bartram, D. (2013) 'Happiness and "economic migration": a comparison of Eastern European migrants and stayers', *Migration Studies*, 1: 156–75.
Basch, L., Glick Schiller, N. and Blanc, C.S. (1994) *Nations Unbound: Transnational Projects, Postcolonial Predicaments, and Deterritorialized Nation-states*. New York: Routledge.
Basok, T. (2003) 'Mexican seasonal migration to Canada and development: a community-based comparison', *International Migration*, 41 (2): 3–26.
Bassel, L. (2012) *Refugee Women: Beyond Gender Versus Culture*. London: Routledge.
Bauböck, R. (1994a) *The Integration of Immigrants*. Strasbourg: Council of Europe.
Bauböck, R. (1994b) *Transnational Citizenship: Membership and Rights in International Migration*. Cheltenham: Edward Elgar.
Bauböck, R. (2003) 'Towards a political theory of migrant transnationalism', *International Migration Review*, 37: 700–23.
Baumann, G. (1996) *Contesting Culture: Discourses of Identity in Multi-ethnic London*. Cambridge: Cambridge University Press.
Baumann, M. (2000) 'Diaspora: genealogies of semantics and transcultural comparison', *NUMEN*, 47: 313–37.
Baycan-Levent, T., Nijkamp, P. and Sahin, M. (2008) *External Orientation of Second Generation Migrant Entrepreneurs: A Sectoral Study on Amsterdam*. Amsterdam: Vrije Universities.
Beale, C.L. (1977) 'The recent shift of United States population to nonmetropolitan areas, 1970–1975', *International Regional Science Review*, 2: 113–22.
Beck, R. (1996) *The Case Against Immigration: The Moral, Economic, Social and Environmental Reasons for Reducing U.S. Immigration Back to Traditional Levels*. New York: Norton.
Benson, M. and O'Reilly, K. (2009) 'Migration and the search for a better way of life: a critical exploration of lifestyle migration', *Sociological Review*, 57: 608–25.

Bertossi, C. (2011) 'National models of integration in Europe', *American Behavioral Scientist*, 55: 1561–80.
Birks, J.S., Seccombe, I.J. and Sinclair, C.A. (1986) 'Migrant workers in the Arab Gulf: the impact of declining oil revenues', *International Migration Review*, 20: 799–814.
Blake, M. (2002) 'Distributive justice, state coercion, and autonomy', *Philosophy & Public Affairs*, 30: 257–96.
Blitz, B.K. (2005) 'Refugee returns, civic differentiation, and minority rights in Croatia 1991–2004', *Journal of Refugee Studies*, 18: 362–86.
Bloch, A. (2002) *The Migration and Settlement of Refugees in Britain*. Basingstoke: Palgrave Macmillan.
Bloch, A. (2005) *The Development Potential of Zimbabweans in the Diaspora: A Survey of Zimbabweans Living in the UK and South Africa*. Migration Research Series, #17. Geneva: International Organization for Migration.
Bloch, A. and Schuster, L. (2005) 'At the extremes of exclusion: deportation, detention, and dispersal', *Ethnic and Racial Studies*, 28: 491–512.
Bloemraad, I. (2006) *Becoming a Citizen: Incorporating Immigrants and Refugees in the United States and Canada*. Berkeley, CA: University of California Press.
Bloemraad, I., Korteweg, A. and Yurdakul, G. (2008) 'Citizenship and immigration: multiculturalism, assimilation, and challenges to the nation-state', *Annual Review of Sociology*, 34: 153–79.
Boccagni, P. (2011) 'The framing of return from above and below in Ecuadorian migration: a project, a myth, or a political device?', *Global Networks*, 11: 461–80.
Bonacich, E. (1973) 'A theory of middleman minorities', *American Sociological Review*, 38 (5): 583–94.
Bonifazi, C. and Heins, F. (2000) 'Long-term trends of internal migration in Italy', *International Journal of Population Geography*, 6 (2): 111–32.
Booth, W.J. (1997) 'Foreigners: insiders, outsiders and the ethics of membership', *Review of Politics*, 59: 259–92.
Borjas, G.J. (1985) 'Assimilation, changes in cohort quality, and the earnings of immigrants', *Journal of Labor*, 3: 463–89.
Borjas, G.J. (1987) 'Self-selection and the earnings of immigrants', *American Economic Review*, 77: 531–53.
Bosniak, L. (2008) *The Citizen and the Alien: Dilemmas of Contemporary Membership*. Princeton, NJ: Princeton University Press.
Bourdieu, P. (1986) 'The forms of capital', in J.G. Richardson (ed.), *Handbook of Theory and Research for the Sociology of Education*. New York: Greenwood Press, pp. 241–58.
Boyd, M. (1989) 'Family and personal networks in international migration: recent developments and new agendas', *International Migration Review*, 23 (3): 638–70.
Boyd, M. and Pikkov, D. (2005) *Gendering Migration, Livelihood, and Entitlements: Migrant Women in Canada and the United States*. Geneva: United Nations Research Institute for Social Development.
Brah, A. (1996) *Cartographies of Diaspora: Contesting Identities*. London: Routledge.
Breton, R. (1964) 'Institutional completeness of ethnic communities and the personal relations of immigrants', *American Journal of Sociology*, 70: 193–205.
Brimelow, P. (1996) *Alien Nation: Common Sense about America's Immigration Disaster*. New York: HarperPerennial.
Brochmann, G. (1996) *European Integration and Immigration from Third Countries*. Oslo: Scandinavian University Press.
Brotherton, D.C. and Barrios, L. (2011) *Banished to the Homeland: Dominican Deportees and Their Stories of Exile*. New York: Columbia University Press.
Brubaker, R. (1992a) *Citizenship and Nationhood in France and Germany*. Cambridge, MA: Harvard University Press.

Brubaker, R. (1992b) 'Citizenship struggles in Soviet successor states', *International Migration Review*, 26: 269–91.
Brubaker, R. (2003) 'The return of assimilation? Changing perspectives on immigration and its sequels in France, Germany, and the United States', in C. Joppke and E. Morawska (eds), *Toward Assimilation and Citizenship: Immigrants in Liberal Nation-states*. Basingstoke: Palgrave Macmillan, pp. 39–58.
Brubaker, R. (2004) *Ethnicity Without Groups*. Cambridge, MA: Harvard University Press.
Brubaker, R. (2005) 'The "diaspora" diaspora', *Ethnic and Racial Studies*, 28 (1): 1–19.
Buchanan, P.J. (2006) *State of Emergency: The Third World Invasion and Conquest of America*. New York: St. Martin's Press.
Burnett, J. (2004) 'Community, cohesion and the state', *Race & Class*, 45 (3): 1–18.
Burt, R.S. (1995) *Structural Holes: The Social Structure of Competition*. Cambridge, MA: Harvard University Press.
Cabrera, L. (2010) *The Practice of Global Citizenship*. Cambridge: Cambridge University Press.
Calavita, K. (2005) *Immigrants at the Margins: Law, Race, and Exclusion in Southern Europe*. Cambridge: Cambridge University Press.
Calavita, K. (2006) 'Gender, migration, and law: crossing borders and bridging disciplines', *International Migration Review*, 40: 104–32.
Caldwell, C. (2009) *Reflections on the Revolution in Europe: Can Europe Be the Same with Different People in It?* London: Allen Lane.
Carens, J.H. (1987) 'Aliens and citizens: the case for open borders', *Review of Politics*, 49: 251–73.
Carens, J.H. (1992) 'Migration and morality: a liberal egalitarian perspective', in B. Barry and R.E. Goodin (eds), *Free Movement: Ethical Issues in the Transnational Migration of People and of Money*. London: Harvester Wheatsheaf, pp. 25–47.
Carens, J.H. (1999) 'A reply to Meilander: reconsidering open borders', *International Migration Review*, 33: 1082–97.
Carens, J.H. (2008) 'The rights of irregular migrants', *Ethics and International Affairs*, 22: 163–86.
Carter, A. (2001) *The Political Theory of Global Citizenship*. London: Routledge.
Cassarino, J.-P. (2004) 'Theorising return migration: the conceptual approach to return migrants revisited', *IJMS: International Journal on Multicultural Societies*, 6: 253–79.
Castles, S. (1986) 'The guest-worker in Europe: an obituary', *International Migration Review*, 20: 761–78.
Castles, S. (2003a) 'Towards a sociology of forced migration and social transformation', *Sociology*, 37 (1): 13–34.
Castles, S. (2003b) 'A fair migration policy – without open borders', *openDemocracy*, 29 December.
Castles, S. (2006) 'Guestworkers in Europe: a resurrection?', *International Migration Review*, 40: 741–66.
Castles, S. (2010) 'Understanding global migration: a social transformation perspective', *Journal of Ethnic and Migration Studies*, 36: 1565–86.
Castles, S., Booth, H. and Wallace, T. (1984) *Here for Good: Western Europe's New Ethnic Minorities*. London: Pluto Press.
Castles, S. and Davidson, A. (2000) *Citizenship and Migration: Globalization and the Politics of Belonging*. Basingstoke: Macmillan.
Castles, S. and Kosack, G. (1985) *Immigrant Workers and Class Structure in Western Europe*. Oxford: Oxford University Press.
Castles, S. and Miller, M.J. (2009) *The Age of Migration: International Population Movements in the Modern World*. London: Macmillan Press.
Cave, D. (2011) 'Better lives for Mexicans cut allure of going north', *New York Times*, 6 July.
Cave, D. (2012) 'Migrants' new paths reshaping Latin America', *New York Times*, 23 January.

Cave, D. (2013) 'For migrants, new land of opportunity is Mexico', *New York Times*, 21 September.
Cerase, F.P. (1974) 'Expectations and reality: a case study of return migration from the United States to Southern Italy', *International Migration Review*, 8: 245–62.
Chang, G. (2000) *Disposable Domestics: Immigrant Women Workers in the Global Economy*. Boston, MA: South End Press.
Chavez, L.R. (1998) *Shadowed Lives: Undocumented Immigrants in American Society*, Fort Worth, TX: Harcourt Brace College Publishers.
Cheong, P.H., Edwards, R., Goulbourne, H. and Solomos, J. (2007) 'Immigration, social cohesion and social capital: a critical review', *Critical Social Policy*, 27: 24–49.
Chin, C.B.N. (1998) *In Service and Servitude: Foreign Female Domestic Workers and the Malaysian 'Modernity' Project*. New York: Columbia University Press.
Chiswick, B.R. (1999) 'Are immigrants favorably self-selected?', *American Economic Review*, 89 (2): 181–5.
Clark, N. (2013) *Detecting and Tackling Forced Labour in Europe*. York: Joseph Rowntree Foundation.
Cohen, A. (1974) *Two-dimensional Man: An Essay on the Anthropology of Power and Symbolism in Complex Society*. Berkeley, CA: University of California Press.
Cohen, R. (1987) *The New Helots: Migrants in the International Division of Labour*. Brookfield, VT: Gower Pub. Co.
Cohen, R. (1996) 'Diasporas and the nation-state: from victims to challengers', *International Affairs*, 72: 507–20.
Cohen, R. (1997a) 'Shaping the nation, excluding the other: the deportation of migrants from Britain', in J. Lucassen and L. Lucassen (eds), *Migration, Migration History, History: Old Paradigms and New Perspectives*. Bern: Peter Lang, pp. 351–73.
Cohen, R. (1997b) *Global Diasporas: An Introduction*. London: UCL Press.
Cohen, R. (2006) *Migration and Its Enemies: Global Capital, Migrant Labour and the Nation-state*. Aldershot: Ashgate.
Cohen, R. and Deng, F.M. (1998) *Masses in Flight: The Global Crisis of Internal Displacement*. Washington, DC: The Brookings Institution.
Cohen, S., Grimsditch, H. and Hayter, T. (2003) 'No one is illegal', www.noii.org.uk; original website now defunct; Canadian version available at www.nooneisillegal.org.
Cohen, Y. (2009) 'Migration patterns to and from Israel', *Contemporary Jewry*, 29: 115–25.
Cole, D. (2003) *Enemy Aliens: Double Standards and Constitutional Freedoms in the War on Terrorism*. New York: New Press, distributed by W.W. Norton & Co.
Constable, N. (2007) *Maid to Order in Hong Kong: Stories of Migrant Workers*. Ithaca, NY: Cornell University Press.
Conway, D. and Potter, R.B. (2007) 'Caribbean transnational return migrants as agents of change', *Geography Compass*, 1: 25–45.
Conway, D. and Potter, R.B. (eds) (2009) *Return Migration of the Next Generations: 21st Century Transnational Mobility*. Farnham: Ashgate Publishing.
Cornelius, W. (1992) 'From sojourners to settlers: the changing profile of Mexican immigration to the United States', in J.A. Bustamante (ed.), *US–Mexico Relations: Labor Market Interdependence*. Stanford, CA: Stanford University Press, pp. 155–95.
Cornelius, W.A. and Martin, P.L. (1993) 'The uncertain connection: free trade and rural Mexican migration to the United States', *International Migration Review*, 27: 484–512.
Cornell, S.E. and Hartmann, D. (2007) *Ethnicity and Race: Making Identities in a Changing World*. Thousand Oaks, CA: Pine Forge Press.
Coutin, S.B. (2007) *Nations of Emigrants: Shifting Boundaries of Citizenship in El Salvador and the United States*. Ithaca, NY: Cornell University Press.
Coutin, S.B. (2010) 'Exiled by law: deportation and the inviability of life', in N. De Genova and N. Peutz (eds), *The Deportation Regime: Sovereignty, Space, and the Freedom of Movement*. Durham: Duke University Press, pp. 351–70.

Craig, G. and O'Neill, M. (2013) 'It's time to move on from "race"? The official "invisibilisation" of minority ethnic disadvantage', *Social Policy Review*, 25: 90–108.
Craig, R.B. (1971) *The Bracero Program: Interest Groups and Foreign Policy*. Austin, TX: University of Texas Press.
Crul, M., Schneider, J. and Lelie, F. (eds) (2012) *The European Second Generation Compared: Does the Integration Context Matter?* Amsterdam: Amsterdam University Press.
Curran, S.R., Garip, F., Chung, C.Y. and Tangchonlatip, K. (2005) 'Gendered migrant social capital: evidence from Thailand', *Social Forces*, 84: 225–56.
Daly, M. and Silver, H. (2008) 'Social exclusion and social capital: a comparison and critique', *Theory and Society*, 37 (6): 537–66.
Dang, A., Goldstein, S. and McNally, J. (1997) 'Internal migration and development in Vietnam', *International Migration Review*, 31: 312–37.
Dauvergne, C. (2008) *Making People Illegal: What Globalization Means for Migration and Law*. Cambridge: Cambridge University Press.
Davis, B., Stecklov, G. and Winters, P. (2002) 'Domestic and international migration from rural Mexico: disaggregating the effects of network structure and composition', *Population Studies*, 56: 291–310.
De Haan, A., Brock, K. and Coulibaly, N. (2002) 'Migration, livelihoods and institutions: contrasting patterns of migration in Mali', *Journal of Development Studies*, 38: 37–58.
De Haas, H. (2005) 'International migration, remittances and development: myths and facts', *Third World Quarterly*, 26 (8): 1269–84.
De Haas, H. (2007) *Remittances, Migration and Social Development: A Conceptual Review of the Literature*. Geneva: United Nations Research Institute for Social Development (Social Policy and Development Programme Papers, #34).
De Haas, H. (2010) 'Migration and development: a theoretical perspective', *International Migration Review*, 44: 227–64.
De Jong, G.F. (2000) 'Expectations, gender, and norms in migration decision-making', *Population Studies: A Journal of Demography*, 54; 307–19.
Deng, F.M. (2006) 'Divided nations: the paradox of national protection', *Annals of the American Academy of Political and Social Science*, 603: 217–25.
Dinerman, I.R. (1982) *Migrants and Stay-at-Homes: A Comparative Study of Rural Migration from Michoacan, Mexico*. La Jolla, CA: Center for U.S.–Mexican Studies, UCSD.
DiNicola, A. (2007) 'Research into human trafficking: issues and problems', in M. Lee (ed.), *Human Trafficking*. Portland, OR: Willan Publishing, pp. 49–72.
Doomernik, J., Koslowski, R., Laurence, J., Maxwell, R., Michalowski, I. and Thranhardt, D. (2009) *No Shortcuts: Selective Migration and Integration*. Washington, DC: Transatlantic Academy.
Dow, M. (2005) *American Gulag: Inside U.S. Immigration Prisons*. Berkeley, CA: University of California Press.
Dowling, S., Moreton, K. and Wright, L. (2007) *Trafficking for the Purposes of Labour Exploitation: A Literature Review*. London: Home Office (UK).
Dreby, J. (2009) 'Gender and transnational gossip', *Qualitative Sociology*, 32: 33–52.
Dreby, J. (2010) *Divided by Borders: Mexican Migrants and Their Children*. Berkeley, CA: University of California Press.
Dufoix, S. (2008) *Diasporas*. Berkeley, CA: University of California Press.
Dumon, W.A. (1989) 'Family and migration', *International Migration*, 27: 251–70.
Durand, J., Massey, D.S. and Parrado, E.A. (1999) 'The new era of Mexican migration to the United States', *Journal of American History*, 86: 518–36.
Durmelat, S. and Swamy, V. (2013) 'Second generation migrants: Maghrebis in France', in I. Ness (ed.), *The Encyclopedia of Global Human Migration*. Hoboken, NJ: Wiley-Blackwell.
Dustmann, C. and Weiss, Y. (2007) 'Return migration: theory and empirical evidence from the UK', *British Journal of Industrial Relations*, 45: 236–56.

Dwyer, P., Lewis, H., Scullion, L. and Waite, L. (2011) *Forced Labour and UK Immigration Policy: Status Matters*. York: Joseph Rowntree Foundation.
Easterlin, R.A. (2001) 'Income and happiness: towards a unified theory', *Economic Journal*, 111: 465–84.
Ebbi, O.N.I. and Das, P.K. (2008) *Global Trafficking in Women and Children*. Boca Raton, FL: CRC Press.
Eckstein, S. (2010) 'Immigration, remittances, and transnational social capital formation: a Cuban case study', *Ethnic and Racial Studies*, 33: 1648–67.
Ehrenreich, B. and Hochschild, A. (2003) *Global Woman: Nannies, Maids and Sex Workers in the New Economy*. London: Granta.
El-Khawas, M.A. (2004) 'Brain drain: putting Africa between a rock and a hard place', *Mediterranean Quarterly*, 15 (4): 37–56.
Ellermann, A. (2005) 'Coercive capacity and the politics of implementation', *Comparative Political Studies*, 38: 1219–44.
Ellermann, A. (2008) 'The limits of unilateral migration control: deportation and inter-state cooperation', *Government and Opposition*, 43: 168–89.
Ellermann, A. (2009) *States Against Migrants: Deportation in Germany and the US*. Cambridge: Cambridge University Press.
Ellermann, A. (2010) 'Undocumented migrants and resistance in the liberal state', *Politics & Society*, 38: 408–29.
Entzinger, H. (1990) 'The lure of integration', *European Journal of International Affairs*, 4: 54–73.
Entzinger, H. (2007) 'Open borders and the welfare state', in A. Pécoud and P. de Guchteneire (eds), *Migration Without Borders: Essays on the Free Movement of People*. Paris and New York: UNESCO Publishing/Berghahn Books.
Espenshade, T.J. (1995) 'Unauthorized immigration to the United States', *Annual Review of Sociology*, 21: 195–216.
Espenshade, T.J. (2001) 'High-end immigrants and the shortage of skilled labor', *Population Research and Policy Review*, 20: 135–41.
Everett, M. (1999) 'Human rights and evictions of the urban poor in Colombia', *Land Lines*, 11: 6–8.
Faist, T. (2000) *The Volume and Dynamics of International Migration and Transnational Social Spaces*. Oxford: Clarendon Press.
Faist, T. (2007) 'Dual citizenship: change, prospects and limits', in T. Faist (ed.), *Dual Citizenship in Europe: From Nationhood to Societal Integration*. Abingdon: Ashgate Publishing, pp. 171–200.
Faist, T. (2010) 'Diaspora and transnationalism: what kind of dance partners?', in R. Bauböck and T. Faist (eds), *Diaspora and Transnationalism: Concepts, Theories and Methods*. Amsterdam: Amsterdam University Press, pp. 9–34.
Favell, A. (1998) *Philosophies of Integration: Immigration and the Idea of Citizenship in France and Britain*. New York: St. Martin's Press.
Favell, A. (2005) 'Integration nations: the nation-state and research on immigrants in western Europe', in E. Morawska and M. Bommes (eds), *International Migration Research: Constructions, Omissions, and the Promises of Interdisciplinarity*. Aldershot: Ashgate, pp. 41–67.
Fawcett, J.T. (1989) 'Networks, linkages, and migration systems', *International Migration Review*, 23: 671–80.
Fekete, L. (2005) 'The deportation machine: Europe, asylum and human rights', *Race & Class*, 47: 64–78.
Fernández-Kelly, P. and Massey, Douglas S. (2007) 'Borders for whom? The role of NAFTA in Mexico–U.S. migration', *Annals of the American Academy of Political and Social Science*, 610: 98–118.
Fielding, A.J. (1982) 'Counter-urbanization in western Europe', *Progress in Planning*, 17: 1–52.

Fischer, P.A. and Straubhaar, T. (1996) *Migration and Economic Integration in the Nordic Common Labor Market*. Copenhagen: Nordic Council of Ministers.

Fix, M. (1991) *The Paper Curtain: Employer Sanctions' Implementation, Impact, and Reform*. Lanham, MD: Rowman & Littlefield.

Foner, N. (1997a) 'The immigrant family: cultural legacies and cultural changes', *International Migration Review*, 31: 961–74.

Foner, N. (1997b) 'What's new about transnationalism? New York immigrants today and at the turn of the century', *Diaspora*, 6 (3): 355–75.

Foner, N. (2007) 'How exceptional is New York? Migration and multiculturalism in the empire city', *Ethnic and Racial Studies*, 30: 999–1023.

Francis, E. (2002) 'Gender, migration and multiple livelihoods: cases from eastern and southern Africa', *Journal of Development Studies*, 38: 167–90.

Freeman, G.P. (1994) 'Can liberal states control unwanted migration?', *Annals of the American Academy of Political and Social Science*, 534: 17–30.

Freeman, G.P. (2004) 'Immigrant incorporation in Western democracies', *International Migration Review*, 38: 945–69.

Frey, W.H. (1996) 'Immigration, domestic migration, and demographic Balkanization in America: New Evidence for the 1990s', *Population and Development Review*, 22: 741–63.

Frisch, M. (1967) *Öffentlichkeit als Partner (The Public Sphere as Partner)*. Frankfurt am Main: Suhrkamp.

Fussell, E. (2010) 'The cumulative causation of international migration in Latin America', *Annals of the American Academy of Political and Social Science: Continental Divides – International Migration in the Americas*, 630: 162–77.

Fussell, E. and Massey, D.S. (2004) 'The limits to cumulative causation: international migration from Mexican urban areas', *Demography*, 41: 151–72.

Gans, H.J. (1979) 'Symbolic ethnicity: the future of ethnic groups and cultures in America', *Ethnic and Racial Studies*, 2: 1–20.

Gans, H.J. (1998) 'Toward a reconciliation of "assimilation" and "pluralism": the interplay of acculturation and ethnic retention', in C. Hirschman, P. Kasinitz and J. DeWind (eds), *The Handbook of International Migration: The American Experience*. New York: Russell Sage Foundation, pp. 161–71.

Gans, H.J. (1999) 'The possibility of a new racial hierarchy in the twenty-first century United States', in M. Lamont (ed.), *The Cultural Territories of Race*. Chicago, IL and New York: University of Chicago Press and Russell Sage Foundation, pp. 371–90.

Gavrilis, G. (2008) *The Dynamics of Interstate Boundaries*. Cambridge: Cambridge University Press.

GCIM (Global Commission on International Migration) (2005) *Migration in an Interconnected World: New Directions for Action*. Geneva: Global Commission on International Migration.

Gellner, E. (1983) *Nations and Nationalism*. Ithaca, NY: Cornell University Press.

Ghosh, B. (ed.) (2000) *Return Migration: Journey of Hope or Despair?* Geneva: International Organization for Migration.

Gibney, M.J. (2004) *The Ethics and Politics of Asylum: Liberal Democracy and the Response to Refugees*. Cambridge: Cambridge University Press.

Gibney, M.J. (2008) 'Asylum and the expansion of deportation in the United Kingdom', *Government and Opposition*, 43: 146–67.

Gibney, M.J. and Hansen, R. (2003) 'Deportation and the liberal state: the involuntary return of asylum seekers and unlawful migrants in Canada, the UK, and Germany', *New Issues in Refugee Research*, Working Paper Series No. 77.

Gilbert, D. (2006) *Stumbling on Happiness*. New York: HarperCollins.

Gilroy, P. (1993) *The Black Atlantic: Modernity and Double Consciousness*. London: Verso.

GISTI (2011) *Le Regroupement Familial (Family Reunification)*. Paris: Les Cahiers Juridiques, Éditions du GISTI.

Gitlin, T. (1995) *The Twilight of Common Dreams: Why America Is Wracked by Culture Wars*. New York: Metropolitan Books.

Giuliano, P. and Ruiz-Arranz, M. (2009) 'Remittances, financial development, and growth', *Journal of Development Economics*, 90: 144–52.
Glazer, N. (1994) 'The closing door', in N. Mills (ed.), *Arguing Immigration: Are New Immigrants a Wealth of Diversity ... or a Crushing Burden?* New York: Simon & Schuster, pp. 37–47.
Glazer, N. and Moynihan, D.P. (1963) *Beyond the Melting Pot: The Negroes, Puerto Ricans, Jews, Italians, and Irish of New York City*. Cambridge, MA: MIT Press.
Global Commission on International Migration (2005) *Migration in an Interconnected World: New Directions for Action*. Geneva: Global Commission on International Migration.
Gmelch, G. (1980) 'Return migration', *Annual Review of Anthropology*, 9: 135–59.
Goering, J.M. (1989) 'Introduction and overview to special issue, the "explosiveness" of chain migration: research and policy issues', *International Migration Review*, 23 (4): 797–812.
Goodhart, D. (2013) *The British Dream: Success and Failure in Immigration since the War*. London: Atlantic.
Gordon, M.M. (1964) *Assimilation in American Life: The Role of Race, Religion and National Origins*. New York: Oxford University Press.
Granovetter, M.S. (1995) *Getting a Job: a Study of Contacts and Careers*. Chicago, IL: University of Chicago Press.
Grasmuck, S. and Pessar, P.R. (1991) *Between Two Islands: Dominican International Migration*. Berkeley, CA: University of California Press.
Greenwood, M.J., Hunt, G.L. and Kohli, U. (1997) 'The factor-market consequences of unskilled immigration to the United States', *Labour Economics*, 4: 1–28.
Gregory, R.G. (1993) *South Asians in East Africa: An Economic and Social History, 1890–1980*. Boulder, CO: Westview Press.
Griffith, D. (2006) *American Guestworkers: Jamaicans and Mexicans in the U.S. Labor Market*. State College, PA: Pennsylvania State University Press.
Griffiths, D., Sigona, N. and Zetter, R. (2005) *Refugee Community Organisations and Dispersal: Networks, Resources and Social Capital*. Bristol: Policy Press.
Guarnizo, L.E. (2003) 'The economics of transnational living', *International Migration Review*, 37: 666–99.
Guarnizo, L.E., Portes, A. and Haller, W. (2003) 'Assimilation and transnationalism: determinants of transnational political action among contemporary migrants', *American Journal of Sociology*, 108: 1211–48.
Hahamovitch, C. (2003) 'Creating perfect immigrants: guestworkers of the world in historical perspective', *Labor History*, 44: 69–94.
Hall, P.A. (1996) 'Introducing African American studies – systematic and thematic principles', *Journal of Black Studies*, 26: 713–34.
Hall, S. (1995) *Nationality, Migration Rights and Citizenship of the Union*. Dordrecht: Martinus Nijhoff Publishers.
Halliday, J. and Coombes, M. (1995) 'In search of counterurbanisation: some evidence from Devon on the relationship between patterns of migration and motivation', *Journal of Rural Studies*, 11: 433–46.
Hammar, T. (1990) *Democracy and the Nation State: Aliens, Denizens, and Citizens in a World of International Migration*. Aldershot: Avebury.
Hanafi, S. and Long, T. (2010) 'Governance, governmentalities, and the state of exception in the Palestinian refugee camps of Lebanon', *Journal of Refugee Studies*, 23: 134–59.
Handelman, D. (1977) 'The organization of ethnicity', *Ethnic Groups*, 1: 187–200.
Hansen, R. (2000) *Citizenship and Immigration in Post-war Britain: The Institutional Origins of a Multicultural Nation*. Oxford: Oxford University Press.
Hansen, R. (2003) 'Citizenship and integration in Europe', in C. Joppke and E. Morawska (eds), *Toward Assimilation and Citizenship: Immigrants in Liberal Nation-states*. Basingstoke: Palgrave Macmillan, pp. 87–109.

Hartmann, B. (2009) 'From climate refugees to climate conflict: who is taking the heat for global warming?', in M.A.M. Salih (ed.), *Climate Change and Sustainable Development: New Challenges for Poverty Reduction*. Cheltenham: Edward Elgar, pp. 142–55.

Hathaway, J.C. (2007) 'Forced migration studies: could we agree just to "date"?', *Journal of Refugee Studies*, 20: 349–69.

Hayter, T. (2000) *Open Borders: The Case Against Immigration Controls*. London: Pluto Press.

Heinburg, J.D., Harris, J.K. and York, R.L. (1989) 'Process of exempt immediate relative immigration to the United States', *International Migration Review*, 23: 839–55.

Heming, L., Waley, P. and Rees, P. (2001) 'Reservoir resettlement in China: past experience and the Three Gorges Dam', *Geographical Journal*, 167: 195–212.

Herbert, U. (1990) *A History of Foreign Labor in Germany, 1880–1980: Seasonal Workers, Forced Laborers, Guest Workers*. Ann Arbor, MI: University of Michigan Press.

Hing, B.O. (2006) *Deporting Our Souls: Values, Morality, and Immigration Policy*. Cambridge: Cambridge University Press.

Hondagneu-Sotelo, P. (1994) *Gendered Transitions: Mexican Experiences of Immigration*. Berkeley, CA: University of California Press.

Hondagneu-Sotelo, P. (2003) *Gender and U.S. Immigration: Contemporary Trends*. Berkeley, CA: University of California Press.

Hondagneu-Sotelo, P. and Cranford, C. (1999) 'Gender and migration', in J. Saltzman Chafetz (ed.), *Handbook of the Sociology of Gender*. New York: Kluwer, pp. 105–26.

Huang, S., Yeoh, B.S.A. and Noor Abdul, R. (2005) *Asian Women as Transnational Domestic Workers*. Singapore: Marshall Cavendish Academic.

Ibrahim, V. (2011) 'Ethnicity', in S.M. Caliendo and McIlwain, C.D. (eds), *The Routledge Companion to Race and Ethnicity*. Abingdon: Routledge, pp. 12–20.

ICRC (International Committee of the Red Cross) (2009) *Internal Displacement in Armed Conflict: Facing up to the Challenges*. Geneva: ICRC.

IOM (International Organization for Migration) (2005) *World Migration 2005: Costs and Benefits of International Migration*. Geneva: International Organization for Migration.

Ireland, P. (2004) *Becoming Europe: Immigration, Integration, and the Welfare State*. Pittsburgh, PA: University of Pittsburgh Press.

Isaacs, H.R. (1975) *Idols of the Tribe: Group Identity and Political Change*. New York: Harper & Row.

Isbister, J. (1996) 'Are immigration controls ethical?', *Social Justice*, 23: 54–67.

Jacobson, D. (1996) *Rights Across Borders: Immigration and the Decline of Citizenship*. Baltimore, MD: Johns Hopkins University Press.

Jacobson, M.F. (1999) *Whiteness of a Different Color: European Immigrants and the Alchemy of Race*. Cambridge, MA: Harvard University Press.

Jasso, G. and Rosenzweig, M.R. (1986) 'Family reunification and the immigration multiplier: U.S. immigration law, origin-country conditions, and the reproduction of immigrants', *Demography*, 23: 291–311.

Jasso, G. and Rosenzweig, M.R. (1989) 'Sponsors, sponsorship rates and the immigration multiplier', *International Migration Review*, 23: 856–88.

Jasso, G. and Rosenzweig, M.R. (1995) 'Do immigrants screened for skills do better than family reunification immigrants?', *International Migration Review*, 29 (1): 85–111.

Jenson, J. (2007) 'The European Union's citizenship regime: creating norms and building practices', *Comparative European Politics*, 5: 53–69.

Jileva, E. (2002) 'Larger than the European Union: the emerging EU migration regime and enlargement', in S. Lavenex and E.M. Uçarer (eds), *Migration and the Externalities of European Integration*. Lanham, MD: Lexington Books, pp. 75–89.

Johnson, K.R. (2007) *Opening the Floodgates: Why America Needs to Rethink Its Borders and Immigration Laws*. New York: New York University Press.

Johnston, R., Trlin, A., Henderson, A. and North, N. (2006) 'Sustaining and creating migration chains among skilled immigrant groups: Chinese, Indians and South Africans in New Zealand', *Journal of Ethnic and Migration Studies*, 32: 1227–50.

Joly, D. (1996) *Haven or Hell? Asylum Policies and Refugees in Europe*. Basingstoke: Macmillan.
Joly, D., Nettleton, C. and Poulton, H. (1992) *Refugees: Asylum in Europe?* London: Minority Rights Publications.
Jones, H. and Findlay, A. (1998) 'Regional economic integration and the emergence of the East Asian international migration system', *Geoforum*, 29: 87–104.
Jones, R.C. (1998) 'Remittances and inequality: a question of migration stage and geographic scale', *Economic Geography*, 74: 8–25.
Joppke, C. (1998) *Challenge to the Nation-state: Immigration in Western Europe and the United States.* Oxford: Oxford University Press.
Joppke, C. (1999a) *Immigration and the Nation-state: The United States, Germany, and Great Britain*. Oxford: Oxford University Press.
Joppke, C. (1999b) 'How immigration is changing citizenship: a comparative view', *Ethnic and Racial Studies*, 22: 629–52.
Joppke, C. (2007) 'Beyond national models: civic integration policies for immigrants in western Europe', *West European Politics*, 30: 1–22.
Joppke, C. (2010) *Citizenship and Immigration*. Cambridge: Polity.
Joppke, C. (2012) *The Role of the State in Cultural Integration: Trends, Challenges, and Ways Ahead*. Washington, DC: Migration Policy Institute working paper.
Joppke, C. and Lukes, S. (1999) 'Introduction: multicultural questions', in C. Joppke and S. Lukes (eds), *Multicultural Questions*. Oxford: Oxford University Press, pp. 1–24.
Joppke, C. and Morawska, E. (2003) 'Integrating immigrants in liberal nation-states: policies and practices', in C. Joppke and E. Morawska (eds), *Toward Assimilation and Citizenship: Immigrants in Liberal Nation-states*. Basingstoke: Palgrave Macmillan, pp. 1–36.
Kalra, V.S. and Kapoor, N. (2009) 'Interrogating segregation, integration and the community cohesion agenda', *Journal of Ethnic and Migration Studies*, 35: 1397–415.
Kalra, V., Kaur, R. and Hutnyk, J. (2005) *Diaspora and Hybridity*. London: SAGE.
Kamphoefner, W.D. (1987) *The Westfalians: From Germany to Missouri*. Princeton, NJ: Princeton University Press.
Kanaiaupuni, S.M. (2000) 'Reframing the migration question: an analysis of men, women, and gender in Mexico', *Social Forces*, 78: 1311–47.
Kandel, W. and Massey, D.S. (2002) 'The culture of Mexican migration: a theoretical and empirical analysis', *Social Forces*, 80: 981–1004.
Kanstroom, D. (2007) *Deportation Nation: Outsiders in American History*. Cambridge, MA: Harvard University Press.
Kasinitz, P., Waters, M.C., Mollenkopf, J.H. and Holdaway, J. (2008) *Inheriting the City: The Children of Immigrants Come of Age*. New York and Cambridge, MA: Russell Sage Foundation and Harvard University Press.
Kay, D. and Miles, R. (1992) *Refugees or Migrant Workers?: European Volunteer Workers in Britain, 1946–1951*. London: Routledge.
Kesler, C. and Bloemraad, I. (2010) 'Does immigration erode social capital? The conditional effects of immigration-generated diversity on trust, membership, and participation across 19 countries, 1981–2000', *Canadian Journal of Political Science*, 43: 319–47.
Khoser, K. (2000) 'Return, readmission and reintegration: changing agendas, policy frameworks and operational programmes', in B. Ghosh (ed.), *Return Migration: Journey of Hope or Despair?* Geneva: International Organization for Migration, pp. 57–99.
Khoser, K. (2001) *The Return and Reintegration of Rejected Asylum Seekers and Irregular Migrants*. Geneva: International Organization for Migration.
King, R. (2000) 'Generalizations from the history of return migration', in B. Ghosh (ed), *Return Migration: Journey of Hope or Despair?*, Geneva, International Organization for Migration, pp. 7–55.
King, R. and Christou, A. (2010) 'Cultural geographies of counter-diasporic migration: perspectives from the study of second-generation "returnees" to Greece', *Population, Space and Place*, 16: 103–19.

King, R., Christou, A. and Ahrens, J. (2011) '"Diverse mobilities": second-generation Greek-Germans engage with the homeland as children and as adults', *Mobilities*, 6: 483–501.

King, R. and Skeldon, R. (2010) '"Mind the gap!" Integrating approaches to internal and international migration', *Journal of Ethnic and Migration Studies*, 36: 1619–46.

Kivisto, P. (2002) *Multiculturalism in a Global Society*. New York: Wiley-Blackwell.

Kivisto, P. (2003) 'Social spaces, transnational immigrant communities, and the politics of incorporation', *Ethnicities*, 3: 5–28.

Kivisto, P. (2012) 'We really are all multiculturalists now', *Sociological Quarterly*, 53: 1–24.

Kivisto, P. and Faist, T. (2010) *Beyond a Border: The Causes and Consequences of Contemporary Immigration*. London: Pine Forge Press.

Klugman, J. and Medalho Pereira, I. (2009) 'Assessment of national migration policies: an emerging picture on admissions, treatment and enforcement in developing and developed countries', SSRN eLibrary, ssrn.com/abstract=1595435.

Knudsen, A. (2009) 'Widening the protection gap: the "politics of citizenship" for Palestinian refugees in Lebanon, 1948–2008', *Journal of Refugee Studies*, 22: 51–73.

Kofman, E. (2004) 'Family-related migration: a critical review of European studies', *Journal of Ethnic and Migration Studies*, 30 (2): 243–62.

Kofman, E., Phyzacklea, A., Raguram, P. and Sales, R. (2000) *Gender and International Migration in Europe. Employment, Welfare and Politics*. London: Routledge.

Korinek, K., Entwisle, B. and Jampaklay, A. (2005) 'Through thick and thin: layers of social ties and urban settlement among Thai migrants', *American Sociological Review*, 70: 779–800.

Koslowski, R. (2000) *Migrants and Citizens: Demographic Change in the European State System*. Ithaca, NY: Cornell University Press.

Kundnani, A. (2007) 'Integrationism: the politics of anti-Muslim racism', *Race & Class*, 48: 24–44.

Kunz, R. (2008) '"Remittances are beautiful"? Gender implications of the new global remittances trend', *Third World Quarterly*, 29: 1389–409.

Kwong, P. (1997) *Forbidden Workers: Illegal Chinese Immigrants and American Labor*. New York: New Press.

Kyle, D. (2000) *Transnational Peasants: Migrations, Networks, and Ethnicity in Andean Ecuador*. Baltimore, MD: Johns Hopkins University Press.

Kyle, D. and Siracusa, C. (2005) 'Seeing the state like a migrant: why so many non-criminals break immigration laws', in W. van Schendel and I. Abraham (eds), *Illicit Flows and Criminal Things: States, Borders, and the Other Side of Globalization*. Indianapolis, IN: Indiana University Press, pp. 153–77.

Kymlicka, W. (2001a) *Politics in the Vernacular: Nationalism, Multiculturalism and Citizenship*. Oxford: Oxford University Press.

Kymlicka, W. (2001b) 'Territorial boundaries: a liberal egalitarian perspective', in D. Miller and S.H. Hashmi (eds), *Boundaries and Justice: Diverse Ethical Perspectives*. Princeton, NJ: Princeton University Press, pp. 249–75.

Kymlicka, W. (2012) *Multiculturalism: Success, Failure, and the Future*. Washington, DC: Migration Policy Institute.

Kymlicka, W. and Norman, W. (2000) 'Citizenship in culturally diverse societies: issues, contexts, concepts', in W. Kymlicka and W. Norman (eds), *Citizenship in Diverse Societies*. Oxford: Oxford University Press, pp. 1–41.

Lahav, G. (1997) 'International versus national constraints in family-reunification migration policy', *Global Governance*, 3: 349–72.

Lahav, G. (1998) 'Immigration and the state: the devolution and privatisation of immigration control in the EU', *Journal of Ethnic and Migration Studies*, 24: 675–94.

Lahav, G. (2004) *Immigration and Politics in the New Europe: Reinventing Borders*. Cambridge: Cambridge University Press.

Laitin, D.D. (1998) *Identity in Formation: The Russian-speaking Populations in the Near Abroad*. Ithaca, NY: Cornell University Press.

Landolt, P., Autler, L. and Baires, S. (1999) 'From Hermano Lejano to Hermano Mayor: the dialectics of Salvadoran transnationalism', *Ethnic and Racial Studies*, 22: 290–315.

Layton-Henry, Z. (1990) *The Political Rights of Migrant Workers in Europe*. London: SAGE.

Lee, H. (2009) 'The ambivalence of return: second-generation Tongan returnees', in D. Conway and R.B. Potter (eds), *Return Migration of the Next Generations: 21st Century Transnational Mobility*. Farnham: Ashgate Publishing, pp. 41–58.

Lee, M. (2007) *Human Trafficking*. Portland, OR: Willan Publishing.

Legoux, L. (2012) 'Le morcellement de la catégorie statistique "réfugié"' (The fragmentation of the statistical category 'refugee'), *e-Migrinter*, 9: 64–78.

Legrain, P. (2007) *Immigrants: Your Country Needs Them*. New York: Little Brown.

Levitt, P. (1998) 'Social remittances: migration-driven local-level forms of cultural diffusion', *International Migration Review*, 32 (4): 926–48.

Levitt, P. (2001) *The Transnational Villagers*. Berkeley, CA: University of California Press.

Levitt, P. (2009) 'Roots and routes: understanding the lives of the second generation transnationally', *Journal of Ethnic and Migration Studies*, 35: 1225–42.

Liang, Z., Chunyu, M.D., Zhuang, G. and Ye, W. (2008) 'Cumulative causation, market transition, and emigration from China', *American Journal of Sociology*, 114: 706–37.

Light, I.H. and Gold, S.J. (2000) *Ethnic Economies*. San Diego, CA: Academic Press.

Lin, N. (1999) 'Building a network theory of social capital', *Connections*, 22 (1): 28–51.

Lipton, M. (1980) 'Migration from rural areas of poor countries: the impact on rural productivity and income distribution', *World Development*, 8: 1–24.

Lister, R. (2003) *Citizenship: Feminist Perspectives*. New York: New York University Press.

Liu, J.M., Ong, P.M. and Rosenstein, C. (1991) 'Dual chain migration: post-1965 Filipino immigration to the United States', *International Migration Review*, 25: 487–513.

Liu-Farrer, G. (2011) *Labour Migration from China to Japan: International Students, Transnational Migrants*. London: Taylor & Francis.

Loescher, G. (2001) 'Protection and humanitarian action in the post-cold war era', in A.R. Zolberg and P. Benda (eds), *Global Migrants, Global Refugees*. New York: Berghahn Books, pp. 171–205.

Loescher, G. (2005) *Protracted Refugee Situations: Domestic and International Security Implications*. London: International Institute for Strategic Studies.

López, M.P. (2008) 'Immigration law Spanish-style: a study of Spain's normalización of undocumented workers', *Georgetown Immigration Law Review*, 21 (4): 2007.

Lozano-Ascencio, F., Roberts, B. and Bean, F. (1999) 'The interconnections of internal and international migration: the case of the United States and Mexico', in L. Pries (ed.), *Migration and Transnational Social Spaces*. Aldershot: Ashgate, pp. 138–61.

Lucas, R.E.B. and Stark, O. (1985) 'Motivations to remit: evidence from Botswana', *Journal of Political Economy*, 93: 901–18.

Lugo, A. (2008) *Fragmented Lives, Assembled Parts: Culture, Capitalism, and Conquest at the U.S.–Mexico Border*. Austin, TX: University of Texas Press.

MacDonald, J.S. and MacDonald, L.D. (1964) 'Chain migration: Ethnic neighborhood formation and social networks', *Milbank Memorial Fund Quarterly*, 42: 82–97.

Mahler, S.J. (1995) *American Dreaming: Immigrant Life on the Margins*. Princeton, NJ: Princeton University Press.

Mahler, S.J. and Pessar, P.R. (2006) 'Gender matters: ethnographers bring gender from the periphery toward the core of migration studies', *International Migration Review*, 40: 27–63.

Mahroum, S. (2005) 'The international policies of brain gain: a review', *Technology Analysis & Strategic Management*, 17: 219–30.

Mai, N. (2012) 'The fractal queerness of non-heteronormative migrants working in the UK sex industry', *Sexualities*, 15: 570–85.

Malkki, L. (1992) 'National geographic: the rooting of peoples and the territorialization of national identity among scholars and refugees', *Cultural Anthropology*, 7: 24–44.

Malpani, R. (2009) 'Criminalizing human trafficking and protecting the victims', in B. Andrees and P. Belser (eds), *Forced Labor: Coercion and Exploitation in the Private Economy*. Boulder, CO: Lynne Rienner Publishers, pp. 129–49.

Marfleet, P. (2006) *Refugees in a Global Era*. Basingstoke: Palgrave Macmillan.

Marfleet, P. and Blustein, D.L. (2011) '"Needed not wanted": an interdisciplinary examination of the work-related challenges faced by irregular migrants', *Journal of Vocational Behavior*, 78: 381–9.

Marrus, M.R. (2002) *The Unwanted: European Refugees from the First World War Through the Cold War*. Philadelphia, PA: Temple University Press.

Marshall, T.H. (1950) *Citizenship and Social Class and Other Essays*. Cambridge: Cambridge University Press.

Martin, P.L. (1998) 'Economic integration and migration: the case of NAFTA', *UCLA Journal of International Law and Foreign Affairs*, 3: 419–32.

Martin, P.L. (2003) *Bordering on Control: Combating Irregular Migration in North America and Europe*. Geneva: International Organization for Migration.

Martin, P.L. (2004) 'Germany: managing migration in the twenty-first century', in W.A. Cornelius, P.L. Martin and J.F. Hollifield (eds), *Controlling Immigration: A Global Perspective*, 2nd edn. Stanford, CA: Stanford University Press, pp. 221–53.

Martin, P.L. (2009) *Importing Poverty? Immigration and the Changing Face of Rural America*. New Haven, CT: Yale University Press.

Martin, P.L., Abella, M.I. and Kuptsch, C. (2006) *Managing Labor Migration in the Twenty-first Century*. New Haven, CT: Yale University Press.

Martin, P.L. and Miller, M.J. (1980) 'Guestworkers: lessons from western Europe', *Industrial and Labor Relations Review*, 33: 315–30.

Martin, P.L. and Miller, M.J. (2000) *Employer Sanctions: French, German and US Experiences*. International Migration Papers, #36. Geneva: International Labour Office.

Martiniello, M. (1994) 'Citizenship of the European Union: a critical view', in R. Bauböck (ed.), *From Aliens to Citizens: Redefining the Status of Immigrants in Europe*. Aldershot: Avebury, pp. 29–47.

Martiniello, M. and Lafleur, J.-M. (2008) 'Towards a transatlantic dialogue in the study of immigrant political transnationalism', *Ethnic and Racial Studies*, 31: 645–63.

Marx, K. (1978 [1885]) *Capital: A Critique of Political Economy* (Volume 2). London: Penguin.

Massey, D.S. (1990) 'The social and economic origins of immigration', *Annals of the American Academy of Political and Social Science*, 510: 60–72.

Massey, D.S. (1998) *Worlds in Motion: Understanding International Migration at the End of the Millennium*. Oxford: Clarendon Press.

Massey, D.S. (1999) 'International migration at the dawn of the twenty-first century: the role of the state', *Population and Development Review*, 25: 303–22.

Massey, D.S. (2010a) 'Social-structure, household strategies, and the cumulative causation of migration', *Population Index*, 56: 3–26.

Massey, D.S. (2010b) 'Immigration statistics for the twenty-first century', *Annals of the American Academy of Political and Social Science*, 631: 124–40.

Massey, D.S., Alarcón, R., Durand, J. and González, H. (1987) *Return to Aztlan: The Social Process of International Migration from Western Mexico*. Berkeley, CA: University of California Press.

Massey, D.S., Arango, J., Hugo, G., Kouaouci, A., Pellegrino, A. and Taylor, J.E. (1998) *Worlds in Motion: Understanding International Migration at the End of the Millennium*. Oxford: Clarendon Press.

Massey, D.S., Durand, J. and Malone, N.J. (2003) *Beyond Smoke and Mirrors: Mexican Immigration in an Era of Economic Integration*. New York: Russell Sage Foundation.

Massey, D.S. and Espinosa, K.E. (1997) 'What's driving Mexico–U.S. migration? A theoretical, empirical, and policy analysis', *American Journal of Sociology*, 102: 939–99.
McDowell, L. (2003) 'Workers, migrants, aliens, or citizens? State constructions and discourses among post-war European labour migrants in Britain', *Political Geography*, 22: 863–86.
McGhee, D. (2005) 'Patriots of the future? A critical examination of community cohesion strategies in contemporary Britain', *Sociological Research Online*, 10 (3).
Mckay, J. (1982) 'An exploratory synthesis of primordial and mobilizationist approaches to ethnic phenomena', *Ethnic and Racial Studies*, 5: 395–420.
Meilaender, P.C. (1999) 'Liberalism and open borders: the argument of Joseph Carens', *International Migration Review*, 33: 1062–81.
Menjívar, C. (2000) *Fragmented Ties: Salvadoran Immigrant Networks in America*. Berkeley, CA: University of California Press.
Menz, G. and Caviedes, A. (2010) *Labour Migration in Europe*. Basingstoke: Palgrave Macmillan.
Migdal, J. (ed.) (2004) *Boundaries and Belonging: States and Societies in the Struggle to Shape Identities and Local Practices*. Cambridge: Cambridge University Press.
Migration Policy Institute (2011) *The Global Remittances Guide*. MPI Data Hub, http://www.migrationinformation.org/datahub/remittances.cfm.
Miller, D. (2000) *Citizenship and National Identity*. Cambridge: Polity Press.
Miller, D. (2007) *National Responsibility and Global Justice*. Oxford: Oxford University Press.
Miller, M.J. (1981) *Foreign Workers in Western Europe: An Emerging Political Force*. New York: Praeger.
Miller, M.J. and Martin, P. (1982) *Administering Foreign Worker Programs*. Lexington: Lexington Books.
Min, P.G. (2008) *Ethnic Solidarity for Economic Survival: Korean Greengrocers in New York City*. New York: Russell Sage Foundation.
Moch, L.P. (2003) *Moving Europeans: Migration in Western Europe since 1650*, 2nd edn. Bloomington, IN: Indiana University Press.
Modood, T. (2005) 'Remaking multiculturalism after 7/7', *openDemocracy*, 29 September.
Modood, T. and Salt, J. (eds) (2011) *Global Migration, Ethnicity and Britishness*. Basingstoke: Palgrave Macmillan.
Monforte, P. and Dufour, P. (2011) 'Mobilizing in borderline citizenship regimes: a comparative analysis of undocumented migrants' collective actions', *Politics & Society*, 39: 203–32.
Mooney, E. (2005) 'The concept of internal displacement and the case for internally displaced persons as a category of concern', *Refugee Survey Quarterly*, 24 (3): 9–26.
Morokvasic, M. (1984) 'Birds of passage are also women', *International Migration Review*, 18: 886–907.
Morawska, E. (1991) 'Return migrations: theoretical and research agenda', in R. Vecoli and S.M. Sinke (eds), *A Century of European Migrations, 1830–1930*. Urbana, IL: University of Illinois Press, pp. 277–92.
Morawska, E. (1994) 'In defense of the assimilation model', *Journal of American Ethnic History*, 13: 76–87.
Morawska, E. (2003) 'Immigrant transnationalism and assimilation: a variety of combinations and the analytic strategy it suggests', in C. Joppke and E. Morawska (eds), *Toward Assimilation and Citizenship: Immigrants in Liberal Nation-states*. Basingstoke: Palgrave Macmillan, pp. 133–76.
Myrdal, G. (1957) *Economic Theory and Underdeveloped Regions*. New York: Harper Torchback.
Nagel, J. (1994) 'Constructing ethnicity: creating and recreating ethnic identity and culture', *Social Problems*, 41 (1): 152.
Nagel, T. (2005) 'The problem of global justice', *Philosophy & Public Affairs*, 33: 113–47.
Nathans, E. (2004) *The Politics of Citizenship in Germany: Ethnicity, Utility and Nationalism*. Oxford: Berg.

Newland, K. (2009) *Circular Migration and Human Development*. Human Development Research Paper 2009/42 New York: United Nations Development Programme.

Newland, K. and Tanaka, H. (2010) *Mobilizing Diaspora Entrepreneurship for Development*. Washington, DC: Migration Policy Institute.

Newton, L. (2008) *Illegal, Alien, or Immigrant: The Politics of Immigration Reform*. New York: New York University Press.

Ngai, M.M. (2004) *Impossible Subjects: Illegal Aliens and the Making of Modern America*. Princeton, NJ: Princeton University Press.

Nobles, M. (2000) *Shades of Citizenship: Race and the Census in Modern Politics*. Stanford, CA: Stanford University Press.

Noiriel, G. (1998) 'Surveiller les déplacements ou identifier les personnes? Contribution à l'histoire du passeport en france de la ie à la iiie république' (The supervision of movements or the identification of people? A contribution to a history of the passport in France from the First to the Third Republic), *Genèses*, 30: 77–100.

Nyers, P. (2003) 'Abject cosmopolitanism: the politics of protection in the anti-deportation movement', *Third World Quarterly*, 24: 1069–93.

O'Connell-Davidson, J. (2005) *Children in the Global Sex Trade*. Cambridge: Polity.

O'Connell-Davidson, J. (2006) 'Will the real sex slave please stand up?', *Feminist Review*, 83: 4–22.

O'Dowd, L. and Wilson, T.M. (1996) 'Frontiers of sovereignty in the new Europe', in L. O'Dowd and T.M. Wilson (eds), *Borders, Nations and States: Frontiers of Sovereignty in the New Europe*. Aldershot: Ashgate, pp. 1–17.

O'Neil, K. (2003) *Brain Drain and Gain: The Case of Taiwan*. Washington, DC: Migration Policy Institute.

O'Neill, M. (2010) *Asylum, Migration and Community*. Bristol: Policy Press.

Oboler, S. (1995) *Ethnic Labels, Latino Lives: Identity and the Politics of (Re)presentation in the United States*. Minneapolis, MN: University of Minnesota Press.

Ohmae, K. (1990) *The Borderless World: Power and Strategy in the Global Marketplace*. New York: HarperCollins.

Okin, S.M. (1999) *Is Multiculturalism Bad for Women?* Princeton, NJ: Princeton University Press.

Ong, A. (1987) *Spirits of Resistance and Capitalist Discipline: Factory Women in Malaysia*. Albany, NY: State University of New York Press.

Ong, A. (1999) *Flexible Citizenship: The Cultural Logics of Transnationality*. Durham, NC: Duke University Press.

Østergaard-Nielsen, E. (2003) 'The politics of migrants' transnational political practices', *International Migration Review*, 37: 760–86.

Ouchu, J.O. and Crush, J. (2001) 'Contra free movement: South Africa and the SADC migration protocols', *Africa Today*, 48: 139–58.

Outshoorn, J. (2005) 'The political debates on prostitution and trafficking of women', *Social Politics*, 12: 141–55.

Padilla, F.M. (1985) *Latino Ethnic Consciousness: The Case of Mexican Americans and Puerto Ricans in Chicago*. Notre Dame, IN: University of Notre Dame Press.

Papademetriou, D. and Martin, P.L. (1991) *The Unsettled Relationship: Labor Migration and Economic Development*. New York: Greenwood Press.

Parreñas, R.S. (2001) *Servants of Globalization: Women, Migration, and Domestic Work*. Stanford, CA: Stanford University Press.

Parreñas, R.S. (2011) *Illicit Flirtations: Labor, Migration, and Sex Trafficking in Tokyo*. Palo Alto, CA: Stanford University Press.

Passel, J.S. (2007) *Growing Share of Immigrants Choosing Naturalization*. Washington, DC: Pew Hispanic Center Report.

Patterson, O. (1977) *Ethnic Chauvinism: The Reactionary Impulse*. New York: Stein & Day.
Pécoud, A. and de Guchteneire, P. (2006) 'International migration, border controls, and human rights: Assessing the relevance of a right to mobility', *Journal of Borderland Studies*, 21: 69–86.
Pedersen, P. J., Pytlikova, M. and Smith, N. (2008) 'Selection and network effects – migration flows into OECD countries 1990–2000', *European Economic Review*, 52 (7): 1160–86.
Pedraza, S. (1991) 'Women and migration: the social consequences of gender', *Annual Review of Sociology*, 17: 303–25.
Perruchoud, R. (1989) 'Family reunification', *International Migration*, 27: 509–24.
Pessar, P.R. (1999) 'Engendering migration studies: the case of new immigrants in the United States', *American Behavioral Scientist*, 42: 577–600.
Petersen, W. (1981) 'Concepts of ethnicity', in S. Therstrom (ed.), *The Harvard Encyclopedia of American Ethnic Groups*. Cambridge, MA: Harvard University Press, pp. 234–42.
Pevnick, R. (2011) *Immigration and the Constraints of Justice: Between Open Borders and Absolute Sovereignty*. Cambridge and New York: Cambridge University Press.
Pew Research Center (2013) *Second-generation Americans: A Portrait of the Adult Children of Immigrants*. Washington, DC: Pew Research Center.
Pilkington, A. (2007) 'In defence of both multiculturalism and progressive nationalism: a response to Mike O'Donnell', *Ethnicities*, 7: 269–77.
Piore, M.J. (1979) *Birds of Passage: Migrant Labor and Industrial Societies*. Cambridge: Cambridge University Press.
Piper, N. (2006) 'Gendering the politics of migration', *International Migration Review*, 40: 133–64.
Plant, R. (2012) 'Trafficking for labour exploitation: getting the responses right', in A. Quayson and A. Arhin (eds), *Labour Migration, Human Trafficking and Multinational Corporations*. London: Routledge, pp. 20–37.
Poros, M.V. (2001) 'Linking local labour markets: the social networks of Gujarati Indians in New York and London', *Global Networks*, 1 (3): 243–60.
Poros, M.V. (2011) *Modern Migrations: Gujarati Indian Networks in New York and London*. Stanford, CA: Stanford University Press.
Poros, M.V. (2013) 'India, migrants to British Africa', in I. Ness (ed.), *The Encyclopedia of Global Human Migration*. Hoboken, NJ: Wiley-Blackwell.
Portes, A. (ed.) (1995) *The Economic Sociology of Immigration: Essays on Networks, Ethnicity, and Entrepreneurship*. New York: Russell Sage Foundation.
Portes, A. (1998) 'Social capital: its origins and applications in modern sociology', *Annual Review of Sociology*, 24: 1–24.
Portes, A. (2000) 'The two meanings of social capital', *Sociological Forum*, 15: 1–12.
Portes, A. (2003) 'Conclusion: theoretical convergencies and empirical evidence in the study of immigrant transnationalism', *International Migration Review*, 37: 874–92.
Portes, A., Fernández-Kelly, P. and Haller, W. (2009) 'The adaptation of the immigrant second generation in America: a theoretical overview and recent evidence', *Journal of Ethnic and Migration Studies*, 35 (7): 1077–104.
Portes, A., Guarnizo, L.E. and Landolt, P. (1999) 'The study of transnationalism: pitfalls and promise of an emergent research field', *Ethnic and Racial Studies*, 22 (2): 217–37.
Portes, A. and Rumbaut, R. (1996) *Immigrant America: A Portrait*. Berkeley, CA: University of California Press.
Portes, A. and Rumbaut, R.G. (2001) *Legacies: The Story of the Immigrant Second Generation*. Berkeley, CA and New York: University of California Press and Russell Sage Foundation.
Portes, A. and Sensenbrenner, J. (1993) 'Embeddedness and immigration: notes on the social determinants of economic action', *American Journal of Sociology*, 98: 1320–50.
Portes, A. and Zhou, M. (1993) 'The new second generation: segmented assimilation and its variants', *Annals of the American Academy of Political and Social Science*, 530: 74–96.

Price, M. and Benton-Short, L. (2008) *Migrants to the Metropolis: The Rise of Immigrant Gateways*. Syracuse, NJ: Syracuse University Press.
Putnam, R. (2000) *Bowling Alone: The Collapse and Revival of American Community*. New York: Simon & Schuster.
Putnam, R.D. (2007) '*E pluribus unum*: diversity and community in the twenty-first century (The 2006 Johan Skytte Prize Lecture)', *Scandinavian Political Studies*, 30: 137–74.
Putnam, R.D., Leonardi, R. and Nanetti, R.Y. (1993) *Making Democracy Work: Civic Traditions in Modern Italy*. Princeton, NJ: Princeton University Press.
Ratha, D., Mohapatra, S. and Silwal, A. (2010) *Outlook for Remittance Flows 2010–11*. Washington, DC: World Bank (Migration and Development Brief, 23 April).
Ratha, D. and Shaw, W. (2007) *South–South Migration and Remittances*. Washington, DC: World Bank Development Prospects Group, Working Paper No. 102.
Rawls, J. (1971) *A Theory of Justice*. Cambridge, MA: Belknap Press.
Rawls, J. (1999) *The Law of Peoples*. Cambridge, MA: Harvard University Press.
Redfield, R., Linton, R. and Herskovits, M.J. (1936) 'Memorandum for the study of acculturation', *American Anthropologist*, 38: 149–52.
Reichert, J. (1981) 'The migrant syndrome: seasonal US wage labor and rural development in central Mexico', *Human Organization*, 40: 56–66.
Reichert, J. (1982) 'A town divided – economic stratification and social-relations in a Mexican migrant community', *Social Problems*, 29: 411–23.
Reitz, J.G. (2009) 'Behavioural precepts of multiculturalism: empirical validity and policy implications', in J.G. Reitz, R. Breton, K.K. Dion and K.L. Dion (eds), *Multiculturalism and Social Cohesion: Potentials and Challenges of Diversity*. London: Springer, pp. 157–71.
Repak, T.A. (1994) 'Labor recruitment and the lure of the capital: central American migrants in Washington, DC', *Gender and Society*, 8 (4): 507.
Richmond, A.H. (1994) *Global Apartheid: Refugees, Racism, and the New World Order*. Oxford: Oxford University Press.
Repak, T.A. (1995) *Waiting on Washington: Central American Workers in the Nation's Capital*. Philadelphia, PA: Temple University Press.
Riley, J.L. (2008) *Let Them In: The Case for Open Borders*. New York: Gotham Books.
Robinson, D. (2008) 'Community cohesion and the politics of communitarianism', in J. Flint and D. Robinson (eds), *Community Cohesion in Crisis? New Dimensions of Diversity and Difference*. Bristol: Policy Press, pp. 15–33.
Robinson, V. and Carey, M. (2000) 'Peopling skilled international migration: Indian doctors in the UK', *International Migration*, 38: 89–107.
Rogers, R. (1985) *Guests Come to Stay: The Effects of European Labor Migration on Sending and Receiving Countries*. Boulder, CO: Westview Press.
Rogers, R. (1997) 'Migration return policies and countries of origin', in K. Hailbronner, D.A. Martin and H. Motomura (eds), *Immigration Admissions: The Search for Workable Policies in Germany and the United States*. New York: Berghahn Books, pp. 147–204.
Romero, F. (2008) *Hyperborder: The Contemporary U.S.–Mexico Border and Its Future*. New York: Princeton Architectural Press.
Romero, S. (2010) 'In Venezuela, a new wave of foreigners', *New York Times*, 7 November.
Roosens, E. (1989) *Creating Ethnicity: the Process of Ethnogenesis*. Newbury Park, CA: SAGE Publications.
Rosenhek, Z. (2000) 'Migration regimes, intra-state conflicts and the politics of exclusion and inclusion: migrant workers in the Israeli welfare state', *Social Problems*, 47: 49–67.
Ruhs, M. and Chang, H.-J. (2004) 'The ethics of labor immigration policy', *International Organization*, 58: 69–102.
Ruiz, I. and Vargas-Silva, C. (2011) 'Another consequence of the economic crisis: a decrease in migrants' remittances', *Applied Financial Economics*, 20: 171–82.

Rumbaut, R. (1999) 'Assimilation and its discontents: ironies and paradoxes', in C. Hirschman, P. Kasinitz and J. DeWind (eds), *The Handbook of International Migration: The American Experience*. New York: Russell Sage Foundation, pp. 172–95.

Rumbaut, R.G. (1997) 'Assimilation and its discontents: between rhetoric and reality', *International Migration Review*, 31: 923–60.

Ryan, L. (2010) 'Becoming Polish in London: negotiating ethnicity through migration', *Social Identities*, 16: 359–76.

Sachs, J. (2007) 'Climate change refugees', *Scientific American*, 296: 43.

Sadiq, K. (2009) *Paper Citizens: How Illegal Immigrants Acquire Citizenship in Developing Countries*. Oxford: Oxford University Press.

Safran, W. (1991) 'Diasporas in modern societies: myths of homeland and return', *Diaspora*, 1 (1): 83–99.

Sahlins, P. (2004) *Unnaturally French: Foreign Citizens in the Old Regime and After*. Ithaca, NY: Cornell University Press.

Sales, R. (2007) *Understanding Immigration and Refugee Policy: Contradictions and Continuities*. Bristol: Policy Press.

Salt, J., Clarke, J. and Wanner, P. (2005) *International Labour Migration*. Strasbourg: Council of Europe.

Sassen, S. (1988) *The Mobility of Labor and Capital: A Study in International Investment and Labor Flow*. Cambridge: Cambridge University Press.

Sassen, S. (1999) *Guests and Aliens*. New York: New Press.

Sassen, S. (2008) *Territory, Authority, Rights: From Medieval to Global Assemblages*. Princeton, NJ: Princeton University Press.

Sassen-Koob, S. (1984) 'Notes on the incorporation of third-world women into wage-labor through immigration and off-shore production', *International Migration Review*, 18: 1144–67.

Saunders, R. (2003) *The Concept of the Foreign: An Interdisciplinary Dialogue*. Lanham, MD: Lexington Books.

Saxenian, A. (1999) *Silicon Valley's New Immigrant Entrepreneurs*. San Francisco, CA: Public Policy Institute of California.

Saxenian, A. (2005) 'From brain drain to brain circulation: transnational communities and regional upgrading in India and China', *Studies in Comparative International Development*, 40 (2): 35–61.

Scarpa, S. (2008) *Trafficking in Human Beings: Modern Slavery*. Oxford: Oxford University Press.

Schachter, J.P., Franklin, R.S. and Perry, M.J. (2003) *Migration and Geographic Mobility in Metropolitan and Nonmetropolitan America: 1995 to 2000*. Washington, DC: U.S. Census Bureau.

Schlesinger, A.M. (1992) *The Disuniting of America: Reflections on a Multicultural Society*. New York: W. W. Norton & Co Inc.

Schuck, P.H. (1998) *Citizens, Strangers, and In-betweens: Essays on Immigration and Citizenship*. Boulder, CO: Westview Press.

Schuster, L. and Solomos, J. (2004) 'Race, immigration and asylum: New Labour's agenda and its consequences', *Ethnicities*, 4: 267.

Schwenken, H. (2013) 'Circular migration and gender', in I. Ness (ed.), *The Encyclopedia of Global Human Migration*. Oxford: Blackwell Publishing Ltd, pp. 1–5.

Seglow, J. (2005) 'The ethics of immigration', *Political Studies Review*, 3: 317–34.

Semyonov, M. and Gorodzeisky, A. (2008) 'Labor migration, remittances and economic well-being of households in the Philippines', *Population Research and Policy Review*, 27: 619–37.

Semyonov, M. and Lewin-Epstein, N. (1987) *Hewers of Wood and Drawers of Water: Noncitizen Arabs in the Israeli Labor Market*. Ithaca, NY: ILR Press.

Shachar, A. (2009) *The Birthright Lottery: Citizenship and Global Inequality*. Cambridge, MA: Harvard University Press.

Shelley, L. (2007) 'Human trafficking as a form of transnational crime', in M. Lee (ed.), *Human Trafficking*. Portland, OR: Willan Publishing, pp. 116–37.

Shils, E. (1957) 'Primordial, personal, sacred, and civil ties: some particular observations on the relationship of sociological research and theory', *British Journal of Sociology*, 8 (1): 130–45.

Shukra, K., Back, L., Keith, M., Khan, A. and Solomos, J. (2004) 'Race, social cohesion and the changing politics of citizenship', *London Review of Education*, 2: 187–95.

Shuval, J. and Leshem, E. (1998) 'The sociology of migration in Israel: a critical view', in E. Leshem and J. Shuval (eds), *Immigration to Israel: Sociological Perspectives*. London: Transaction Publishers, pp. 3–50.

Silberman, R. (1992) 'French immigration statistics', in D.L. Horowitz and G. Noiriel (eds.), *Immigrants in Two Democracies: French and American Experiences*. New York: New York University Press, pp. 112–23.

Simmel, G. (1964 [1908]) *The Sociology of Georg Simmel*, compiled and translated by Kurt Wolff. Glencoe, IL: Free Press of Glencoe.

Simon, P. (2012) *French National Identity and Integration: Who Belongs to the National Community?* Washington, DC: Migration Policy Institute.

Skeldon, R. (1997) *Migration and Development: A Global Perspective*. Harlow: Longman.

Skeldon, R. (2006) 'Interlinkages between internal and international migration and development in the Asian region', *Population Space and Place*, 12 (1): 15–30.

Smith, R.C. (2003) 'Diasporic memberships in historical perspective: comparative insights from the Mexican, Italian and Polish cases', *International Migration Review*, 37: 724–59.

Smith, R.C. (2006) *Mexican New York: Transnational Lives of New Immigrants*. Berkeley, CA: University of California Press.

Smith, R.C. (2008) 'Contradictions of diasporic institutionalization in Mexican politics: the 2006 migrant vote and other forms of inclusion and control', *Ethnic and Racial Studies*, 31: 708–41.

Solimano, A. (2010) *International Migration in the Age of Crisis and Globalization: Historical and Recent Experiences*. Cambridge: Cambridge University Press.

Solinger, D.J. (1999) 'Citizenship issues in China's internal migration: comparisons with Germany and Japan', *Political Science Quarterly*, 114 (3): 455–78.

Sonnino, E. (1995) 'La Popolazione Italiana Dall' Espansione Al Contenimento' (The Italian population: from expansion to containment), in *Storia dell' Italia Repubblicana*. Torino: Einaudi, pp. 529–85.

Soysal, Y.N. (1994) *Limits of Citizenship: Migrants and Postnational Membership in Europe*. Chicago, IL: University of Chicago Press.

Spener, D. (2009) *Clandestine Crossings: Migrants and Coyotes on the Texas–Mexico Border*. Ithaca, NY: Cornell University Press.

Sriskandarajah, D. (2005) *Reassessing the Impacts of Brain Drain on Developing Countries*. Washington, DC: Migration Policy Institute.

Sriskandarajah, D. and Cooley, L. (2009) 'Stemming the flow? The causes and consequences of the UK's "closed door" policy towards Romanians and Bulgarians', in J. Eade and Y. Valkanova (eds), *Accession and Migration: Changing Policy, Society, and Culture in an Enlarged Europe*. Farnham: Ashgate Publishing, pp. 31–55.

Staring, R. (2004) 'Facilitating the arrival of illegal immigrants in the Netherlands: irregular chain migration versus smuggling chains', *Journal of International Migration and Integration*, 5: 273–94.

Stark, O. (1991) *The Migration of Labor*. Oxford: Basil Blackwell.

Stark, O. and Bloom, D. (1985) 'The new economics of labor migration', *American Economic Review*, 72: 173–78.

Stark, O. and Taylor, J. E. (1989) 'Relative deprivation and international migration', *Demography*, 26: 1–14.

Stark, O., Taylor, J.E. and Yitzhaki, S. (1988) 'Migration, remittances and inequality: a sensitivity analysis using the extended Gini index', *Journal of Development Economics*, 28: 309–22.

Stea, D., Zech, J. and Gray, M. (2010) 'Change and non-change in the US–Mexico borderlands after NAFTA', in I.W. Zartman (ed.), *Understanding Life in the Borderlands: Boundaries in Depth and in Motion*. Athens, GA: University of Georgia Press, pp. 105–30.

Sutcliffe, B. (1998) 'Freedom to move in the age of globalization', in D. Baker, G. Epstein and R. Pollin (eds), *Globalization and Progressive Economic Policy*. Cambridge: Cambridge University Press, pp. 325–36.

Talavera, V., Núñez-Mchiri, G.G. and Heyman, J. (2010) 'Deportation in the US–Mexico borderlands: anticipation, experience and memory', in N. De Genova and N. Peutz (eds), *The Deportation Regime: Sovereignty, Space, and the Freedom of Movement*. Durham, NC: Duke University Press, pp. 166–95.

Tan, K.-C. (2004) *Justice Without Borders: Cosmopolitanism, Nationalism, and Patriotism*. Cambridge: Cambridge University Press.

Tannenbaum, M. (2007) 'Back and forth: immigrants' stories of migration and return', *International Migration*, 45: 147–75.

Tapinos, G.P. (2000) 'Globalisation, regional integration, international migration', *International Social Science Journal*, 52: 297–306.

Taran, P., Ivakhnyuk, I., Pereira Ramos, M. da C. and Tanner, A. (2009) *Economic Migration, Social Cohesion and Development: Towards an Integrated Approach*. Strasbourg: Council of Europe.

Taylor, C. (1992) *Multiculturalism and the Politics of Recognition: An Essay*. Princeton, NJ: Princeton University Press.

Taylor, J.E. (1999) 'The new economics of labour migration and the role of remittances in the migration process', *International Migration*, 37 (1): 63–88.

Thernstrom, S. (1992) 'American ethnic statistics', in D. Horowitz (ed.), *Immigrants in Two Democracies: French and American Experiences*. New York: New York University Press, pp. 80–111.

Thomas, B. (1954) *Migration and Economic Growth: A Study of Great Britain and the Atlantic Economy*. Cambridge: Cambridge University Press.

Thompson, L.M. (1985) *The Political Mythology of Apartheid*. New Haven, CT: Yale University Press.

Torpey, J. (2000) *The Invention of the Passport: Surveillance, Citizenship, and the State*. Cambridge: Cambridge University Press.

Triandafyllidou, A. (2010) 'Irregular migration in Europe in the early 21st century', in A. Triandafyllidou and A. Lundqvist (eds), *Irregular Migration in Europe: Myths and Realities*. Farnham: Ashgate Publishing Group, pp. 1–22.

Truong, T.-D. (2003) 'Gender, exploitative migration, and the sex industry: a European perspective', *Gender, Technology and Development*, 7: 31–52.

Tsuda, T. (2003) *Strangers in the Ethnic Homeland: Japanese Brazilian Return Migration in Transnational Perspective*. New York: Columbia University Press.

Turton, D. (2003) *Refugees, Forced Resettlers and 'Other Forced Migrants': Towards a Unitary Study of Forced Migration*. Geneva: UNHCR.

UNESCO (1950) *Statement on the Race Question*. Paris: UNESCO.

UNHCR (2010) *2009 Global Trends: Refugees, Asylum-seekers, Returnees, Internally Displaced and Stateless Persons*. Geneva: UNHCR.

UNHCR (2011) *Asylum Levels and Trends in Industrialized Countries, 2010*. Geneva: UNHCR.

United Nations (1998) *Recommendations on Statistics of International Migration*. New York: United Nations.

United Nations Population Division (2009) *Trends in International Migrant Stock: The 2008 Revision*. New York: United Nations.

van Liempt, I. (2011) '"And then one day they all moved to Leicester": the relocation of Somalis from the Netherlands to the UK explained', *Population, Space and Place*, 17: 254–66.
van Schendel, W. and Itty, A. (eds) (2001) *Illicit Flows and Criminal Things: States, Borders, and the Other Side of Globalization*. Bloomington, IN: Indiana University Press.
Verduzco, G. and De Lozano, M.I. (2011) 'Migration from Mexico and Central America to the United States: human insecurities and paths for change', in T.-D. Truong and D. Gasper (eds), *Transnational Migration and Human Security*. London: Springer, pp. 41–56.
Verduzco, G. and Unger, K. (1998) 'The impact of migration on economic development in Mexico', in OECD (ed.), *Migration, Free Trade and Regional Integration in North America*. Paris: OECD Publishing, pp. 103–17.
Vermeulen, G., Van Damme, Y. and De Bondt, W. (2010) *Organised Crime Involvement in Trafficking in Persons and Smuggling of Migrants*. Antwerp: Maklu Uitgevers N.V.
Vertovec, S. (1999) 'Conceiving and researching transnationalism', *Ethnic and Racial Studies*, 22: 1–11.
Vertovec, S. (2007a) *Circular Migration: The Way Forward in Global Policy?* Oxford: University of Oxford, International Migration Institute.
Vertovec, S. (2007b) 'Superdiversity and its implications', *Ethnic and Racial Studies*, 30: 1024–54.
Vertovec, S. (2009) *Transnationalism*. Abingdon: Routledge.
Vertovec, S. and Wessendorf, S. (2010) 'Introduction: assessing the backlash against multiculturalism in Europe', in S. Vertovec and S. Wessendorf (eds), *The Multiculturalism Backlash: European Discourses, Policies and Practices*. London: Routledge, pp. 1–31.
Waldinger, R. (1999) *Still the Promised City?: African-Americans and New Immigrants in Postindustrial New York*. Cambridge, MA: Harvard University Press.
Waldinger, R. (2003) 'The sociology of immigration: second thoughts and reconsiderations', in J.G. Reitz (ed.), *Host Societies and the Reception of Immigrants*. La Jolla, CA: Center for Comparative Immigration Studies, UCSD, pp. 21–43.
Waldinger, R. and Lichter, M.I. (2003) *How the Other Half Works: Immigration and the Social Organization of Labor*. Berkeley, CA: University of California Press.
Waldinger, R. and Reichl, R. (2007) 'Today's second generation: getting ahead or falling behind?', in M. Fix (ed.), *Securing the Future: US Immigrant Integration Policy, a Reader*. Washington, DC: Migration Policy Institute, pp. 17–41.
Walters, W. (2002) 'Deportation, expulsion, and the international police of aliens', *Citizenship Studies*, 6: 265–92.
Walzer, M. (1983) *Spheres of Justice: A Defense of Pluralism and Equality*. New York: Basic Books.
Ware, V. (2009) 'The ins and out of Anglo-Saxonism: the future of white decline', in M. Perryman (ed.), *Breaking up Britain: Four Nations after a Union*. London: Lawrence & Wishart, pp. 133–49.
Warner, W.L. and Srole, L. (1945) *The Social Systems of American Ethnic Groups*. New Haven, CT: Yale University Press.
Waters, M.C. (1999) *Black Identities: West Indian Immigrant Dreams and American Realities*. New York and Cambridge, MA: Russell Sage Foundation and Harvard University Press.
Waters, M.C., Tran, V.C., Kasinitz, P. and Mollenkopf, J.H. (2010) 'Segmented assimilation revisited: types of acculturation and socioeconomic mobility in young adulthood', *Ethnic and Racial Studies*, 33: 1168–93.
Weber, M. (1968 [1922]) *Economy and Society: An Outline of Interpretive Sociology*. New York: Bedminster Press.
Weber, M. (2003 [1927]) *General Economic History*. Mineola, NY: Dover Publications.
Weiss, T.G. (2003) 'Internal exiles: what next for internally displaced persons?', *Third World Quarterly*, 24: 429–47.

Wihtol de Wenden, C. (2007) 'The frontiers of mobility', in A. Pécoud and P. de Guchteneire (eds), *Migration Without Borders: Essays on the Free Movement of People*. Paris and New York: UNESCO Publishing and Berghahn Books, pp. 51–64.

Wilkinson, R.C. (1983) 'Migration in Lesotho: some comparative aspects, with particular reference to the role of women', *Geography*, 68: 208–24.

Wong, D. (2005) 'The rumor of trafficking: border controls, illegal migration, and the sovereignty of the nation-state', in W. van Schendel and I. Abraham (eds), *Illicit Flows and Criminal Things: States, Borders, and the Other Side of Globalization*. Bloomington, IN: Indiana University Press, pp. 69–100.

Woolcock, M. (1998) 'Social capital and economic development: toward a theoretical synthesis and policy framework', *Theory and Society*, 27: 151–208.

World Bank (2011) *Migration and Remittances Factbook*. Washington, DC: World Bank.

Worley, C. (2005) '"It's not about race. It's about the community": New Labour and "community cohesion"', *Critical Social Policy*, 25: 483–96.

Wright, M. and Bloemraad, I. (2012) 'Is there a trade-off between multiculturalism and socio-political integration? Policy regimes and immigrant incorporation in comparative perspective', *Perspectives on Politics*, 10: 77–95.

Xiang, B. (2006) *Global 'Body Shopping': An Indian Labor System in the Information Technology Industry*. Princeton, NJ: Princeton University Press.

Yu, B. (2008) *Chain Migration Explained: The Power of the Immigration Multiplier*. New York: LFB Scholarly Publishers.

Yuval-Davis, N., Anthias, F. and Kofman, E. (2005) 'Secure borders and safe haven and the gendered politics of belonging: beyond social cohesion', *Ethnic and Racial Studies*, 28: 513–35.

Zachariah, K.C. (2002) *Gulf Migration Study: Employment, Wages and Working Conditions of Kerala Emigrants in the United Arab Emirates*, Thiruvananthapuram, Kerala: Centre for Development Studies.

Zelinsky, W. (1971) 'The hypothesis of the mobility transition', *Geographical Review*, 61 (2): 219–49.

Zelinsky, W. (1983) 'The impasse in migration theory', in P. Morrison (ed.), *Population Movements: Their Forms and Functions in Urbanization and Development*. Liège: Ordina Editions, pp. 19–46.

Zetter, R. (1988) 'Refugees, repatriation, and root causes', *Journal of Refugee Studies*, 1: 99–106.

Zolberg, A.R., Suhrke, A. and Aguayo, S. (1989) *Escape from Violence: Conflict and the Refugee Crisis in the Developing World*. New York: Oxford University Press.

Zolberg, A.R. and Woon, L.L. (1999) 'Why Islam is like Spanish: cultural incorporation in Europe and the United States', *Politics & Society*, 27: 5–38.

